CW00738779

Cinema of the Dark Side

Atrocity and the Ethics of Film Spectatorship

Shohini Chaudhuri

EDINBURGH
University Press

© Shohini Chaudhuri, 2014

Edinburgh University Press Ltd
The Tun – Holyrood Road
12 (2f) Jackson's Entry
Edinburgh EH8 8PJ
www.euppublishing.com

Typeset in Monotype Ehrhardt by
Servis Filmsetting Ltd, Stockport, Cheshire,
and printed and bound in Great Britain by
CPI Group (UK) Ltd, Croydon CR0 4YY

A CIP record for this book is available from the British Library

ISBN 978 0 7486 4263 2 (hardback)
ISBN 978 1 4744 0042 8 (paperback)
ISBN 978 0 7486 9461 7 (webready PDF)
ISBN 978 1 4744 0043 5 (epub)

The right of Shohini Chaudhuri to be identified as author of
this work has been asserted in accordance with the Copyright,
Designs and Patents Act 1988 and the Copyright and Related
Rights Regulations 2003 (SI No. 2498).

Contents

Acknowledgements

M y heartfelt thanks go to those who generously offered help, encouragement and lively dialogue by reading draft chapters: Ruth Blakeley, John Cant, Matthew Carter, Sabine El Chamaa, Nina Fischer, Fabian Freyenhagen, Jeffrey Geiger, Catherine Grant, Joanne Harwood, John Masterson, Éadaoin O'Brien, Colin Samson, Marina Warner and Hugh Whitby. A number of other people I talked to about this project have also inspired my choices and approach, among them Michele Aaron, Sanja Bahun, Eamonn Carrabine, Hydar Dewachi, Carlos Gigoux, John Haynes, John Horne, Clive Johnson, Jay Prosser, Vera Svihalkova and John Wrathall.

Thanks to my local Amnesty group in London, particularly Hugh Whitby, who got me involved in the first place, and Deepa Shah, our group chair. I owe a great deal to Dick Blackwell, who set up the Centre for Psychotherapy and Human Rights (CPHR) to combine therapy for survivors of political violence with research into the causes and contexts of that violence. The ideas in this book evolved with my work with both Amnesty and CPHR. An early version of Chapter 3 was presented as a public lecture jointly convened by CPHR and the Institute of Group Analysis in London in 2012.

While writing the book, I have drawn constant inspiration from my students, my colleagues and the interdisciplinary environment at the University of Essex, including its Human Rights Centre. In particular, I would like to acknowledge students on my third-year module Cultural Ideology and Film and the MA in Refugee Care, who have helped me to develop these ideas further through their response to some of this material. Also many thanks to Lyndsey Stonebridge (University of East Anglia) and Les Back (Goldsmiths) for launching Humanities in Human Rights, a skills exchange programme funded by the Arts and Humanities Research Council, which offered an engaged forum in which to present ideas from this book's Introduction.

The research was supported by two terms of study leave granted by the

University of Essex, for which I am extremely grateful. The lengthy writing process was made easier by the understanding and advice of Gillian Leslie and the editorial team at Edinburgh University Press. I also thank Jonathan Wadman for his meticulous work in copy-editing the manuscript. Meanwhile, Oliver Craske enabled me to keep going with his love and support throughout, and by being my first reader and editor.

An earlier version of Chapter 1 appeared in *Screening the Past* 37 (2013). A section of Chapter 4 was previously published in Sandra Ponzanesi and Marguerite Waller (eds), *Postcolonial Cinema Studies* (Routledge, 2012) and has been greatly expanded and revised.

Figures

Introduction

In the science fiction film *Children of Men* (2006), set in a future dystopian Britain, a propaganda film plays on a TV screen on a train. Images of disasters and atrocities around the world appear in a rapid-fire parody of TV news headlines. The news consists entirely of bad things happening to other people in other places. The apocalyptic montage climaxes as Big Ben chimes over the headline 'Only Britain soldiers on'.

In today's world, atrocity images circulate with apparent ease and instantaneity via 24-hour TV news, the Internet and mobile phone cameras. Yet mainstream news remains strictly regulated, by considerations of not only what is 'acceptable' for public viewing but also what is 'newsworthy' and friendly to government interests. Though terrorism at home and abroad frequently makes the headlines, mainstream Western news media often present atrocities overseas as unfortunate but inevitable, directly emanating from the region's troubled history or geography. News reports provide brief, remote glimpses seemingly disconnected from their viewers, and therefore easily accepted as background to their lives, highlighting the disparity between those who watch and those who suffer. Through decisions of selection, prioritisation, inclusion and exclusion, the news helps to shape an 'imagined picture' of the world (Calhoun 2010: 33).

This book is a comparative study of 21st-century cinematic images of atrocity. It asserts that cinema can counter the desensitising impact of such news images. It finds its immediate historical and political context in the post-9/11 climate, when global terrorism has become a universal fear and concern. But rather than the terrorism of groups such as Al-Qaeda, which is promoted as the prime threat to human life by Western governments and news media, its focus is the cinematic treatment of *state* terror, which routinely destroys many more lives through the arms trade, aerial bombardment, enforced disappearance, torture, genocide and population displacements, resulting in an unstable, asymmetric world that this book interprets not as a natural division (the West versus 'the rest') but as a legacy of colonial histories maintained by present-day politics.

National security is frequently offered as a justification for state terror, but this conceals other agendas at work, namely promoting the interests of elites which, for Western democracies, are intertwined with ensuring the free flow of capital in order to maintain their power and influence in the world. Though the USA has primacy in the global capitalist system, other powerful states share similar competitive interests, while their client states also benefit from this system: a form of neo-imperialism following similar aims and methods to older colonialisms characterised by resource extraction and labour exploitation and enforced by a rule of terror which crushed rebellions through torture and collective punishments. As the work of Edward Herman and Noam Chomsky and Mark Curtis has shown, massive human rights violations are committed in pursuit of these agendas. For these writers, the media perform the role of 'perception management' (Curtis 2004: 101), which projects powerful groups as moral forces for good and keeps their agendas partially hidden so as to 'manufacture consent' (Herman and Chomsky 2002).

Cinema occupies part of this broader media landscape, disseminating images that construct how we think and feel about atrocities. Films help to shape prevailing normative perceptions, but they can also question those perceptions and build different ones. This book seeks to use film to interrogate aspects of geopolitical realities. In its analysis, it points towards to a new conceptualisation of human rights cinema in which human rights morality is repositioned within an ethical framework that reflects upon the causes and contexts of atrocities, and invites viewers to question their own relation to those histories.

A few days after 9/11, US Vice-President Dick Cheney declared: 'We also have to work . . . the dark side.' This provides the book's central metaphor. A portent of what was to come, Cheney's words hinted at the dirty tactics that the USA (along with its allies) has come to refer to and justify as a global 'War on Terror' – which encompasses everything from conflicts in Afghanistan and Iraq to kidnappings, torture and targeted killings by drones and special forces. The metaphor of the dark side, originating from *Star Wars* (1977), positions the USA as a force for good, legitimating the unleashing of the darkest forces to battle a new, ruthless enemy. The 'dark side' is not a new phenomenon, however, as it is shaped by and echoes past forms of violence from the Cold War back to colonial history.

This book takes a transnational approach in its study of cinematic images of state-sponsored atrocity in the shadow of these post-9/11 developments, using them to evoke other landscapes of state terror and allow connections to emerge across multiple contexts. While films are often about national histories, this book is not about their negotiation of particular national pasts. Rather, it reveals links between histories that might not otherwise be apparent and meanings that risk being exclusively considered within the confines of national cinema studies. The book's transnational scope enables thematic comparisons, as well as highlighting the role of film production and distribution in determining which atrocities we know about and the kinds of knowledge that are produced.

Most films discussed in the book, either through their production or distribution arrangements or through their narrative styles, belong to the mainstream – what might be called popular world cinema. This includes some films that are not 'obvious' human rights films, among them the science fiction films covered in Chapter 4. The book analyses a necessarily limited but diverse range of films to show that the topic merits different approaches. Even relatively mainstream films are capable of challenging dominant perceptions, thereby throwing into relief the far larger number of films that don't.

The rest of this Introduction highlights the various critical discourses with which the book engages, firstly drawing on film theory and critical theory to show what have been perceived as some of the ethical problems raised by human rights representations. This book is invested in human rights activism and film studies debates on the ethics of spectatorship, yet it also seeks to challenge some of the orthodoxies of both these discourses. In film studies debates, those orthodoxies include the emphasis on Brechtian aesthetics, the dynamics of the gaze, trauma, and Levinasian ethics. The Introduction then outlines the concepts of the image, ethics and politics that define my approach, grouping these into three sections: reflection on causes and contexts of atrocity, a reconfigured framework of morality and ethics, and embodied spectatorship.

HUMAN RIGHTS REPRESENTATIONS AND THE ETHICS OF SPECTATORSHIP: PROBLEMS AND DEBATES

Human rights organisations and activists have long recognised the power of film for evidence, advocacy and awareness-raising. A film can offer personal stories and background, making human rights 'tangible by eyewitness experience' (Claude and Weston 2006: xii). Films are frequently used as part of human rights campaigns and, since the 1990s, a film festival network specialising in human rights has mushroomed worldwide. A definition of the human rights film is offered by the Charter of the Human Rights Film Network, a consortium of human rights film festivals established in 2004: 'Human rights films, in our view, are films that reflect, inform on and provide understanding of the actual state of past and present human rights violations, or the visions and aspirations concerning ways to redress those violations' (Human Rights Film Network n.d.). At the heart of activists' use of film is the belief that, by exposing human rights abuses around the world, film can bring about change or prevention: a belief in cinema's transformative power to break through spectators' ignorance, indifference or denial. The assumption is that representation promotes recognition, which, in turn, promotes the responsibility to act. Yet, as Jacques Rancière reminds us, though a film may open up new possibilities for politicisation, there is 'no straight path' from viewing to 'understanding of the state of the world, and none from intellectual awareness to political action' (2010: 143). Nor can you simply counter biased opinions with a statement of facts.

Activist use of film is mostly concerned with content: post-screening panel discussions at human rights film festivals, for example, are dominated by the issues raised by a film, rather than its aesthetic choices. This overlooks the relationship between form and content, and between film and its institutional contexts. These are precisely the focus of film studies debates, which problematise some of the major assumptions of human rights, including its ideal of 'witnessing'.

Film famously played a role as a witness when it was used (for the first time) as legal evidence at the Nuremberg trials. Footage of Nazi camps shot by US and Soviet film crews was used as irrefutable proof that those atrocities had occurred (Delage and Goodrich 2013: 3). Watching is integral to human rights monitoring and its forms of collective activism, as signalled by names of organisations such as Human Rights Watch and Witness. The latter, one of several institutions that provide filmmaking equipment and training to people whose rights are at risk, is renowned for the slogan 'See it, film it, change it'. The ethos behind human rights witnessing is that 'seeing is believing', creating the impression that all you have to do is get a camera, record abuses, and get the images 'out there'.

Film studies has a different stance towards the activity of watching. Here, a central preoccupation has been 'Who is looking at whom and how?' (Downing and Saxton 2010: 20). Feminist critiques of cinema have traditionally centred on the objectifying male gaze and the voyeuristic character of film spectatorship, since film indulges a desire to look from a privileged vantage-point, without being seen ourselves. The visual gaze is associated with mastery and control, as in concepts of the male gaze and the imperial gaze (Mulvey 1989; Pratt 1992). This has led to an emphasis on the dynamics of the gaze in debates on the ethics of spectatorship. For example, Libby Saxton explores the motif of the view through the spyhole into Holocaust gas chambers, which necessitates a camera placement that aligns us with a Nazi: a sadistic-voyeuristic subject position, like the spyhole shot in *Schindler's List* (1993), where naked Jewish women are glimpsed in their abject terror. It implies, she says, an illusion of mastery and control over 'a vulnerable on-screen other who can neither return our gaze nor acquiesce in our looking' (Saxton 2008: 75).

Sophia Wood (2012) has argued that although atrocity films, including Nazi camp footage, appear to position spectators as 'witnesses', they also position us as voyeurs of other people's suffering. For her, the discourse of 'witnessing' is a pretext for voyeurism. To assert that images purporting to bear witness perpetuate another kind of violence is a common rhetorical move. Many critical accounts insist that we shouldn't look at atrocity images – instead, we should look away – or that some images shouldn't be shown. However, these questions of propriety and limits belong to the domain of morality rather than ethics (for the distinction between morality and ethics, see below).

Despite the disparity between the human rights discourse of witnessing and film theories of the gaze, one concern that they share is how to break viewers' assumed passivity or indifference in order to rouse them into action, particularly in the Brechtian model of spectatorship frequently invoked in arguments for a more politically or ethically progressive cinema. Brechtian self-reflexivity fosters critical distance from representations and provides audiences with moments to reflect on their roles as witnesses. For Michele Aaron, a self-reflexive film like *Funny Games* (1997) reminds spectators of their investment in watching 'unconscionable' content, holding them 'accountable' for it (Aaron 2007: 89, 118), while Saxton identifies films that 'disturb the voyeuristic-sadistic gaze', offering 'alternative viewing positions' that promote 'more responsible and self-conscious ways of looking' (Saxton 2008: 22, 73).

While these film scholars raise important issues, reminding us that there is no neutral position from which we look, the Brechtian model presents a number of assumptions that are critiqued in this book: that the spectator is by default passive, that emotions are antithetical to critical reflection, and that cinematic identification is solely based on optical point of view. As adopted into film theory, the Brechtian model offers a purely cerebral notion of spectatorship that neglects its embodied aspects and results in critics judging merely a handful of films to be capable of generating meaningful effects.

In the arena of human rights film, documentary is the privileged genre, due to its 'emphasis on "truth"' (Torchin 2012b: 2), stemming from belief in the camera's truth-value as well as in the transparency of this evidence. A similar preoccupation with film's access to 'truth' or empirical reality underlies film theory. For André Bazin (1967), what distinguishes cinema from other art forms is its 'objectivity', derived from the photographic medium's ability to capture reality through an indexical link to real-world objects. But the camera is not just a recording apparatus; it is also a means of expression. A film, whether documentary or otherwise, is never objective; it is always partial and selective, offering a set of perspectives or perceptions on reality. As Linda Williams writes, 'the truth figured by documentary cannot be a simple unmasking or reflection. It is a careful construction, an intervention in the politics and the semiotics of representation' (1993: 20).

Truth-telling is demanded by testimony, usually a first-person narrative relating suffering and injustice. In Shoshana Felman and Dori Laub's account of Holocaust testimony, the endeavour to bear witness is marked by impossibility. In their well-known statement, the Holocaust is an 'event without a witness', meaning that not only were the bulk of its witnesses exterminated, but the experience traumatically dislocated survivors' memories (Felman and Laub 1991: 80). The paradox of this discourse of trauma as testimony is that the 'truthfulness' of the victim's account lies precisely in its dislocation, evidence that the traumatic subject has 'contaminated' its mode of narration.

The notion that historical trauma induces a crisis of representation has generated prevalent discourses of unrepresentability or inadequacy of representation. The trauma paradigm is indebted to Cathy Caruth's work (1995), itself inspired by Felman and Laub as well as by studies of post-traumatic stress disorder (PTSD). Its widespread influence is evident in scholarly writing that explores how cinematic cultures work through traumatic pasts, often mapping historical trauma onto the exclusive concerns of national identity and the national cinema that is their specialist subject of study.

While recognition of traumatic realities for victims of historical atrocities is undoubtedly important, this book breaks with the trauma paradigm, which it finds problematic for a number of reasons. In its inward focus on victimised subjectivity, trauma reduces the significance of events to the history of specific individuals or a group. This prevents interrogation of the larger issues of *why* those events happened, which would situate them in a longer history of structures of violence. Trauma interprets violence through a subjective logic that can render a conflict's political background unintelligible. Moreover, a PTSD diagnosis can be given to perpetrators, who claim they suffered too. While, as I argue in the chapters to follow, the perpetrator's perspective can be illuminating of the 'atrocity-producing situation', there is a danger that films can assist in the cultural process of turning perpetrators into victims by adopting a post-traumatic mode of narration. The trauma paradigm is further problematic because it expects artworks to reflect a model of traumatised subjectivity, thereby valorising a specific canon of works that 'bear witness' to the 'unrepresentable', as elaborated in Chapter 2.

In the Latin American genre of *testimonio*, we find more politicised notions of testimony as a narrative seeking political justice, denouncing a current oppression or setting straight the official historical record (Yúdice 1996: 44). The book draws on this understanding of testimony as acknowledging histories of violence and countering official and cultural denial about their extent and impact. The literature around this genre also usefully emphasises how *testimonio* requires an interlocutor, in this case, the filmmaker, who helps transmit the account to an audience.

The fact that marginalised voices depend on those in authority to be given a platform forces us to recognise that images and other testimonies don't speak for themselves, despite their apparent immediacy. They depend on rhetorical strategies and delivery contexts: the filmmakers' choices of subject, perspective, aesthetics and intended audience; the circuits of distribution and exhibition, including factors of access and gatekeepers; and audiences, who approach films with their own interpretative choices and unpredictable responses (Hesford 2011; Torchin 2012a). These inform the articulation of truth claims and shape response. Though the Internet has offered new opportunities for distribution and exposure, enabling anyone to upload their films and share them with world audiences, attention still needs to be directed to those films. Often it is a privileged filmmaker who 'speaks' on behalf of an oppressed subject, while self-representation, though 'an important form of self-agency', can be entangled in the same 'global politics of recognition and economic distribution' (Hesford 2011: 155).

Human rights images draw on a powerful but often problematic iconography of suffering intended to move spectators to compassion, giving 'exemplary' victims, such as women, children and the elderly, prominent status. According to Wendy Hesford, the field of human rights has not yet substantially engaged in a critical way with 'the visual rhetorics of recognition, identification, witnessing, and agency that inform its practice' (2011: 191). Her term 'human rights spectacle' comprises a variety of image-making practices, from NGO campaign materials to independent documentary films depicting war, genocide, rape, gender inequality, poverty and illness in other (non-Western) parts of the world. In order to generate viewer sympathy or empathy, Hesford claims, these deploy a visual rhetoric that perpetuates repressive Western ideologies, maintaining power relations over victims in a way that does not benefit them. Western viewers are interpolated as benevolent rescuers, like present-day civilising missions, repeating the colonial view of other societies as repressive or barbaric. Chandra Talpade Mohanty (1988) has criticised the characterisation of Third World women as passive victims waiting to be 'saved'. Hesford makes a similar point about images of endangered children, represented in a way that denies them any agency.

Though they are distinct and developed separately, human rights (which are meant to protect individuals from state power and domination) and humanitarianism (a movement dedicated to alleviating others' suffering) have become increasingly intertwined. Both have been co-opted by powerful states to justify their neo-imperialistic enterprises. As Slavoj Žižek (2005) observes, 'human rights' has become the ideology of military intervention in countries where economic and strategic interests are at stake. Military intervention on humanitarian grounds – labelled 'the military-humanitarian complex' (Douzinas 2007: 64) – results in many further human rights violations, contradicting claims of 'protecting' civilian populations.

Both contemporary politics and human rights representations play on what Luc Boltanski (1999) calls the 'politics of pity', a phrase borrowed from Hannah Arendt (1990), and contrasted by both of them with a more favourable 'politics of justice'. Media images of distant suffering tend to evoke indignation against perpetrators, sympathy with victims and their benefactors, or aesthetic contemplation – positions that, with the exception of aesthetic contemplation (which has other problems), are more or less hypocritical. As Susan Sontag says, 'so far as we feel sympathy, we feel we are not accomplices to what caused the suffering. Our sympathy proclaims our innocence as well as our impotence' (2003: 91). Driven by a fantasy of benevolence, self-piety or even schadenfreude, these forms of compassion create a separation between oneself and the situation of the oppressed; this is why, Sontag suggests, neither compassion nor outrage can direct a course of action.

'Compassion fatigue' is seen as a prevalent phenomenon and problem by charities, filmmakers and journalists, hence the demand for ever more sensationalist images (Moeller 1999). In her work on atrocity photography, Barbie Zelizer makes the point that we rely on the media to bear witness to atrocity, yet its extensive coverage has not prevented atrocities from recurring. The claim that we do not know what is happening cannot be made today, as it was with regard to Nazi atrocities, as evidence is constantly before us through ubiquitous atrocity images (Zelizer 1998: 203). One reason why we react indifferently to contemporary atrocities, Zelizer argues, is the use of the Holocaust as an interpretive framework. Images of contemporary atrocities recycle iconic Holocaust images, such as gaunt faces behind barbed wire and corpses piled in open graves. Repetition of the same sorts of image makes them familiar, no longer shocking, and neutralises our capacity to attend to the specificities of both the Holocaust and current atrocities, which are turned into generic, universal phenomena like '*a* mass burial, *a* shower, *a* survivor' (ibid.: 14, original emphasis). By this means, photography accomplishes the opposite of what was intended, 'atrocity's normalization' (ibid.: 212). What has occurred is a severing of the link between bearing witness and responsibility – we remember in order to forget.

Holocaust imagery has become part of the genre iconography of films about other historical atrocities, as Madeleine Hron (2012) has analysed in her study of Rwandan genocide films. Cinematic images create parallels between different atrocities, recalling Zelizer's statement 'Collectively held images . . . act as signposts, directing people who remember to preferred meanings by the fastest route' (1998: 7). I am struck by how the famous photograph of the boy in the Warsaw Ghetto recurs in films about different contexts; it appears in both *Hotel Rwanda* (2004) and *Waltz with Bashir* (*Vals Im Bashir*, 2008), for example (see

Chapters 2 and 5). Originally a Nazi trophy photograph, it now designates injustices of various kinds, suggesting that images gain as well as lose meaning when they are recirculated. My film analysis points to a different reading of 'signposting', especially in the science fiction films in Chapter 4, where imaginative links are made between normalised present-day forms of violence and past violence. This signposting is often used critically to highlight 'family resemblances' between different types of violence – how they share some features in common, while others are different: similarities rather than equivalences.[1]

Theodor Adorno proclaimed in 1949 that 'to write poetry after Auschwitz is barbaric', a statement often interpreted as a ban on all representations of atrocity (1981: 34). Yet, as he clarifies in a later reformulation in his *Negative Dialectics*, silence is not an alternative. Here, Adorno announces that Hitler has imposed a 'new categorical imperative . . . upon unfree mankind: to arrange their thoughts and actions so that Auschwitz will not repeat itself, so that nothing similar will happen' (1973: 65).[2] This is a perspective that I hold to be compatible with this book's aim of demonstrating that cinema has a role in making ethical comparisons between different historical atrocities. Yet, it is from thinkers like Adorno that we have inherited the belief that popular culture, including cinema, suppresses critical thinking and that film, from the outset, trivialises any serious topic it might approach, thwarting attempts at fostering critical thought and resistance (Adorno 2000: 168). Here is his statement on genocide representation:

> The so-called artistic representation of the sheer physical pain of people beaten to the ground by rifle butts contains, however remotely, the power to elicit enjoyment out of it . . . When genocide becomes part of the cultural heritage in the themes of committed literature, it becomes easier to continue to play along with the culture which gave birth to murder. (Adorno 1982: 312)

The worry is that representations of violence mimic violence, or aestheticise it, transfiguring it into a beautiful and thrilling spectacle. Similar arguments are made about films – that they glamorise atrocity by their meticulous depiction of it, undercutting their own human rights 'message'. What most debates about the aestheticisation of violence miss, however, is that *all* images aestheticise, mediate, transform. A non-aestheticising alternative does not exist; rather, the question is *how* images transform.

Numbing or perverse pleasure, the two types of inappropriate response to atrocity images identified by critics, can result from particular aesthetic choices. Let me demonstrate this through a scene in *The Matrix* (1999), where Neo and Trinity enter a high-security building, dressed in black trenchcoats and sunglasses, armed to the teeth. Firing a torrent of bullets, they stride past security guards, killing hordes of them. This is presented to us through the familiar conventions of screen violence: slow motion, rapid cutting and a rock soundtrack, with little focus on the victims and a great deal of focus on Neo and Trinity's heroism and cool glamour – as Alison Young has pointed out (2010: 26), their violence is justified as morally righteous. All this creates a viewing experience that generates pleasurable identification with violence, so that we do not realise that what we are watching is actually a massacre.

Through their aesthetic strategies, filmmakers make decisions about whose death and suffering should be acknowledged and whose should be permitted or pass unnoticed. Similar strategies are at work in news media, which distinguish between 'worthy' and 'unworthy' victims, the latter being victims of the government's own policies (or their allies) and therefore receiving blander coverage (Herman and Chomsky 2002: lxiii). A case in point is media coverage of the 1991 Gulf War and the censoring of images of foreign civilian casualties in the 'War on Terror', including from drone strikes. As Jean Baudrillard has pointed out, the Gulf War was fought by a US-led coalition using aerial bombardment with computer-generated images of the battlefield, where the 'enemy only appears as a computerised target' (Baudrillard 1995: 62). This aided in the dehumanisation of the 'enemy' not only for combatants but also for the Western public, watching the same images transmitted 'live' on TV news. The ideology of 'clean, technological war' distances viewers from the suffering and promotes the image of a moral and just war.

The Gulf War and subsequent conflicts bear out Paul Virilio's assertion that *'the history of battle is primarily the history of radically changing fields of perception'* (1989: 7, original emphasis) together with links both he and Baudrillard make between war and cinema, making the 'logistics of perception' (ibid.: 4) central to both. In the use of virtual reality environments in operational warplanes, they identified a major feature of the so-called paradigm of 'new war', distinguished from the old war of confrontation between armies, yet which is similar to old colonial wars in its aim of exercising domination over 'the refractory forces on the planet' (Baudrillard 1995: 86).

The electronic battlefield of automated war affords combatants huge psychological distance from those they are maiming and killing. Zygmunt Bauman regards this as an extension of the rational project that included the Holocaust. The architects of the 'Final Solution' had to find ways of overcoming what Arendt called 'that "animal pity by which all normal men are affected in the presence of physical suffering"', namely means of distancing perpetrators from victims so as to facilitate the violence and reduce moral qualms (Bauman 2000: 184). This involved creating techniques of moral indifference, such as distancing perpetrators from the 'face' of their victims through technology and bureaucracy; in this way, causal connections between one's own actions and suffering are hidden.

As a counterpoint, Bauman invokes Emmanuel Levinas's philosophy in which ethical behaviour is elicited by the presence of the face, which conveys a sense of the Other's vulnerability. For Levinas (1969), this ethical obligation emanates from God, a radical alterity ('the altogether-other') that lies beyond the face of the Other yet towards which it gestures. An encounter with the face of the other, therefore, is an embrace of alterity. Yet, even for Levinas, there are those whose alterity has no appeal: the Palestinian has no face, he once suggested in an interview, and therefore their vulnerability does not pose the obligation not to kill (1989: 294). Unlike many other studies of the ethics of spectatorship, this book does not draw on a Levinasian approach. It is more interested in the political contexts through which otherness is *constructed*: how categories of people are othered, so that they may be subjugated and beaten down, or so that their suffering and death become acceptable.

Even films with an explicit human rights agenda can perpetuate indifference, as Elizabeth Goldberg highlights in her study of fiction films that aim to tell 'the truth' about previously silenced histories of oppression. These are films about distant conflicts, privileging the stories of white/Western protagonists, played by Western stars, and what *they* did against the backdrop of collective struggles. Through what Goldberg calls a 'split narrative' and a *Bildungsroman* format, the Western subject is prioritised over other subjects – racial Others, who are perceived as disposable and relegated to the background. For Goldberg, the problem with this genre is not its failure to reflect historical 'truth' but 'its use of the spectacle of tortured bodies within a classic Hollywood structure' that reinforces assumed Western superiority and hegemony (Goldberg 2007: 30).

One of her examples is a scene in *Salvador* (1986), where the protagonist Boyle and another photojournalist, in search of a photo opportunity, ascend a hill where bodies of the disappeared have been unceremoniously dumped. Ostensibly, the film denounces these atrocities, highlighting Boyle's moral awakening and accusations against the US government for its complicity with the repressive regime. Visually, and at the level of the protagonists, however, it confirms an imperialistic logic, depicting the spectacle of dead and dying bodies as the background to the Western characters' quest – these human rights violations being placed, Goldberg claims, in service to the film's genre, not 'as testimonials to their own occurrence' (Goldberg 2001: 259).

REFLECTION ON CAUSES AND CONTEXTS OF ATROCITY

Human rights is a discourse of moral protest. It says: 'That's terrible – we must stop this.' However, for Slavoj Žižek, the SOS call to 'do something' inculcates a false sense of urgency. In this emphasis on immediate action, he reads an anti-theoretical impulse ('There is no time to reflect: we have to act now'). Instead, he suggests, 'there are situations when the only truly "practical" thing to do is to resist the temptation to engage immediately and to "wait and see" by means of a patient, critical analysis' (Žižek 2009: 6). Though the view that sometimes it is better to reflect and do nothing would be anathema to most human rights activists, such reflection might help to strengthen activism.

By reflecting, Žižek means analysing what he calls 'the complex interaction of the three modes of violence': subjective violence (carried out by agents), the symbolic violence of language, and the objective violence of our economic and political systems. 'One should resist', he writes, 'the fascination of subjective violence', that of 'evil' individuals and other clearly recognisable agents, and criminal and terrorist acts, because it is merely 'the most visible' of these three modes (ibid.: 10). A kind of decoy, the spectacle of physical violence can prevent us from thinking about the broader causes and contexts of violence; we do not see the other types of violence because they are so routine and therefore invisible. Indeed, Žižek compares systemic violence to the universe's dark matter – matter that is unseen, but without which the universe would not behave in the way it does.

An anthropologist who has studied political violence, Nancy Scheper-Hughes similarly remarks that an exclusive focus on the physical violence of atrocity is not only voyeuristic but 'misses the point' of 'the larger project of witnessing, critiquing, and writing against violence, injustice, and suffering' (Scheper-Hughes and Bourgois 2004: 1). When violence is regarded as the product of economic, political and social relations, its critique consists in making inequality, exploitation and injustice visible, rather than simply advocating compassion for suffering, tolerance and respect for otherness. In this book, I am interested in how film representation moves beyond an appeal to spectacular violence and icons of victimisation that elicit compassion for an oppressed Other. Although films necessarily foreground subjective violence, they can also allude to other, less obvious types of violence; and the extent to which they connect the three modes of violence determines their complexity. This means remaining alert to other possibilities within films, their ability to trace everyday or systemic violence, or the continuity between that everyday violence and eruptions of direct violence.

A key concern of this book is how films reflect on the ways in which people give their consent to atrocities or become part of systems of violence. Among the thinkers who have given me my bearings in this regard is Hannah Arendt, for whom the 'banality of evil' – a phrase that emphasises the ordinariness of perpetrators, rejecting the idea that they are simply sadistic 'monsters' – was one of the major features and lessons to be drawn from the Holocaust. While atrocity is usually conceived as an abnegation of morality, Arendt highlighted how it is often justified by its perpetrators as a moral act, forming part of socially permissible behaviour under given circumstances. Robert Jay Lifton's term 'atrocity-producing situation', an environment in which brutalities are sanctioned and normalised, aptly encapsulates this alteration of morality. Lifton first elaborated the concept in his study of US Vietnam War veterans and later updated it for the Iraq War (Lifton 1973; Lifton 2004). As colonial processes have been central to fashioning present-day forms of violence, they are prominent in my analysis, forming the paradigmatic atrocity-producing situation.

The imperialist enterprise involved a 'rethinking of the category of the human' (Calhoun 2010: 38). Atrocities were committed against indigenous populations in the Americas, Asia, Africa and Australasia as part of colonial exploitation because they were regarded as lesser humans. As Upendra Baxi points out, this politics of cruelty was consistent with the European Enlightenment tradition in which the French Declaration of the Rights of Man and Citizen (1789) and the US Bill of Rights (1791) were embedded. According to its criteria, the human was defined by 'the capacity to *reason* and autonomous moral *will*', and variously 'excluded "slaves", "heathens", "barbarians", colonized peoples, indigenous populations, women, children, the impoverished, and the insane' (Baxi 2008: 44). Inaugurated by the Universal Declaration of Human Rights (1948), contemporary human rights, in contrast, are defined by their inclusivity, based on values of a common humanity, therefore assuming that all human lives have equal value. Yet, questions of 'who counts as human?' persist, as political exclusions from the ideal of common humanity are all too evident. For example, when the state is the safeguard of its citizens' rights, those who are stateless refugees fall through the net, treated as less than human, as Arendt observed in *The Origins of Totalitarianism* (see Chapter 4).

Another ambiguity is whether states remain beholden to their human rights obligations when they act outside their own territory, including in occupied territory. Consistent with the underlying principle of universality, human rights obligations ought to be applicable across territorial borders (Lubell 2010: 261). Yet when states wage conflicts abroad they regularly flout human rights. Extraterritoriality, the spatial topography of empire, where the same rules and restraints do not seem to apply, will turn out to be a common theme in this book. Such extraterritorial operations have become increasingly significant in the 'War on Terror', yet another fracturing of human rights universality.

A RECONFIGURED FRAMEWORK OF MORALITY AND ETHICS

The terms 'morality' and 'ethics' are often used as synonyms. In this book, however, morality refers to the domain of normative values, manifesting in socially formed laws and codes of conduct.[3] Morality exists in multiple forms and differs from one set of circumstances to another. In contrast, ethics explores the conditions under which morality is constructed under different circumstances; it is a meta-reflection on the moral framework.

Human rights constitute one site in which norms are constructed and enforced, embodying both law and morality. Even when states are in breach of its norms, they tend to deny it in order to maintain their moral standing in the international community, opening up a gap between their stated and their actual behaviour. The contemporary human rights regime comprises not only human rights law (which protects the rights of individuals under a state's authority) but also international humanitarian law (known as the 'law of war', which places restraints on armed conflict – for example, the Geneva Conventions) and international criminal law (which is concerned with crimes against humanity, genocide and aggression). Although they have different origins and purposes, each of these branches of law consists of a similar set of prohibitions, and several acts are the subject of more than one body of law, for example torture and enforced disappearance, as will be seen in chapters to follow. David Scheffer (2006) has proposed the collective term 'atrocity crimes' for a range of large-scale crimes involving a systematic or widespread assault on populations which currently fall under different legal fields, including genocide and crimes against humanity. 'Atrocity crimes' epitomises the definition of atrocity in this book.

As well as offering a rich experience of specific scenarios in which human rights issues are encountered, cinema is another site, beyond the law, in which norms are constructed and reconstructed. I argue that films adopt either a predominantly moral or a predominantly ethical approach in the construction of their cinematic world. For example, they can construct a moral universe in which we give consent to certain kinds of violence, which then become acceptable. Essential to this is their 'structure of sympathy' (a term derived from cognitive theorist Murray Smith), which establishes allegiance with characters, a moral kinship based on 'traits we *wish* or *desire* to possess' (Smith 1999: 218, original emphasis). In this way, films encourage spectators to root for characters and desire particular narrative outcomes. The mainsprings of classic narrative – causality, closure, coherence – often work towards creating a *moral* tale of good and evil which is unsuited to a properly *ethical* treatment of the subject of atrocity. In Chapters 1 and 2, films with tidy resolutions and narrative *teloi* towards moral punishment or redemption are contrasted with films that withdraw from viewers the certainty of a normative moral universe and thereby offer greater space for ethical reflection.

Whereas the endeavours of human rights monitoring and activism lie in checking whether rights are confirmed or denied – 'naming and shaming' offending governments – a shift from a moral to an ethical perspective 'bring[s] to light what their confirmation or denial mean' (Rancière 2010: 68). Although it is usually governments that place orders for heinous policies, ordinary people are also involved, to the extent that we 'assent to them, often by our silence', or support them in other ways, making us 'complicit in what is done in our collective name' (Gregory 2004: 29). This book develops what Nouri Gana calls 'complicity as a locus of analysis and a modality of critique' (2008: 37). It explores how films implicate spectators by 'set[ting] in motion an imaginative and empathizing process through which viewers can determine for themselves the degree to which they might be unwittingly involved as subjects in historical circumstances that might not initially qualify even as objects of remote concern for them' (ibid.: 36). Therefore, it asks how films make us engage with a past (or present) that we didn't think we were part of. How do they invite us to confront the causes and contexts of violence and suffering? How do they build new perceptions or confirm existing ones?

EMBODIED SPECTATORSHIP

As noted earlier, Brechtian aesthetics has predominated as *the* model of ethical or political cinema. Some of the films I discuss contain features that Brecht ascribes to his epic theatre: they offer spectators a different 'picture of the world', make them 'face something', bring them to 'the point of recognition' and turn 'the human' into 'an object of enquiry', rather than taking it for granted (Brecht 1964: 37). However, they rarely break their artifice through self-reflexivity and by no stretch of the imagination can they be thought of as 'Brechtian'. Stylistically, they share affinity with what Brecht called 'dramatic theatre' – in providing spectators with 'sensations', involving us in the 'experience', they engage our emotions and empathy.

Underlying the Brechtian suspicion of emotions is the belief that they passively absorb us in the spectacle. Yet the findings of film theory over the last twenty years suggest that spectatorship is not a passive condition. As Jacques Rancière elucidates in *The Emancipated Spectator*, the spectator is an active interpreter, feeling and understanding, composing their own version of what they see with various elements before them; as spectators, we 'all the time link what we see to what we have seen and said, done and dreamed' (2009: 17). Moreover, new technologies that have emerged over the last two decades have fostered new forms of viewing experience. Laura Mulvey (2006) has even reconsidered her earlier account of spectatorship in the light of DVD technology. With new technologies, the flow of a film can be arrested so that, even when we watch a film that is constructed rather conventionally, we engage with it differently and more actively.

The films discussed in this book are closer to two alternative models of political cinema offered by Rancière and Gilles Deleuze. Rancière defines the political as making a space political that was not before; political art is that which 're-configure[s] the fabric of sensory experience' in order to 'make the invisible visible', disrupt established relations and, conversely, relate what was 'previously unrelated' (Rancière 2010: 140, 141). Rancière is speaking of fictional creations that 're-fram[e] the real' in ways that create 'new forms of perception' of what is given to us *as* the real (ibid.: 141). This encapsulates film's ability to create a shift of perspective: how it can be ethico-political without making overt political statements and make audiences think without telling them what to think.

Deleuze suggests two ways in which cinema provokes thought. Firstly, its images produce a sensory affect that triggers conscious reflection, which then alters how we perceive the images when we revisit them, either during our film viewing or later on, resulting in another 'affective shock' (Deleuze 1989: 161). Secondly, the sheer external affective force of cinematic images is capable of confronting us with what has remained 'unthinkable' and alien to our habitual thought (ibid.: 179). For Deleuze, cinema's affective qualities are what produce reflection and insight. Far from reacting with a 'distanced gaze' at the spectacle, we respond viscerally to cinema's technological stimuli. The film is an 'event', consisting of light, colour (even in black-and-white films, which rely on variations of shade), movement and sound, that acts upon us (Powell 2005: 55).

Although the face in close-up is celebrated for its affective power, Deleuze gives equal prominence to the 'affects of things', such 'the "point" of Jack the Ripper's knife' which is 'no less an affect than the fear which overcomes his features' (1992: 97). Affects also reside in colours; for example, 'the atmospheric colour which pervades all the others' (Deleuze 1986: 118). Drawing an analogy with painting, Deleuze differentiates between what the image represents and the image itself, which possesses its own visceral force (Deleuze 1989: xii; Deleuze 2004: 25). In a self-portrait by Van Gogh, it is the thick brushstrokes, jarring colours and swirling forms that seize viewers, before they react to it as a representation of the artist. Deleuze claims that cinema's movement-images are similarly sensational, not to be confused with the sensationalism of what is depicted.

Deleuze distinguishes clichéd, predictable emotions from affects that arise from 'the unexpected, the unrecognized, the unrecognizable' (2000: 369). Previous discussion has highlighted the play on moral sentiment (the 'politics of pity') as one of the ideological effects of human rights representations, which obtains a further political value in serving to justify foreign policies. This book, therefore, analyses *how* films use emotion, not merely for sentimental function, but also to generate new affects. Indeed, it argues for cinema's capacity to produce new connections and disrupt habitual perceptions, laying the basis for breaking coercive habits of thinking and behaving as part of a collective social transformation.

In its film analysis, this book also draws on the work of scholars who have adapted Deleuze's ideas in inspirational ways such as Daniel Frampton, Laura Marks, Anna Powell and Alison Young, along with other theorists of embodied spectatorship such as Vivian Sobchack and Jennifer Barker, whose conceptual framework is derived from phenomenology. If film provokes thought it is because film itself 'thinks', Daniel Frampton argues in his book *Filmosophy*. Filmmakers make decisions that 'affect our reception of the film; *decisions* that we can understand as the thinking of the film' (Frampton 2006: 117, original emphasis). A film tells us what it 'thinks' about its characters and subjects through choices of framing, editing, colour, sound, camera movement and focus – a form of thinking that we understand affectively. The film's thinking is not reducible to its makers' intentions, however, since the film that filmgoers experience is a mechanical, transsubjective entity that has its own being and becoming. At the same time, the viewer's own affective thinking mingles with the film and shapes their encounter with it, which accounts for the fact that different people can experience the same images in startlingly different ways dependent on how images interact with their own embodied histories and circuit of images they have previously encountered.

As Frampton writes, 'with a greater sense of the thinking that a film can do [and provoke] we can see all sorts of subversions of meanings without resort[ing] to calling them Brechtian devices' (ibid.: 175). The notion of film-thinking gives value to smaller, less bombastic formal gestures, countering the idea that Brechtian self-reflexivity is the only way a film can be thought-provoking. Through this inclusive approach, *all* films can be recognised as 'thoughtful', though some think with greater subtlety than others. Such small subversions are significant, because they exist within the films and anyone can encounter them through attentive viewing.

Although much film criticism tends to privilege the camera, and hence the gaze, 'Film-thinking *inhabits* and *is* its world, rather than simply "looking" at it as the "camera" rhetoric persuades' (ibid.: 99, original emphasis). While our natural human inclination is to place ourselves at the centre of perception, Deleuze highlights how cinema puts 'perception into things' (1986: 81). Cinema shows us objects from perspectives we could never inhabit ourselves. It tears sounds and images from their referents in the real world, and juxtaposes them in impossible or unexpected ways, such as the superimposition of a man inside a beer glass in *Man with a Movie Camera* (*Chelovek s kinoappa-ratom*, 1929). Because cinema frees us from natural perception, it can show us what we overlook in reality, enabling us to notice the unnoticed.

The digital is thought to break the indexical link to the real world or pro-filmic reality, thus engendering, it is alleged, profoundly different relationships between object, image and viewer. Yet sound and vision in film have always been constructed. The alterations of digital imaging affect how we perceive a character or event but so, too, do other cinematic devices such as lighting, colour, composition, editing and sound. Rather than regard the constructed-ness of cinematic aesthetics as less ethical or less 'true', this book highlights the complex negotiation between image and reality. As Frampton writes, 'film *uses* the real; but it takes it and immediately moulds it and then refigures it and puts it back in front of the filmgoer as interpretation, as re-perception' (2006: 4). It creates its own world, a 'cousin' of our reality that allows us to understand that reality differently.

Although cinema is an audio-visual medium, Laura Marks has offered a comprehensive account of it as a multisensory experience by combining phe-nomenological and Deleuzian approaches. Through haptic visuality (vision based on touch) and synaesthesia (perception that mobilises two or more senses simultaneously), film can appeal to touch, smell and taste. Marks's chosen texts are intercultural experimental films that question the visual regis-ter's ability to yield knowledge, often obscuring vision in 'protective gestures toward the people and places they represent' (Marks 2000: 178). In contrast to the objectifying logic of the visual gaze, these 'less ocularcentric ways of seeing' are implicitly more ethical (ibid.: 136). Though Marks is sceptical of mainstream cinema, which she believes presents a commodified version of sensuous knowledge or misguidedly attempts to create 'a total sensory envi-ronment' (Marks 2002: 20), her arguments are relevant in many ways to the films covered in this book. Sensory images trigger and disturb our memories and provoke us to think about the past (and present) in new ways.

For Vivian Sobchack, 'the film experience is meaningful not to the side of our bodies but because of our bodies' (2004b: 60). Her emphasis on the body as the means by which we know and make sense of the world derives from the phenomenologist Maurice Merleau-Ponty. In *The Tactile Eye*, Jennifer Barker has developed Sobchack's insights, foregrounding film's tactile qualities and its ability to summon viewers' own embodied histories as sites of reception and understanding. Our bodily investment in the screen image calls us to ask 'Where are we in this picture?', to place 'ourselves in relation to others and to history' (Barker 2009: 7).

Together, these theorists offer productive ways of exploring how films implicate us in histories we may not have experienced ourselves and point to strategies that address (though do not entirely overcome) the problems of representation outlined above. This book argues that this kind of affective thinking, which immerses us into the image, is a more profound way of understanding than just thinking *about* the issues.

OUTLINE OF THE BOOK

This book is not a survey of films about historical atrocities. Neither is it an empirical study of how real audiences have responded to these films, although it does refer to their reception contexts. Rather, it explores the relationship between spectator and image through an analysis of the images themselves. Every moment on screen is the result of decisions taken by filmmakers and alternative paths not taken, determining the kinds of knowledge about past and present atrocities a film conveys to its audiences and the viewing experiences it creates. Every aesthetic choice is also an ethical choice, the actual counterpart of a potentially infinite set of possibilities.

The purpose of film analysis is to 'reveal the ingredients' that 'made you understand the film in a certain way' (Frampton 2006: 181). In this book, that includes contextual as well as textual details, as films cannot be properly understood without reference to the historical conditions of their production and reception. Having used the films to inform my analysis of broader issues, my aim is to alert readers to potential ways of engaging or interacting with the films when they subsequently view them or others like them. Each chapter deals with the filmic treatment of specific atrocity crimes – torture, genocide, enforced disappearance, deportation and apartheid respectively. The book does not just use films to illustrate these human rights 'issues', but explores how films 'think' about each form of state violence and produce either moral or ethical confrontations with those events through their aesthetic choices. The analyses are intended to be provocative for the purpose of stimulating thought and debate.

Chapter 1 elaborates the book's argument about morality and ethics by discussing documentaries and fictional dramas about torture and the 'War on Terror', including *Zero Dark Thirty* (2012), *Taxi to the Dark Side* (2007) and *Standard Operating Procedure* (2008). It argues that *Zero Dark Thirty* adheres to a moral script about 9/11 and its aftermath, justifying the self-appointed forces of good going over to 'the dark side'. By constructing such a moral universe, the film helps to normalise torture and other illicit practices, making them acceptable. *Taxi to the Dark Side* creates another kind of moral universe, inspiring pity for the dark side's victims and outrage towards the policy's architects. However, *Standard Operating Procedure*, though criticised for its lack of moral perspective, stands out as the most 'ethical' of these films, as it engages us at multiple sensory levels and explores how moral norms are reconstructed in the 'atrocity-producing situation'.

Many people derive their historical knowledge from movies. Chapter 2 addresses this issue through a discussion of fictional films about the Holocaust and the Rwandan genocide. Historical dramas frequently offer up tales of good versus evil that reassure viewers about their moral place in the world, as in the 'one good man' motif exemplified in *Schindler's List*. Though academic criticism has critiqued these tendencies, it also has a predominantly moralistic outlook, preoccupied with taboos and limits. This chapter argues that such moralism, which presents perpetrators as antithetical to everything that we, the viewers, stand for, impedes ethical reflection. Inspired by the philosophy of Hannah Arendt, it attempts to shift the debate by investigating how films enable or prevent insights into how genocide happens through the wider population's complicity. It elaborates Arendt's 'boomerang thesis', which questions traditional interpretations of the Holocaust as a 'unique' event, suggesting links between colonialism, the Holocaust and contemporary atrocities, and applies these insights in its readings of *The Boy in the Striped Pyjamas* (2008), *Hotel Rwanda*, *Sometimes in April* (2005) and *The Night of Truth* (*La Nuit de la vérité*, 2004).

Chapter 3 explores concerns with memory in films about the disappearances in Chile and Argentina, which encompass thrillers, poetic, performative and animated documentaries, and surreal narratives: *Imagining Argentina* (2003), *Chronicle of an Escape* (*Crónica de una fuga*, 2006), *Nostalgia for the Light* (*Nostalgia de la luz*, 2010), *The Blonds* (*Los rubios*, 2003), *Abuelas* (2011) and *Post Mortem* (2010). As these films are aimed at least partly at transnational audiences, the chapter asks how they foster audience identification with memories they have never had. It draws on Michael Rothberg's concept of 'multi-directional memory' to argue that these films contain powerful associations, evoking other histories of the disappeared in ways that disrupt and unsettle the memories we hold as individuals and communities. One of the links it explores is between the Latin American 'dirty wars' and the 'War on Terror', in which enforced disappearance has returned on a global scale.

Whereas the previous chapters are concerned with the multisensory character of spectatorship and response to atrocity images, Chapters 4 and 5 deal with another aspect of our embodied reality: spatial relationships. This part of the book focuses on how different bodies inhabit space, *become* othered and racialised – encounters shaped by colonial histories. Theorists such as Henri Lefebvre (1991) and Doreen Massey (2005) have pointed out that space is socially produced, continually remade and organised according to power structures. In today's world, 'matters of space, territories, borders' remain 'crucial' to 'issues of power' (Rancière 2010: 149). From Michael Shapiro's work (2009), which asserts cinema's ability to map spaces of geopolitical violence, these chapters develop the analytical tool of 'spatial mapping'. Films map and produce space, enter into real spaces and create imaginary ones. In so doing, they can reveal the pervasive character of state violence, providing images of structural violence without the representation of spectacular violence or sentimental affects; instead, viewers are invited to infer their own links from the mise-en-scène.

Science fiction films that have dramatised issues of immigration, detention and deportation form the focus of Chapter 4, which argues that, far from being about the future, science fiction is a historiographic mode which can situate current oppressive realities in a longer history of violence. In their mises-en-scène, *Children of Men*, *District 9* (2009) and *Monsters* (2010) make links between wealthy states' present-day treatment of immigrants and the historical atrocities of the 'War on Terror', Nazi concentration camps and apartheid. Combining location shooting with CGI, these films create a recognisable world, a slightly altered version of our own reality, which provokes us to scrutinise an oppressive geopolitical order. A coda on the science fiction blockbuster *Elysium* (2013), which shares similar features, both reinforces and qualifies the chapter's argument about the genre's critical potential.

Chapter 5 focuses on space as an instrument of everyday violence in the Israeli–Palestinian conflict and explores how the cinematic use of space reveals social divisions and enables us to perceive the conflict differently from how news media present it. It shows how the trauma narrative invoked in *Waltz with Bashir* fits with the dominant perspective on the war, while spatial meanings illuminate the conflict's political and historical background. Those spatial meanings form part of the dramatic intent of fictional films such as *Close to Home* (*Karov La Bayit*, 2005), *Lemon Tree* (*Etz Limon*, 2008) and *Paradise Now* (2005), and various documentaries about the Israel–West Bank wall. In *Waltz with Bashir*, however, they derive from its video game-like portrayal of the war.

In the Conclusion, I recap the book's main insights in the light of *The Act of Killing* (2012), a critically acclaimed documentary about the Indonesian genocide which was released just as this book was being completed.

NOTES

1. The term 'family resemblances', proposed by Wittgenstein (1969) in his study of language, has been applied to similarities between different atrocities by Scheper-Hughes and Bourgois (2004) and Freyenhagen (2013).
2. For elaboration of this aspect of Adorno's thought, see Freyenhagen (2013: 133–61).
3. Distinguishing between morality and ethics is a recognised philosophical practice. This book's distinction is partly inspired by Aaron (2007: 109), who defines morality as 'predefined codes of conduct' and ethics as 'thinking through one's relationship to morality'.

CHAPTER I

Documenting the Dark Side: Fictional and Documentary Treatments of Torture and the 'War on Terror'

Shortly after the 9/11 terrorist attacks, US Vice-President Dick Cheney declared the need for the USA and its allies to work 'the dark side', ushering in an era of globalised torture, rendition and assassinations. This chapter deals with documentaries and fictional dramas that have delved into 'the dark side' of the post-9/11 intelligence world – including *Zero Dark Thirty* (2012), *Taxi to the Dark Side* (2007) and *Standard Operating Procedure* (2008). Each of these three films offers a distinctive perspective on torture and the 'War on Terror', but I argue that *Standard Operating Procedure*, criticised by some for its lack of moral viewpoint, is actually the most ethical of these films.

The Hollywood blockbuster about the hunt for Osama bin Laden, *Zero Dark Thirty*, has also attracted critical controversy, in its case for its apparent endorsement of torture. In the wake of 9/11, debates emerged about the effectiveness of torture in gathering intelligence to prevent future attacks. The capture and killing of bin Laden in May 2011 revived those debates, with Cheney (2011), among others, claiming that the policy of 'enhanced interrogation techniques' that he instigated led to obtaining the name of bin Laden's courier, which in turn enabled the CIA to track down the Al-Qaeda leader. In its narrative *Zero* adheres to the view that torture played a crucial part in locating bin Laden – a view, however, that has been disputed in real life, although the film claims to be 'based on first hand accounts of actual events'. Its screenwriter, Mark Boal, has defended the film on the grounds that it is 'a movie not a documentary', a gesture criticised by Alex Gibney, director of *Taxi*:

> It implies that because 'movies' (unlike Boal, I would include documentaries, for better and for worse, in that category) have an obligation to entertain, they don't have to be nitpickers for accuracy. Yet, on the other hand, Bigelow [Kathryn Bigelow, the film's director] says that this film is

a 'journalistic account'. So which one is it? You can't have it both ways. (Gibney 2012b)

Debates about documentary have tended to revolve around questions of 'truthfulness', questions from which, Gibney suggests, fictionalised 'movies' purporting to be based on historical events are not exempt. In her writing on the documentary filmmaker Errol Morris, Linda Williams has rejected the 'dichotomy of truth and fiction' in these debates, suggesting that 'the choice, rather, is in strategies of fiction for the approach to relative truths' (1993: 20). This book takes as its starting point the view that use of the cinematic medium to articulate historical and political issues is *inherently* transformative, whether in documentary or fiction. Far from a transparent window onto historical and political realities, the art of filmmaking consists in the careful crafting of sounds and images to appeal to spectators' emotions and bodily senses. Therefore, this chapter does not seek to scrutinise 'truth' and 'fiction' in these films, but to shift the debate to the aesthetic choices that lead to either moral or ethical confrontations with historical torture events.

While the terms 'moral' and 'ethical' are often used interchangeably, this book follows a crucial distinction. A moral viewpoint, of which there can be several, expresses normative values about 'right' and 'wrong'. An ethical standpoint reflects on these normative viewpoints and how they are constructed and reconstructed under different circumstances; it is a reflection on morality, revealed from this meta-perspective to be a malleable framework.

In my analysis, I argue that, despite accusations of moral irresponsibility in its account of historical events, *Zero* adheres to a moral script about 9/11 and its aftermath, in which torture and other questionable methods (such as drone strikes and elimination by elite commando squads) are promoted as necessary evils, justifying the self-appointed forces of good going over to 'the dark side' to defeat their enemies. *Taxi to the Dark Side* constructs a different kind of moral universe, focusing on the consequences of 'the dark side' for its victims, inspiring pity for them and outrage towards those who instituted the torture policy. Here, torture is always wrong and, moreover, an ineffective means of intelligence-gathering. *Taxi*'s predominantly moral stance earned it a warm reception among those on the anti-war side of the political spectrum, and it won the 2008 Best Documentary Film Academy Award. However, I also contend that *Standard Operating Procedure* (*SOP*), a documentary that was criticised for its lack of moral perspective, deserves re-evaluation for its exploration of how moral norms are reconstructed in the 'atrocity-producing situation' and its ability to engage us at multiple sensory levels. In my argument, this is where a properly ethical response resides. A term adopted from Robert Jay Lifton (2004), the 'atrocity-producing situation' is an environment in which 'sanctioned brutality becomes the norm' and to which ordinary people are capable of adapting themselves to carry out or give consent to atrocities; the 'War on Terror' is a classic example of such a situation.

The question that drives this discussion of morality and ethics is 'How are we being invited to watch?' While viewers may come to a screening with existing moral viewpoints, affiliated to their social, cultural and political backgrounds, films offer cues for sympathy or allegiance and invite viewers to respond in particular ways. Useful here is Noël Carroll's notion of 'criterial prefocusing', which describes how films make the emotively significant aspects of events and characters stand out for us through narrative structure, dialogue, voiceover narration, sound, lighting and variable framing (Carroll 2010: 6). Through these kinds of technique, films invite the emotional responses that their makers intended us to have – including indignation in response to injustice, admiration of virtue, or disgust towards behaviour regarded as immoral.

However, in this way, films can encourage spectators to accept their moral universe, which may be at odds with their own moral beliefs. In other words, they are capable of manipulating our sympathies and moral judgements. Therefore, it is not just a film's 'accuracy' that we should be worried about but, rather, how it constructs a moral universe through its narrative and aesthetic choices. *Zero*, as a major Hollywood movie, has been more widely seen than other films on the topic.[1] It has the power to create a moral consensus about these events. Importantly, not only does the film create a consensus about a dark past under the Bush administration, it justifies its continuation under a new phase of the 'War on Terror' whose hallmark is targeted killings. My analysis draws attention to the malleability of moral norms as they are constructed and reconstructed in *Zero* and *Taxi* and demonstrates how this malleability is reflected upon in *SOP*.

In order to explore the films' moral and ethical confrontations with post-9/11 events, it is necessary first to consider their political and historical contexts. The chapter, therefore, begins by tracing some of the moral and political discourses around torture; it then analyses how they have been remediated in fictional and documentary treatments.

TORTURE AND THE 'WAR ON TERROR'

Speaking on the NBC television news show *Meet the Press* just five days after 9/11, US Vice-President Dick Cheney employed a metaphor drawn straight from the movies:

> We also have to work . . . sort of the dark side, if you will. We've got to
> spend time in the shadows in the intelligence world. A lot of what needs
> to be done here will have to be done quietly, without any discussion,

using sources and methods that are available to our intelligence agencies, if we're going to be successful. That's the world these folks operate in, and so it's going to be vital for us to use any means at our disposal . . . to achieve our objective. (Cheney 2001)

Invoking the Manichean moral universe of *Star Wars* (1977), his speech positioned the USA and its allies as the forces of good facing an utterly evil enemy and obliged to go over to 'the dark side' in order to defeat it. According to this rhetoric, this new enemy necessitates a new kind of war – a 'War on Terror' – where dirty methods, involving torture, kidnapping and assassinations, are legitimate, their ostensible purpose to prevent the USA from further attacks.

As an initial step, President George W. Bush signed a secret memo on 17 September 2001, the full contents of which remain classified to date, which authorised the CIA to capture and detain suspected terrorists around the world (Scahill 2013: 20). Among the numerous executive orders and memos that followed, a military order of 13 November 2001 enabled any non-US citizen anywhere in the world to be detained indefinitely without trial, apart from by military commissions which do not meet international fair trial standards. This laid the basis for the arbitrary detention of thousands of individuals in Afghanistan and Iraq, as well as for the expansion of the CIA's 'extraordinary rendition' programme. 'Extraordinary rendition' basically means kidnapping and involves the extralegal capture and transfer of prisoners from one country to another. Under this programme, suspects have been clandestinely abducted and flown to CIA 'black sites' and other secret detention facilities around the world, without their fate or whereabouts being disclosed, and away from the scrutiny of international monitors. By acting extraterritorially and collaborating with foreign intelligence agencies, especially in states known for their routine use of torture, the administration aimed to remove prisoners from the protection of US and international laws to sites such as Guantánamo Bay. Chosen for its offshore location in Cuba, the notorious military base is part of a much wider network of 'War on Terror' jails, which has expanded with the complicity of many other countries (including Britain) assisting in prisoner arrest or interrogation, providing refuelling stops for rendition flights and hosting 'black sites' – turning torture and enforced disappearance, even though both are banned under international law, into a globalised system (OSJI 2013).

In international law, torture is forbidden both under the 1949 Geneva Conventions relating to the treatment of prisoners of war and the United Nations Convention against Torture and Other Cruel, Inhuman or Degrading Treatment or Punishment (1984). Under the Bush administration, suspected terrorists were labelled 'unlawful' enemy combatants to exempt them from the protections of the Geneva Conventions (Danner 2004: 105). In the UN

Convention, torture is defined as 'severe pain or suffering' that is 'intentionally inflicted' by a public official (or someone instigated on their behalf) to gain information or a confession, or to intimidate or punish an individual or a third party (UN 1984). The Convention constructs and enshrines a moral standard – that torture is indefensible under any circumstances and against anyone. However, for the Bush administration, this definition of torture was perceived to be adjustable. In keeping with its Latin etymological root meaning 'to twist', torture twists not only bodies but also language, as witnessed in the euphemistic jargon of 'enhanced interrogation techniques', through which administration lawyers sought to give legal sanction to torture, while denying the techniques' status *as* torture (Danner 2004; Mayer 2008; Gregory 2010).

When the photographs from Abu Ghraib prison, Iraq, taken by US military police (MPs) employed as prison guards, were leaked to the media in April 2004, the administration blamed the incidents they showed on the pranks of a few 'bad apples', low-ranking soldiers who were prosecuted and sent to jail. The 'bad apple' narrative suggested that these were isolated incidents, distancing them from official policy. Among the thousands of snapshots of naked Iraqi prisoners hooded and shackled in sexually humiliating poses, lorded over by US soldiers, a few have become notorious: those of Private Lynndie England leading an Iraqi prisoner on a leash, a hooded captive standing on a box in a crucifixion pose (with electric wires dangling from his outstretched arms), and Specialist Sabrina Harman smiling and giving a thumbs-up sign over a dead Iraqi. There are two predominant interpretations of the Abu Ghraib 'scandal'. One domesticates it into US popular culture, locating the source of its cruelty in Internet pornography and campus humiliation rituals (Limbaugh 2004). The other regards it as an instance of exceptional or deviant behaviour, unrepresentative of US values.

However, this is not the first or the last time that the USA has been involved in torture, nor is it an exclusively US story. What happened at Abu Ghraib and other sites is not exceptional but has roots in a much longer history of colonial violence, evoking memories of the British in Kenya, the French in Algeria, the French and the US in Vietnam, US involvement in Latin America, and its history of slavery, lynching and campaigns against Native Americans. In his book *The Colonial Present*, Derek Gregory contends that the 'War on Terror' is nothing 'other than the violent return of the colonial past, with its split geographies of "us" and "them," "civilization" and "barbarism," "Good" and "Evil"' (2004: 11).[2] A phrase that justifies an open-ended war, without temporal or geographical parameters or even clearly defined targets, the 'War on Terror' is also seen by some commentators as filling the US superpower's 'enemy deficit' after the Cold War – recreating a Manichean universe in order to provide a 'license' to expand its global empire (McClintock 2009: 55). The recent wars in Afghanistan and Iraq were both strategically enfolded into the 'War on Terror' – in the case of Iraq, following a spurious link between Saddam Hussein and Al-Qaeda, and his alleged possession of 'weapons of mass destruction'. Similar to the Cold War, these foreign policies seek to preserve US dominance and form part of 'a broader imperial project' of increasing 'its presence and influence in the wider Middle East' (Blakeley 2013: 618).

In Western news media, 9/11 victims are duly mourned, while foreign casualties of the 'War on Terror' are usually hidden from view or masked under the dehumanising imagery and nomenclature of 'terrorists'. As Judith Butler writes, our response to suffering rests upon the creation of certain perceptual frames through which we recognise what is and isn't a grievable life: while some 'ways of framing' 'bring the human into view in its frailty and precariousness', 'allow us to stand for the value and dignity of human life' and 'react with outrage when lives are degraded or eviscerated', others 'foreclose responsiveness' (Butler 2009: 77). In dominant post-9/11 political discourses, 'War on Terror' victims do not appear as grievable lives, only as the faces of terrorists – 'the worst of the worst', to use the epithet with which Bush administration officials famously vilified Guantánamo prisoners. When torture and other brutalities are inflicted against 'evil' people, who are regarded as a threat to lives, they cease to be perceived as horrific; an altered moral universe is ready for its cinematic remediation.

ZERO DARK THIRTY AND OTHER FICTIONAL TREATMENTS OF TORTURE

In their book *Screening Torture*, Michael Flynn and Fabiola F. Salek remark upon a post-9/11 Hollywood trend of cultivating identification with torturers, rather than with their victims. The administration of torture is viewed as necessary and just in films like *The Dark Knight* (2008), or as lacking long-term negative consequences in films like *V for Vendetta* (2005). In Hollywood movies, torture has become professional and efficient (since it is applied selectively and is always effective), in support of 'the myth that torture leads to truthful confessions' (Flynn and Salek 2012: 10). In Flynn and Salek's reckoning, 'these films transmit the concept that torture can be absorbed by civil society, that the consequences for the victims, the perpetrators and the system are insignificant' (ibid.: 12).

Yet perhaps this trend is not as novel as it appears, for it slots into a moral universe familiar to Hollywood filmgoers. As Alison Young writes of Hollywood film violence in general, 'the violence of wrong-doing is wrong, whereas the violence which responds to wrong-doing is righteous' (2010: 24). When carried out against villains, violence is understood as 'retribution', 'punishment' and 'heroism', which makes it seem necessary and admirable, unfettered by legal restraints. Films typically establish a classic binary between 'good guys' and 'bad guys', but even morally and legally compromised heroes, who temporarily go over to 'the dark side', can 'win our admiration because they [ultimately] do the right things' (Carroll 2010: 17).

As Lina Khatib notes, prior to 9/11, Islamic fundamentalism already occupied the place of the villain in Hollywood's imagination of the fight between 'good' and 'evil', East and West, where, 'in contrast to the degeneracy of the Arab/Muslim/fundamentalist Other, the United States stands superior, morally right and unbeatable' (Khatib 2006: 166). Despite some initial trepidation (including awareness of racial stereotyping), post-9/11 film and television have resurrected this characterisation. In TV shows such as *24* (2001–10) or *Spooks* (2002–11), the heroes are intelligence agents pursuing suspects who are often, but not always, Muslims, and willing to torture them in the name of national security. Spectators are encouraged to 'approve' of their use of torture because of the need to extract intelligence swiftly under an immediate, dire security threat: a ticking-bomb scenario. As several commentators have observed, the ticking bomb is a rhetorical device employed to justify torture, yet there is no evidence of imminent terrorist attacks having been prevented by using torture in real life (Blakeley 2011). The idea of the ticking bomb is given dramatic form in *24*'s narrative structure: each season follows a day in the life of Counter Terrorist Unit agent Jack Bauer, and each episode narrates the events of one hour, while an on-screen countdown reminds us of Bauer's 'race against the clock' (Prince 2009: 239).

Although they often show the tortured writhing in agony and screaming, cutting to the wincing reactions of onlookers to confirm the painful spectacle, these fictional representations do not tend to linger on the phenomenon. They deploy a conventional cinematic iconography of torture that emphasises immediate, stereotypical effects, such as convulsions from electro-shock, not effects that take hours to develop or whose signs are not obvious.[3] As Chuck Kleinhans (2009) suggests, action drama's kinetic pace 'allows the audience to recognize, experience, and quickly move on past the torture event'. In other words, the event becomes an 'action-image' (Deleuze 1986) that extends into fast movement rather than unfurling into the duration of a critical image that might implicate the audience, allow them to absorb the painful experience, and ethically confront the consequences and contexts of torture.

'War on Terror' interrogators have been known to turn to films for inspiration and guidance; *24* was regular viewing at Guantánamo Bay, while *The Battle of Algiers* (*La battaglia di Algeri*, 1966), a film about the counter-insurgency war in Algeria which showed French paratroopers using torture against the guerrilla movement FLN, was screened at the Pentagon (Kaufman 2003). The resurgent interest in this film, made by Italian neo-realist director Gillo Pontecorvo in collaboration with former FLN military chief Saadi Yacef, is particularly significant as it acknowledges similarities between the colonial situation of the French in Algeria and recent military occupations, especially in Iraq. However, for the US military its interest mainly lay in its illustration of the benefits of torture in intelligence-gathering. Although this might seem at odds with its other status as a revolutionary training text, *The Battle of Algiers* is similar to *24*, and (as we will see) *Zero Dark Thirty*, in that its torture images are embedded within a narrative structure that shows torture is effective: the torture of an informer is shown to lead the paratroopers to guerrilla leader Ali La Pointe's hideout, enabling them to win the Battle of Algiers, although not the Algerian War itself.

Among post-9/11 fiction films, only a few stand out for their anti-torture stance. One is the Hollywood movie *Rendition* (2007), loosely based on the case of Khalid el-Masri, who was subjected to extraordinary rendition after a CIA mix-up regarding his name (which was similar to that of a suspected terrorist named al-Masri). One narrative strand follows a pregnant mother, Isabella, as she tries to track down what has happened to her husband, Anwar, an Egyptian-American chemical engineer, who has been rendered to a secret prison, where he is brutally tortured on behalf of the USA by the Egyptian secret police. Another thread focuses on the moral conversion of CIA agent Douglas Freeman, whose role is to observe the torture. The film constructs the moral viewpoint that confessions extracted under torture tend to be false. Attesting to Anwar's innocence, Freeman quotes lines from Shakespeare's *Merchant of Venice* ('I fear you speak upon the rack where men enforced do speak anything'). He disobeys his superiors' orders and smuggles Anwar out of prison. *Rendition* encourages us to regard Freeman as a benevolent hero who makes the right moral choice – another clue can be found in his name – in contrast to a corrupt US administration.

The Bollywood thriller *New York* (2009) evokes sympathy with the plight of thousands of Muslims submitted to racial profiling and ill-treatment as 'suspected terrorists' after 9/11. It portrays the breakdown of the detainees' subjectivity through interrogation and the way that US reaction to 9/11 has itself spurred radicalisation into terrorism. It was particularly well received in the Middle East, where Bollywood has been popular for decades. However, *New York* – like *Rendition* – creates moral closure on this painful topic, with a final caption stating President Barack Obama's intention to close the Guantánamo Bay facility, as if that were the end of the story.

Though the Obama administration has distanced itself from 'War on Terror' rhetoric, its security policies form a continuity with, and even an intensification of, the precedent set by the Bush years. Torture techniques and CIA secret prisons may have been banned, but indefinite detention of suspected terrorists has been extended to US citizens, rendition has not been outlawed, and the assassination programme using drones and special forces (also initiated by Cheney) has been expanded. So far, the era has produced two significant new representations of the post-9/11 intelligence world, though both retain essential characteristics of torture as mainstream entertainment. One is the TV series *Homeland* (2011–), where the focus is on a CIA officer facing an 'enemy within', an ex-soldier who has been held captive by Al-Qaeda and who may now constitute a security threat; Obama has declared it to be among his favourite TV shows (Banham 2012). The other is *Zero Dark Thirty*, which, as I argue below, aims to create a moral consensus about this dark chapter of US history.

Zero opens without visuals, just audio that immerses its audience in the sounds of 9/11 victims and rescue workers. The black screen indexes the traumatic nature of these events as resistant to cinematic representation. The film then cues to 'two years later', with a suspect named Ammar being tortured in a CIA 'black site'. The opening soundscape of 9/11 victims primes us to perceive him as a barbaric enemy guilty of helping to plan the attacks, and serves to dissipate moral anxiety about his torture. Waterboarded, forcibly led around like a dog, and confined to a small box, he surrenders information about Osama bin Laden's courier that ultimately leads the protagonist, Maya (who, as in *Homeland*, is a female CIA agent), to discover bin Laden's hideout. Maya can safely take off her hood during interrogation because Ammar will *never* be set free. Chained to the ceiling, covered in his own filth, and subjected to acts of naked bodily humiliation, he is framed as a dehumanised monster. While the dehumanisation is part of the torture, ostensibly to reduce him to a state of helplessness so that he gives up the information, he is 'criterially prefocused' for us not as suffering an injustice (ill-treatment under custody), but as inherently physically and morally disgusting, as underscored by a shot of Maya covering her nose as she enters the locked shed that serves as his cell. We are not invited to perceive torture as an illegal act, just an extreme method, as the Bush administration's jargon of 'enhanced interrogation techniques' would have us believe.

In these opening scenes, Maya's partner Dan, a bearded, seasoned interrogator, leads the interrogations. Together, they form a double act, making Maya look relatively 'clean', since Dan is the one who does the 'hard stuff'. Indeed, throughout the film, Maya never directly tortures anyone, although she orders others to. Legally speaking, this implicates her in a crime, yet the film does not expose it for our moral judgement.

Carl Plantinga has suggested distinctions between 'allegiance' (allying with and rooting for particular characters), 'sympathy' (care and concern for those in danger or suffering from an injustice) and 'liking' (prompted by traits of similarity, affiliation or attractiveness). Among these, allegiance represents 'a deeper and more abiding psychological relationship with a character' (Plantinga 2010: 42). These distinctions are crucial to *Zero*'s effort to make us bond with protagonists involved in insalubrious practices. It encourages us to root for Maya, a woman in a male-dominated intelligence world, who, despite her pale, delicate features, is depicted as smart and determined, and deserving of our admiration and hence our allegiance.

Meanwhile Dan, although portrayed as a torturer, is a likeable character, switching from his tough-guy persona to joking and sharing fruit juice and cigarettes with Ammar. In later scenes, he further transforms into a clean-shaven, suited official at the CIA's Virginia headquarters. However, the film does not generate anxiety about the ambiguities of Dan's character; rather, it uses his likeable traits to cement allegiance with his 'side'. It would have our 'liking' for him intertwine with our knowledge that he is a torturer without inducing any unsettling effects (which is very different, as we will see, from *Standard Operating Procedure*'s treatment of torturers).

Zero is set in multiple locations, making use of titles with real place names in an attempt to ground its depiction in history. The majority of the drama takes place in Pakistan, where Maya has a desk at the US embassy and where bin Laden's hideout is eventually found. Among other locations are CIA 'black sites' (including a shipping container in Poland), military bases and detention centres in Afghanistan, and the CIA's US headquarters. Evoked through the film's global settings, the global torture network is presented as tackling Islamic fundamentalism, a global evil. *Zero* reinforces 'the myth of a unified Islamic fundamentalist world' (Khatib 2006: 175) through its portrayal of various terrorist attacks – such as the 7/7 London bombings, the Islamabad Marriott Hotel bombing, and 9/11 itself – as part of one global conspiracy. Linking together sporadic attacks in different locations gives the impression of a single group behind them, lending moral force to the administration's position that the USA is waging an ongoing war with a ruthless enemy.

At the CIA station at the US embassy in Islamabad, faces of suspects are plastered on the noticeboard, each one unequivocally framed as an evil terrorist. Boundaries between 'us' and 'them' are reinforced by representing the world outside the enclave of the embassy as a hostile environment. Through the windows, Maya and other CIA staff stare at protesters bearing banners condemning 'American terrorism' after their boss's name is leaked in a lawsuit brought by a drone attack victim's family. As presented in the film, the demonstrators are threatening, potentially violent terrorists filled with anti-American sentiment. There is no sense that protest against the drone policy could be justified, though reports have suggested that drone strikes routinely kill substantial numbers of civilians (Benjamin 2013; Scahill 2013). In May 2012, the *New York Times* reported that all males of combatant age within the strike zones are regarded as legitimate targets, 'unless there is explicit intelligence posthumously proving them innocent' (Becker and Shane 2012), an extraordinarily dehumanising formulation that calls into question the strikes' precision calculation and highlights the lack of a clearly defined enemy: one is identified as a terrorist simply by association or by one's neighbourhood, revealing drone warfare as a means of terrorising civilian populations among whom 'terrorists' are thought to be living.

Ammar reveals the crucial lead to bin Laden over lunch, which Maya and Dan tactically present to him as a reward for information he ceded earlier under duress and which he cannot remember; he believes he has already imparted key details and therefore gives them more. Although not actually involving torture, the scene is pivotal to the film's crediting of torture as the source of intelligence that led to bin Laden, contrary to the US Senate Intelligence Committee's findings that intelligence work other than torture was more significant (Pilkington 2012). Later, the film presents Ammar as having offered this information as a consequence of torture methods rather than some other cause, which prompts Obama's officials to doubt it and demand further evidence. Contrary to its record with other targeted killings, the new administration is shown requiring careful and precise corroboration about the target before launching an attack. The other reason it gives for its scepticism is memories of false intelligence of 'weapons of mass destruction' (WMD), which led to the Iraq War.

Zero might, therefore, be seen as morally recuperating the CIA's image following its involvement in shady torture practices and overcoming the bad WMD precedent. Indeed, a memo approved for release in April 2013, revealing details of the agency's requested changes to *Zero*'s draft screenplay, illuminates the CIA's influence over the film and the screenwriter's readiness to alter plot details to portray the agency in a positive light; in exchange, the CIA gave him classified information on the bin Laden operation (Chen 2013). Like *24*, *Zero* features heroes who temporarily go over to 'the dark side' in order to do 'good'. At no point does Maya show any doubt about her mission: she is 100 per cent certain of the reliability of her intelligence; she never makes any mistakes. The plot is driven by a moral motor in which the injustice of the 9/11 attacks and deaths of 3,000 civilians recalled in the opening is redressed through CIA investigation and torture and, finally, the capture of bin Laden. Emphatically, Maya not only wants him captured but dead. The retributive logic of torture and assassination is fully consistent with *Zero*'s moral outlook – the sequence of injustice, revenge and restoration.

The raid on bin Laden's compound is finally carried out as a joint operation between the CIA and US Navy Seals in stealth helicopters, hence the title, 'zero dark thirty', which refers to the early hours after midnight when the mission took place as well as the darkness that shrouds the entire enterprise. The film thus attempts to create a consensus on the Bush years, suggesting that questionable methods were used but that they gave valuable intelligence without which 'the greatest manhunt in history', as billed on the film poster

– the search for bin Laden, *the* worst of the worst – would never have been concluded. Moreover, the mission's success acts as a validation of the Obama administration's emphasis on targeted assassinations, making *Zero*, which is as much about the present as it is about the past, a standard bearer for this policy.

However, this attempt at consensus is complicated by the fact that the film does not give a sense of elevation or joy when justice is restored. At the end, Maya boards a military aircraft, which has been specially hired for her. As she is the only passenger, the pilot asks for her destination. The question hovers over the film's exquisite last shot: Maya's tear-stained face as she realises she has nowhere to go. Nonetheless, her display of sensitivity is entirely self-preoccupied, focusing on the sacrifices *she* has made, having devoted herself to a ten-year search to the exclusion of everything else; we are made to feel sorry for *her*, not for the countless lives destroyed by her methods. The ending does not alter the film's fabricated moral universe, which effectively normalises torture and other extrajudicial measures.

TAXI TO THE DARK SIDE: A DOCUMENTARY IN THE MORAL MODE

The documentaries *Taxi to the Dark Side* and *Standard Operating Procedure* might be seen as an antidote to Hollywood's fictions. However, I would argue that they are intended to work on their viewers emotionally, in a similar way to fiction. Their filmmakers understand that 'issues' alone do not appeal to audiences; therefore, they arrange their material in the form of compelling stories, structure their narratives around popular genre motifs, and reinforce their arguments with emotion-building musical scores, in the hope of attracting viewers who might not otherwise watch such films. In documentary, the compelling story is often found at the end of the production process, in the editing – like 'a screenplay in reverse' (Gibney 2012a). It is, therefore, predominantly through editing that moral and ethical perspectives emerge.

Documentary theorists such as Bill Nichols insist on distinctions between documentary and fiction on the grounds that the documentary gaze is directed at the historical world in which we live and the real people in it, rather than a world imagined by its creators. Yet, though documentaries feature real social actors, the latter are *selected* and *cast* in the films and we engage with them as characters. Documentaries have absorbed fictional conventions; conversely, fiction films have appropriated 'truth'-telling conventions associated with documentary, such as handheld camera, location shooting and natural lighting (techniques that do not themselves guarantee truth but rather stem from the technical constraints of early documentary filmmaking). Documentary and fiction might be plausibly regarded as two forms that have segued into each other.

For Nichols, film style is 'intimately attached to the idea of a moral point of view' (1991: 80). He proposes what he calls an 'axiographics' of documentary, by which he means the values inscribed through a film's spatial organisation, including the filmmaker's presence or absence within the image, the camera's distance from its subject, and the acoustic layering of on- or off-screen voice and sound (ibid.: 77). All of this privileges the observational aspect of filmmaking. The observational documentary values that Nichols espouses are partly redundant to the documentaries considered here, which record their events retrospectively, making extensive use of archival images created by others, along with dramatic reconstructions and computer animation.

A US documentary made in association with the Discovery Channel, *Taxi* tells the story of Dilawar, a 22-year-old Afghan taxi driver, apprehended as a suspected terrorist and detained at Bagram military base, where he was tortured and died of his wounds. From its opening, it 'criterially prefocuses' Dilawar as an innocent victim. A relative gives a character portrait of him as 'a good and honest man'. The film lingers on family photographs, bringing Dilawar's young face close up to the sound of doleful music that underscores the poignancy of his untimely death. The title credits appear over images of a taxi steering its way across the dusty plains: the film's first reconstruction. With interior shots that place us inside the taxi, the film draws the audience into the situation of its central character. 'On December 1st 2002, Dilawar, a young Afghan taxi driver, took three passengers for a ride. He never returned home,' Gibney's voiceover declares, before the graphics configure into the film's title, signifying the tragic collision between Dick Cheney's post-9/11 remark about 'work[ing] the dark side' and the story of this young man.

Following a murder mystery format, the film charts the circumstances of Dilawar's arrest on false charges of firing rockets at US bases. He was turned in by an Afghan militiaman who, it later transpired, had carried out the attacks himself. Within five days of his imprisonment, Dilawar died, having been chained to the ceiling and repeatedly beaten. His death swiftly followed that of another prisoner and was brought to light when *New York Times* journalist Carlotta Gall tracked down Dilawar's family and found a pathology report in which the cause of his death was stated to be homicide, contrary to the initial press release, which declared that both prisoners had died from natural causes.

The film's moral perspective is evident in its use of dramatic contrast between light and dark and repetition as a narrative device. Unlike most of the other interviewees, who are filmed in brightly lit homes or offices, the interviewed military police and interrogators from Bagram are spot-lit in the darkness of a studio, giving a feel for the moral darkness surrounding the prisoner deaths. One of several recurring images established early on is a photograph of Dilawar on the day of his arrest, standing against a height chart with a placard displaying his prisoner number – a framing that we instantly recognise for a 'suspect'. Another is MP Sergeant Thomas Curtis's sketch illustrating how Dilawar was cuffed to the ceiling to deprive him of sleep – a sinister hangman motif that the film accentuates by reversing it out on a black background. These images are repeated with intensifying moral and affective charge, as viewers accumulate more knowledge of the injustice of his imprisonment and death.

Taxi constructs the post-9/11 intelligence world as morally flawed by portraying Dilawar as 'The Wrong Man' – a title given to a section of the film, highlighting, like the 1956 Hitchcock movie, a case of mistaken identity. Later, autopsy photographs from the coroner's inquest are added to its montage, displaying serious injuries to Dilawar's legs from repeated beatings, apparently a standard method to control prisoners even though he was already shackled. In her writing on documentary ethics, Vivian Sobchack has claimed that, in documentary, death is 'experienced as real – even when not as graphically displayed as it often is in fiction', and therefore requires justification when shown (2004a: 241). By introducing these photographs of the dead man into its narrative sequence, *Taxi* saturates them with a pathos that they lacked for those who took them, since they were created as a military record. They confirm that this was a life, restoring what Butler calls a 'quality of grievability'.

To show how torture was justified as a policy, *Taxi* focuses in detail on official memos redefining and implicitly condoning its use, 'follow[ing] the paper trail all the way up to the White House' (Crowdus 2008: 30). It identifies Cheney as 'the primary architect of the new policy' with a clip from the

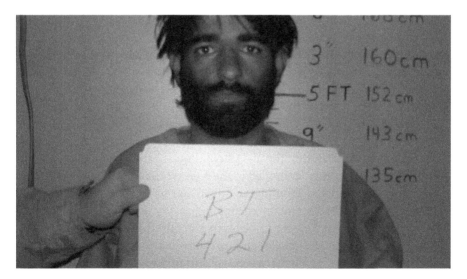

Figure 1.1 *Taxi to the Dark Side* highlights Dilawar's official framing as a 'suspect' and exchanges this with other frames that present him as an innocent whose torture and untimely death is a great injustice.

speech he gave on *Meet the Press*, and features interviews with John Yoo, a lawyer in the Department of Justice, who is named as the torture policy's 'chief draftsman'. Memos written by the administration's lawyers attempted to redefine what counts as torture so as to permit practices such as waterboarding, hooding, stress positions, nudity and sexual humiliation. For example, an August 2002 memo for Alberto Gonzalez, Counsel to the President, defined torture as the deliberate intent to inflict pain equal to that 'accompanying physical injury, such as organ failure, impairment of bodily function, or even death', and 'prohibits only extreme acts' – a phrase that *Taxi* emphasises in close-up in order to show how it legitimated 'lighter' techniques that, nevertheless, are lethal when used together or repeatedly, as it suggests happened to Dilawar.

Unlike the interrogation scenes in mainstream fiction, *Taxi* features a stylised black-and-white re-enactment of a torture scene that attempts to convey the altered states caused by techniques such as sleep deprivation, isolation, sensory deprivation and stress, designed to break down detainees. It is based, according to the film's titles, on the Guantánamo Bay interrogation log for 9/11 suspect Mohammed al-Qahtani. An actor plays al-Qahtani, subject to sexual humiliation by a female interrogator, who invades his space and whispers into his ear 'Your mother is a whore', the words literally floating on screen. Other acts of humiliation include performing 'dog tricks', which the film compares with the photograph of Lynndie England from Abu Ghraib, and being injected with fluid and forced to wet himself. The film does not invite viewers' moral opprobrium for a 'terrorist'. Stroboscopic lighting together with a repetitive melody in this sequence creates startle effects – what the cognitive theorist Murray Smith (1995) calls 'autonomic reactions' – that simulate torture conditions, including temporal distortions. Unlike *Zero*, *Taxi* encourages spectators to imagine what it is like to be subject to these dehumanising procedures. The screen's bright glare provokes empathic or mirror reactions, as we are invited to think and feel about how a prisoner deals with his bodily intimacies exposed to constant surveillance.

Taxi invokes experts such as historian Alfred McCoy, author of *A Question of Torture*, who declares that the al-Qahtani interrogation contains the 'entire genealogy' of CIA torture, compiled in the *Kubark Counter-intelligence Manual* (1963) and disseminated around the world during the Cold War. McCoy explains how the CIA became interested in sensory deprivation experiments by Canadian professor Donald O'Hebb that involved placing volunteers into a cubicle, wearing goggles, gloves and earmuffs to block their senses. O'Hebb found that psychosis could be triggered within forty-eight hours, and the effects could be 'more intolerable' than the direct infliction of pain. In conjunction with this, the film places before us official footage from Guantánamo in which the jumpsuited, gloved and earmuffed detainees are bracketed in such a way that they don't obviously appear to be in pain. When attuned to the embodied form of perception that the film fosters in us, however, we become aware of the possibility of an attack being inflicted on sensory receptors with the aim of breaking down detainees. Through this editorial juxtaposition, the film changes the original meaning of official images connoting a power spectacle of subdued 'evil-doers'.

Throughout, *Taxi* makes extensive use of press images and other archival video and photography. A section entitled 'The Worst of the Worst' begins with a montage of press statements by US government leaders. 'These are among the most dangerous, best-trained, most vicious killers on the face of the earth', declares Donald Rumsfeld. 'They're terrorists, they're bomb makers, they're facilitators of terror, they're members of Al-Qaeda, the Taliban,' adds Cheney, while Bush concludes: 'The only thing I know for certain is that these are bad people.' Juxtaposed with the film's other images, such as military footage of suspects being captured and hooded by US forces in Afghanistan, the leaders' portentous speeches become incriminating evidence of flows of communication from the highest in the administration to interrogators and soldiers on the ground, shaping their perceptions of the enemy as barbaric and evil.

Dilawar's capture along with the three passengers who accompanied him on that fateful taxi ride is illustrated by a dramatically lit photograph of four blindfolded Afghan captives, their hands bound behind their backs, crouching in the sand and surrounded by US soldiers, who cast ominous shadows: a composition of moral protest against injustice which forms one of the film's publicity images. It is not a photograph of this particular incident, yet it is not dismissed by us as 'fake', since it is representative of Dilawar's situation – just as Dilawar is representative, cast among the many thousands arbitrarily detained and interrogated under the aegis of the 'War on Terror' whose fate may be glimpsed through his, countering constructions that vilify them all as 'evil people'.

Ultimately, however, *Taxi* settles for a 'soft' liberal outrage against torture, with a coda featuring Gibney's father, Frank B. Gibney, a navy interrogator during the Second World War and the Korean War, who declares his loss of faith in 'the American government' when the highest officials not only 'countenance' but also 'advocate torture'. He declares: 'All through World War II and the Korean War . . . we had the sense that we were on the side of the good guys.' The film's ending restates ideas of good and evil with this benevolent interrogator's moral message that 9/11 has corrupted America, endorsing its exceptionalist myth and serving to contain the events within an isolated chapter of history. For a more complex treatment of these torture events, we need to turn to *Standard Operating Procedure*.

Figure 1.2 A photograph of Afghan captives provides a composition of moral protest against injustice in *Taxi to the Dark Side*.

STANDARD OPERATING PROCEDURE: A DOCUMENTARY WITHOUT A 'MORAL CENTRE'?

Released by Sony Pictures Classics, *Standard Operating Procedure* (*SOP*) focuses entirely on the Abu Ghraib scandal and its 'bad apples'. It has not received major plaudits like *Taxi*, but has generated much critical debate. Its director, Errol Morris, is renowned for his innovative, postmodern approach, but many critics have found his aesthetic style problematic for this brutal subject matter. One of the most damning responses has come from Bill Nichols (2010), who upbraids Morris for failing to determine responsibility for the Abu Ghraib atrocities and taking 'the sting from terrible images that had shocked the world by . . . fetishizing them' in the film's reconstructions.[4] Morris's non-judgemental approach, he remarks, may have worked in some of his previous films, but is misplaced here, seeming to condone the perpetrators' behaviour, or lessen its evil. Just as the guards portray their role as 'softening up' detainees prior to their interrogation – that is, as not carrying out the real torture that, they claim, happened during interrogations with the CIA and military intelligence – so, Nichols argues, the film aims to 'soften up' its viewers to sympathise with perpetrators in their 'unfortunate plight as scapegoats'. Thus, he accuses Morris's film of lacking the 'moral center' exhibited by *Taxi*.

Likewise, Thomas Austin has criticised *SOP* for failing to conform to the 'politics of pity', the conventional forms of spectator response to distant suffering theorised by Luc Boltanski, which revolve around pity for victims, sympathy with their benefactors and outrage towards perpetrators. This is what, in his view, compromises the film's 'moral and political' potential (Austin 2011: 344). However, as Austin and Nichols are both exclusively preoccupied with the film's *moral* framework (or lack thereof), they miss the essential *ethical* dimension opened up through its aesthetic choices.

Certainly, *SOP* does not offer viewers a secure higher moral ground, as underscored by the absence of guiding voiceover narration and lack of external authorities; neither the forensic expert Brent Pack nor Tim Dugan, the civilian interrogator from the private firm CACI, who appear in the film alongside the 'bad apples', qualify as providing this moral viewpoint, since Pack was involved in the trial and demonstrates a flawed perspective, while Dugan was part of the interrogations, also gesturing to the murky role of private contractors (see Singer 2004).

Nor does *SOP* provide the catharsis of moving beyond events through a heroic redemptive figure, like the 'good' interrogator represented by Gibney's father in *Taxi*. Joe Darby, the soldier who turned in the photos to the military authorities (but not to the media), is noticeably absent. Morris interviewed him but edited him out of the final film. Beginning with a letter that Darby signed as a 'Concerned MP' and submitted with CDs of the incriminating photos, this interview appears as a 'deleted scene' on the DVD release, and in it Darby claims that the activities were confined to a few people (whom he names in his letter), that they should be punished and that this shouldn't go any further. In contrast, the film instructs us that the activities were not confined to this group, more was happening than is shown in the photos, and this is worthy of exposure.

Unlike *Taxi*, *SOP* does not provide an overview of the political context and chains of responsibility to the Pentagon and White House.[5] Rather than blaming the 'bad apples' – who have, already, been blamed – or naming and shaming those who set policies, *SOP* captures the subjectivity of soldiers for whom torture was not simply a policy but a practice that came to be accepted as the norm or 'standard operating procedure'. In its invitation to viewers to consider the subjective dimensions of the 'atrocity-producing situation', it is more complex and ethical (rather than merely moral) than either *Taxi* or *Zero Dark Thirty*.

Moreover, *SOP* is alone among documentaries on the subject – including Rory Kennedy's *Ghosts of Abu Ghraib* (2007) – in questioning the Abu Ghraib photographs' status and function as evidence. As Susan Sontag writes, 'the very notion of atrocity, of war crime, is associated with the expectation of photographic evidence' (2003: 74). A photograph is an indexical trace of the events it records, yet it remains ambiguous, offering partial and selective knowledge; it is not merely a case of 'seeing is believing'. While the photographs *did* serve an important purpose in revealing torture and abuse to the public, 'they prevented people from looking further, oddly enough,' states Morris (Bloom 2008: 11). As Specialist Megan Ambuhl, one of the 'bad apples' interviewed in the film, puts it, 'the pictures only show you a fraction of a second. You don't see forward and you don't see backward. You don't see outside the frame.' This undercuts the photograph's testimonial claim: it only shows you a frozen action; it does not capture the event. Rather, it is full of gaps.

In its three main levels of narration – interviews, photographs and reconstructions – the film recontextualises the photographs and endows them with new possibilities to provoke. Despite the absence of an overarching moral framework, the editing and music provide cues for response to the images, telling us what the filmmakers want us to think and feel about them. Often there is a counterpoint between the image and various layers of soundtrack, including Danny Elfman's musical score, which repeats its melody with variations 'to beckon the viewer to slow down to look at and emotionally react to . . . the Abu Ghraib photos' (Lesage 2009). The photos are used as counterpoint to interview testimony or, alternatively, the interviews 'complicate' what the photos seem to show. Austin remarks that 'there is no consistent epistemological hierarchy governing [these] two sets of sources' (2011: 349), but this deliberately throws viewers upon their own imaginative resources to feel their way through the film rather than relying on a fixed moral framework.

Interrotroning the 'bad apples'

Unlike other documentaries, where interviews are edited to converge into a main argument about events, *SOP*'s interviews with MPs (Sabrina Harman, Lynndie England, Megan Ambuhl, Jeremy Sivits, Javal Davis and others), military and civilian interrogators, and Brigadier General Janis Karpinski illuminate their different viewpoints. This allows the film to explore the situation's complexity and its characters' moral gradations, portraying them as neither wholly 'bad' nor wholly 'good'. Interviewees face the camera in an artificially lit studio backdrop, removed from both military context and their own social milieu – a strategy that Nichols has criticised as decontextualising. This set-up, however, places the audience in the position of a jury, evaluating for themselves the interviewees' stories.

Crucial here is Morris's use of the 'interrotron', a device he invented so that, rather than being present in the same room, his image can be beamed like a teleprompter to his interviewees, allowing them to look simultaneously at him and the camera. Through the direct gaze it facilitates, it constructs a startling intimacy between viewer and interviewee. We tend to associate a direct gaze, whether on camera or in real life, with truth-telling. Shawn Rosenheim has described the interrotron as a device with 'psychoanalytic dimensions', extracting confessions from its subjects (1996: 232). Its function is reliant on close-ups, which magnify micro-movements of facial gestures and expressions, and allow us to scrutinise the faces of the 'bad apples' for signs of guilt, remorse, honesty, pleasure – in other words, for what they *feel* in their recollection of events. We watch them as they reveal themselves to the inter-rotron, prompted by its inert yet expectant presence to search for an answer. The neutral background eliminates perspectival depth, while the film's 2.40:1 anamorphic widescreen format magnifies faces, all of which makes the soldiers' ordinariness stand out.

Why, Nichols wonders, doesn't Morris ask the guards about 'their background and experience prior to arriving at Abu Ghraib – their families, their educational level, their political views and habits'? (Nichols 2010). If the film psychoanalyses its interviewees, it does not focus on their personal psychology. Instead, it psychoanalyses the environment, exploring the conditions that allow such acts to take place, challenging views that they were solely the product of deviant behaviour.

The film emphasises ambiguity, a 'push and pull in our stance toward such characters' (Plantinga 2010: 44). On the one hand, it pulls us towards sympathy for the perpetrators, exploring their own sense of victimisation and the forces that led them to become involved in atrocities. Access to their thoughts and emotions through facial close-ups and voice testimonies enables the soldiers to become personalities for us, whereas their victims do not. On the other hand, this alignment does not result in unqualified allegiance; indeed, it invites unease as we share their emotional recollections testifying to their enjoyment at torturing others, as when Lynndie England smirks when recalling how one prisoner who was forced to masturbate continued to do so mechanically long after others had stopped.

SOP's exclusive focus on perpetrators not only prevents us from taking a higher moral ground – through, for example, pity for victims. It also explores the circumstances of perpetration, allowing us to see *how* it could happen. In a pivotal scene, England relates how some nights she would go up to the 'hard site' (where 'high-value' detainees were kept) and see people in stress positions: 'We thought it was unusual, weird and wrong, but when we first got there the example was already set. That's what we saw. I mean, it was OK.' After 'that's what we saw', England looks off screen, then directly ahead, in central framing, for 'it was OK'. The jump cuts call attention to the alteration of the soldiers' and interrogators' moral bearings in Abu Ghraib prison: how the exceptional came to be accepted as the norm.

Barbara Ehrenreich (2004) has remarked that the fact that women have been involved in torture at Abu Ghraib destroyed her belief in women's moral superiority. Her reaction testifies to the gender crisis that is provoked when women's participation in atrocity is disclosed, largely due to essentialist notions of women as 'soft' and caring. While female CIA agents, portrayed as educated and drawn from a higher social class, are used to promote a more acceptable face of the intelligence world in dramas such as *Homeland* and *Zero Dark Thirty*, *SOP* makes the gender politics of torture explicit in a way that other films don't, highlighting not the essentialist but rather the structural position of women, including the scapegoating of lower-class female soldiers.

When women are torturers, there is an apparent reversal of normative structures of victimisation, since women are traditionally positioned as victims and historically have been so in conditions of war. Contrary to this, the machinery of intelligence-gathering in the 'War on Terror' made a strategic use of women as subordinates, displaying detainees' nakedness to them as a deliberate tactic to degrade and humiliate Muslim men. But these scenarios also humiliated and degraded women. While the photograph of England leading the prisoner on the leash became an icon of the Abu Ghraib scandal, positioning her as a dominatrix figure subjugating the Iraqi man, her interviews reveal the gender politics and the different forces of desire that govern her role in these pictures, which were staged by Specialist Charles Graner, at that time her lover, the master of ceremonies in many of the photographed abuses – exhibiting *his* desire to exert power over both England and the Iraqi, using England as his tool.

While this might seem to exonerate England, *SOP*'s interviews with female soldiers highlight their subordinated role, trapped on the one hand by the goals of intelligence-gathering and the war, and on the other by a desire to fit in and be accepted by their male colleagues. Unlike *Ghosts of Abu Ghraib*, where she also appears, *SOP* foregrounds that Sabrina Harman – famous for the thumbs-up photo – is a lesbian, whose sexuality and gender make her doubly oppressed in the army's homophobic, sexist environment. Along with her aspirations to be a forensic photographer, this is key to her central role in this film, showing that a 'victim' like her could also be a victimiser. The film incorporates letters home to her wife Kelly, read aloud by her in voiceover with significant lines illuminated in close-up: important contemporaneous evidence of her moral thinking, clearly stating her knowledge of acts of wrongdoing, her confusion, despair and outrage that they were being condoned, and her decision to take pictures as 'proof' of what would otherwise be disbelieved.

In interview, Harman candidly explains the thumbs-up snapshot, which was taken by a male colleague, who asked her to pose with the corpse: 'Whenever I get into a photograph, I never know what to do with my hands, so I probably have a thumbs-up because it's just something that automatically happens. Like when you get into a photograph, you want to smile.' Whether or not we believe her explanation, it illuminates aspects of the atrocity-producing situation, for she is unlikely to have produced a thumbs-up photo over the corpse of one of her own comrades; her unthinking inclination to pose with a thumbs-up indicates the extent to which Iraqi prisoners failed to register for her and other soldiers as fellow humans.

The universe of images and the out-of-field

SOP's use of the Abu Ghraib photographs has been pivotal to allegations that it objectifies victims and aestheticises brutal events – rendering them 'beautiful' and more than what they are. However, without this transformative power it would not be able to provoke or haunt viewers in the way it does. In the opening credit sequence, the photographs are shown receding into a black background, as if suspended in the universe, using the dynamics of the CGI movement-image. This presents each photograph as 'an island universe' in itself, the point being that not everything is photographed; only certain images have been captured. The photographs are surrounded by a white border and black background to emphasise their status as snapshots. *SOP* highlights the contingencies of the photographic frame – an artificially isolated, closed system, each act of framing a bracketing or limitation. Each framing, however, is linked to the larger dimensions of space and time – an out-of-field that the film explores in its interviews and reconstructions.

In the military trial against the 'bad apples', the photographs were used as evidence to decide which events were criminal acts and which were 'standard operating procedure'. Shots of a Sony digital camera, held with latex gloves, lay bare the device through which the evidence has been collected and subsequently analysed by forensic expert Brent Pack. Digital technology enables one to calculate the exact time a picture was taken by providing 'metadata' (information about information), which Pack used to align the pictures in a sequential narrative. This is pictured in the film by a CGI timeline, a perspectival grid upon which the photographs taken by each of the three cameras (Harman's, Graner's and Staff Sergeant Ivan Frederick's) travel across the screen and are grouped chronologically. The graphics depict the multiple and fragmented events coalescing into one seamless continuity, resolved into a singular truth.

The sequence is reminiscent of Michelangelo Antonioni's film *Blow-Up* (1966), where the photographer attempts to reconstruct a narrative of events from the 'instants' he has photographed but, as we later discover, it's the 'wrong' story that he creates. Similarly, *SOP* questions Pack's detective narrative impulse, providing an ironic counterpoint through its music, which 'conveys a sense of the mechanical' (Lesage 2009) during his analysis, allowing the audience to perceive for itself the limitations in his perspective when he uses the photographs to separate out 'criminal acts' from 'standard operating procedure'. As the photographs appear one by one, they are rubber-stamped 'criminal act' or 'S.O.P.', including that of the prisoner on the box, holding wires in

Figure 1.3 The hooded man, an iconic image of torture and the 'War on Terror', is stamped 'S.O.P.' ('standard operating procedure') in Errol Morris's film.

his hands (he was told he would be electrocuted if he stepped off the box), now an iconic image of torture and the 'War on Terror'. On the grounds that the wires did not look live, Pack deemed the act to be 'S.O.P.', along with other photographs of nude prisoners wearing women's underwear on their heads, handcuffed to a bed, or stacked in a naked human pyramid. The red lettering of the 'S.O.P.' stamp which the film lays upon these photos highlights the gulf between the official sanctioning of these practices within the CIA and military – despite their obvious depiction of degrading, cruel and humiliating treatment, defying the UN Convention against Torture and the Geneva Conventions – and the moral and ethical response that the film elicits from its viewers.

SOP's use of reconstructions has filled critics with unease. Since they don't show the faces or provide the voices of the Iraqi victims, they seem to give us the privilege and pleasure of looking, without the victims looking back at us. The victims are not shown as realistic figures, but portrayed in fragments, as in an extreme close-up of a general's eyebrow being shaved as a punishment. This is what leads Nichols to criticise the film for voyeuristic and fetishistic strategies. He even contends that the reconstructions provide the guards' point of view, allowing us to occupy the perpetrators' position – like the shot through the spyhole of the 'gas chamber' in *Schindler's List* (1993). However, what is wrong with this reading is that it approaches the film only through a visual-cognitive map, that is, solely from the perspective of the visual gaze, rather than through the tactile, proprioceptive and synaesthetic mapping that these reconstructions encourage.[6] I take my cue for the opposition between visual-cognitive and proprioceptive mapping from Jennifer Barker (who derives it from Brian Massumi's *Parables for the Virtual*). These two types of sensual map are said to coexist and mutually inform or 'interrupt' each other. Synaesthesia is one way that we become aware of the proprioceptive map.

As Barker writes, in another context, 'these images compromise vision (and visual identification), forcing us to experience them as skin and *become* skin in order to make sense of them' (2009: 60, original emphasis). While *SOP*'s reconstructions illustrate details of interview testimony, they avoid representational verisimilitude. Instead, they invite viewers to take in sensory cues in order to understand, through imaginative simulation and other kinds of empathy, events we have never experienced ourselves, or at least not in the same configuration. Through their appeal to viewers' tactile awareness and other sense organs, they question the guards' stance that the acts were harmless, trivial or simply 'standard operating procedure' – making the moral and ethical ramifications of the torture policy palpable to our senses.

Recreating Abu Ghraib on a sound stage far away from the actual prison, the reconstructions utilise extreme close-ups, blurred shots, soft focus, slow motion and the staging of the movement towards the camera. Yet, it is, paradoxically, the images' very constructedness that gives them their power and immediacy: 'sounds and images are "reactivated," multiplied and intensified, precisely by being cut off from their source or origin' (Shaviro 1993: 35). The reconstructions don't present violent events directly but moments close to them, 'staying peripheral in spatial and/or temporal terms' (Austin 2011: 350). They depict conditions in the prison where both prisoners and their guards were vulnerable to fire. Slow-motion imagery of falling mortars and debris emphasises how the prison defied the Geneva Conventions for prisoners of war, which state that prisoners must not be held in a place 'exposed to the fire of a combat zone' (ICRC 1949). Sometimes the reconstructions directly contradict the testimonies: for example, after military interrogator Roman Krol claims that he was charged with the 'trivial' offence of throwing a nerve-ball at a prisoner, an image of a bouncing ball conveys its weight through slow motion and the noise of its impact on the ground. These images require us to 'see' proprioceptively, with a range of inner and outer senses. If we only interpreted them visually, we would not be able to grasp their meaning. These scenes also form a contrast to the depiction of conventional film violence – characters ducking explosions or rains of bullets – where the use of slow motion 'convey[s], paradoxically, a sense of speed' (Young 2010: 38). Here, slow motion encompasses a feeling for the vulnerability of the body under assault.

In the reconstruction of the prisoner on the box, the film focuses in close-up on his feet and upturned fingers to emphasise that his forced standing under conditions of sleep deprivation is still torture, even if the wires were not live and were removed after the photograph was taken (something that Harman claims and Pack accepts on the basis of the photo's visible evidence). Forces exerted by our own bodies, their muscle and bone structure, their desire to sit down and to sleep, can be used to inflict pain upon us:

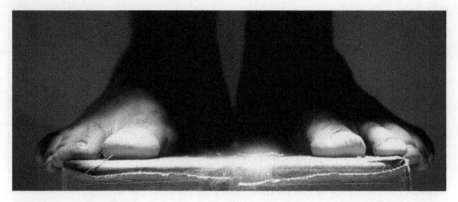

Figure 1.4 A reconstruction in *Standard Operating Procedure* invites viewers to imagine the pain of enforced standing.

> Standing rigidly for eleven hours can produce as violent muscle and spine pain as can injury from elaborate equipment and apparatus, though any of us outside this situation, used to adjusting our body positions every few moments before even mild discomfort is felt, may not immediately recognize this. (Scarry 1985: 47–8)

Torture includes the transformation and deformation of the body under these forces, which are what these reconstructions seek to capture by recomposing the photographs into movement-images.

Another key reconstruction is of the waterboarding carried out by military intelligence, which invites audiences to imagine what this form of torture may be like. It begins with a view from underneath the showerhead that recalls the imagery of *Psycho* (1960). At first droplets fall; then a torrent of water moves in the direction of the viewer's line of vision, becoming a dazzling shimmer as it catches the light – the tactile intensity of the light depicting the force of the water. There is a fade to black, then, with sound effects of plunging, we appear to be immersed underwater, becoming one with the flowing matter. Only after this are we given a shot of water pouring on a face covered in a sack. In other words, before we are *shown* what the practice of waterboarding looks like, we are first invited to imagine what its smothering and sensation of drowning *feel* like. Called a 'no-brainer' by Cheney, waterboarding has been officially denied to be a form of torture and the media have labelled the process 'simulated drowning'. However, Morris depicts it as an *actual* drowning, which it is, accompanied by slow asphyxiation and blackout – as sufferers have described it, a feeling of pain and annihilation that is felt throughout the body, engulfing one's very being, yet that remains unsensed by others and, therefore, unreal to them.

SOP depicts Abu Ghraib as a haunted house populated by 'ghosts'. The film tracks down corridors, past transparent, spectral figures of non-uniformed and unidentified interrogators belonging to the CIA and OGAs (other government agencies), who are literally known as 'ghosts', materialising and disappearing without notice, their job being to interrogate 'ghost detainees', who are never registered in the official log. Crucial here is the story of the death of 'ghost prisoner' Manadel al-Jamadi, who died in the shower while being interrogated, supposedly of a 'heart attack'. His body was later ferried out of the prison, disguised as a patient with an intravenous drip. In interview, Sergeant Anthony Diaz, who was responsible for looking after the prisoner before and after the CIA interrogation, describes the prisoner's blood dripping onto his uniform, making him feel 'part of it' even though he says he himself was not involved in the shower torture; however, in the reconstruction, the horror imagery of blood, viscous and slowly dripping, marks his and others' complicity.

Together with Staff Sergeant Frederick, Harman later went to investigate the body, which had been left, packed with ice inside a body bag, in a locked room. This is when the thumbs-up photo was taken. However, Harman later returned to take more photographs herself. From the injuries al-Jamadi sustained, it was clear to her that attribution of death by 'heart attack' was a ruse. A bandage had been affixed to one of his eyes to conceal some of the damage he had sustained. Those responsible for his death were not held accountable, while an attempt was made to prosecute Harman for taking the photographs, alleging that she had tampered with the evidence although, as she points out in interview, the evidence had already been tampered with. The charges were later dropped because the authorities didn't want the photos to come to light and reveal the cover-up of a murder.

As in its other reconstructions, *SOP* depicts the finding of al-Jamadi's body obliquely – firstly, through imagery of a pool of water collecting outside the door, indirectly evoking the horror, decomposition and stench as the ice-packed corpse defrosts. The scene's key moment is the removal of the bandage from the dead man's eye. The close-up of the wound, combined with the movement-image that endows the still photo with motion, has a tactile force capable of leaving enduring aftertraces on our sensorium. Whereas this series of Abu Ghraib photographs caught the public gaze because of Harman's smile and thumbs-up, which detracted from the murder, the reconstruction refocuses our attention on the crime and the workings of power through denial, a 'radical effacement' that claims 'that there never was [such] a human, there never was a life, and no murder has, therefore, ever taken place' (Butler 2004: 147). Through these reconstructions, which evoke the out-of-field of the photographs, the film provokes us to feel and ponder the atrocities that have *not* been captured – that are not in the frame.

CONCLUSION

In their cinematic recreation of the post-9/11 intelligence world, the documentary and fiction films discussed in this chapter make crucial aesthetic choices that lead to either moral or ethical confrontations with historical events. Although vastly differing in their outlook, *Zero Dark Thirty* and *Taxi to the Dark Side* both exhibit moral viewpoints. Conforming to dominant scripts about 9/11 and its aftermath, *Zero* constructs a moral tale of good and evil that justifies its heroes going over to 'the dark side' in order to achieve their ends. By encouraging spectators to accept their moral universe, such films can play a pivotal role in eliciting public consent to torture and other extra-judicial measures.

Taxi and *Standard Operating Procedure* together create important counter-images against this tendency. Whereas fictional representations often rely on an established image repertoire that presents torture in conventional ways, *Taxi* and *SOP* as documentary films both attempt to articulate their own cinematic vocabulary of pain, drawing upon the multisensory properties of images and appealing to viewers' embodied imaginations to convey the effects of torture upon its victims, including 'clean' techniques where signs are not immediately obvious.

The value and importance of *Taxi* lies in its elucidation of an alternative moral viewpoint. It focuses on the injustices of 'the dark side' to its victims, starting close up with the story of an innocent Afghan, then enlarging the picture to reveal the systematic dehumanisation fostered by 'War on Terror' rhetoric and implementation of a torture policy carried out using standard techniques in detention centres around the world since 9/11.

However, equally, if not more, important is a meta-perspective on moral viewpoints that is attentive to how they are reconfigured in different settings; in my argument, I have called this an ethical standpoint. Although it also elicits moral emotions, *SOP* avoids a standard moral framework based on pity for victims and indignation towards perpetrators. Instead, by uncomfortably aligning viewers with the perpetrator mindset, it makes us reflect on how moral norms are altered in the atrocity-producing situation, where brutal acts become 'standard operating procedure'. It registers further complexity by gesturing to a universe of acts and networks of complicity beyond its frames, the atrocities we do not know about because their images have not been captured and circulated.

Though no longer officially called by that name, the 'War on Terror' is still being waged. To date, Guantánamo Bay prison remains open. Trials by military commission have been reinstated after being revoked, and the Pentagon has asserted the right to detain people indefinitely even if they are cleared by these trials. The use of drones and other targeted killings shares the same principle as extraordinary rendition and indefinite detention in denying individuals a trial or hearing charges brought against them. While CIA secret prisons have been declared closed, rendition remains in force. Far from being confined to a single, unprecedented chapter of US history, 'the dark side', foreshadowed by the colonial past, lingers on, supported by similar underground international endorsement and complicity, lending these films an ongoing relevance.

NOTES

1. *Zero Dark Thirty*'s US box office intake was US$95,720,716, more than doubling its US$40 million budget. Although they performed well for documentaries, *Taxi to the Dark Side* and *Standard Operating Procedure* pale in comparison, at US$274,661 and US$229,117 respectively. *Rendition* (2007), a Hollywood film which takes a different moral standpoint about torture from *Zero Dark Thirty*, also performed far less well, at US$9,736,045, making a huge loss on its estimated $US27.5 million budget. Box office figures are taken from www.boxofficemojo.com. Additional budget estimates are from www.imdb.com.

2. Samuel Huntington's 'clash of civilizations thesis' (1993), which contends that 'fault lines' of future world conflicts will be cultural rather than ideological, with Islam posing the largest threat to the West, foreshadows 'War on Terror' binaries. It became influential among members of the Bush administration.

3. For further discussion of the conventional iconography of torture, see Rejali (2012).

4. Among the articles in *Jump Cut*'s special issue on *SOP* in which Nichols's essay appears, only one (Williams 2010) offers a favourable appraisal of the film.

5. An accompanying book based on Morris's interviews covers the broader context of the Bush administration's policies (see Gourevitch and Morris 2008), as does Morris's commentary on the DVD.

6. Proprioception is defined as 'the sense one uses, based on cues from such organs as one's muscles, tendons and inner ear, to judge one's position relative to one's own body and to the immediately surrounding space'. Synaesthesia refers to the intermingling of different senses; in filmic terms, this can involve exploring how vision in cinematic experience is 'entangled with other senses' (Barker 2008: 241, 243).

CHAPTER 2

History Lessons:
What Audiences (Could) Learn
about Genocide from
Historical Dramas

During classes on the Holocaust, a required element in secondary-level history, UK teachers have found that students repeatedly claim that such events could never happen today (Levenson 2009). So some teachers have proposed that the Rwandan genocide should be included in the national curriculum, inspired by *Hotel Rwanda* (2004). This film marked the first time many audiences heard about the Rwandan genocide, affirming the extent to which people without direct connection to particular historical events find out about them from the movies. This chapter explores fictional films about the Holocaust and the Rwandan genocide – mainly historical dramas, which aspire to be pedagogical vehicles, providing 'lessons' about the past. What do they teach us about genocide and how do they avoid comforting illusions that it belongs to the past or begins and ends with the Nazis?

As this chapter argues, using *Schindler's List* (1993) as its archetypal example, historical dramas tend to be moralistic, offering up tales of good versus evil that foster identification with heroic 'good men', who act as we would wish to act in similar circumstances, or with innocent bystanders, both of which relieve viewers of their own responsibility while reassuring them about their moral place in the world, either as individuals or nations. Critics have objected to the way such movies come to define what audiences know and understand about those events, highlighting cinema's potential to 'rewrite' history in ways that erase its troubling aspects; such distorted knowledge, it is often argued, is hardly better than no knowledge at all. Yet while illuminating some of those tendencies, academic criticism itself has a moralistic tenor, as testified by views on mainstream Holocaust films, which are criticised for trivialising that catastrophe and attacked for their 'inappropriate comparison with other events' and for denying its 'true horror' (Weissman 2004: 12). Discussion tends to revolve around taboos and limits, 'drawing a line' at certain kinds of representations, such as extermination in the gas chambers.

Such moralism, both of the movies and the critics, tends to present perpetrators as 'evil' Others, utterly unlike 'us', the viewers, which can stand in the way of an ethical reflection on the atrocity-producing situation. As Hannah Arendt, herself a Jewish refugee from Nazi Germany, remarked, the moral horror the Holocaust inspired has prevented recognition that it was not a collapse of moral values, but the swift replacement of one set of values by another. Ordinary people, who considered themselves 'decent', easily adapted and '"coordinated" themselves' to a society where it was acceptable to endorse crimes against entire groups of people (Arendt 2003b: 54). They proved capable of trading one set of morals for another 'with no more trouble than it would take to change the table manners of a whole people' (Arendt 2003a: 43). This chapter puts films in dialogue with Arendt's philosophy to explore how their historical story-worlds develop, or avoid, insights into how such events *could* happen through large-scale collaboration and consent to the segregation (and, later, killing) of a targeted group, whereby murderous actions are redefined and justified as moral. It presents the possibility of extracting another kind of 'moral' from these films: the wider public's complicity, including our own, in atrocities that continue to be committed in the here and now.

Occurring in Europe, the self-proclaimed seat of modern civilisation, the Holocaust was carried out in secrecy, at a distance, in an extensive network of concentration camps in Nazi Germany's colonial empire in the east.[1] In contrast, although sharing a number of elements with the Holocaust, including wartime conditions, race politics and large-scale slaughter, the Rwandan genocide occurred in public, without attempts to conceal crimes, distinguished by its so-called intimacy (involving friends, relatives and neighbours) and wide civilian participation. While the Nazis are renowned for their industrial, bureaucratic killing, the Rwandan *génocidaires* used machetes, clubs and hoes to hack their victims to death. Yet the Nazis also used crude methods – shooting, slave labour and starvation – as well as gassing; and, contrary to its construction as atavistic violence, the Rwandan genocide depended on modern means of organisation, involving the media, the army, militias and the government. While the Holocaust is frequently conceptualised as 'unique', a profound rupture with history and tradition, the Rwandan genocide suffered from clichéd presentation as 'tribal rivalry' in international news media, a misperception that obscured the political calculation behind the conflict. Underlying both notions is a Eurocentric worldview that overlooks the colonial histories that interlink the West and its others and that continue to affect present-day global politics.

This chapter draws on Arendt's 'boomerang thesis' of the Holocaust and its reconfigurations by Aimé Césaire and Frantz Fanon, all of which problematise interpretations of the Holocaust as a 'unique' event, suggesting connections between it, colonialism and contemporary atrocities. It elaborates these links through film analyses. Made under the shadow of the 'War on Terror', *The Boy in the Striped Pyjamas* (2008) raises contemporary parallels with US and UK citizens' tacit consent to their governments' detention and torture of 'enemy combatants', suggesting multiple connections between past and present – for example Nazism, British imperialism and the 'War on Terror' – which have been obscured by moral discourses about the film trivialising the Holocaust. *Hotel Rwanda* seeks to expose the complicity of the international community in the Rwandan genocide, yet it upholds the 'one good man' motif and reinforces imperialistic views of the West as a benevolent rescuer. Such moralism is resisted in *Sometimes in April* (2005) and *The Night of Truth* (*La Nuit de la vérité*, 2004), which also explore the circumstances of the Rwandan genocide (and its aftermath). *Sometimes* achieves this through its greater moral complexity in its portrayal of perpetrators and global 'bystanders', while *Night* offers a political (rather than moral) resolution and emphasises African agency.

Like these films, the chapter takes the ethical risk of making comparisons, which emphasises genocide as an ever-present possibility, never relegated to the past. This does not merely arouse guilt and sorrow for what *has been* but, rather, confronts us with what *is still happening*, impressing upon us the urgent need to think through connections between past and present.

THE MORALISM OF HISTORICAL DRAMA

In recounting history, there is always a temptation to simplify, as novelist and Holocaust survivor Primo Levi remarks:

> The need to divide the field into 'we' and 'they' is so strong that this pattern, this bi-partition – friend–enemy – prevails over all others. Popular history, and also the history taught in schools, is influenced by this Manichean tendency which shuns half-tints and complexities. (Levi 1988: 22)

Levi likens this attitude to history to spectator sport, which wants 'winners and losers', 'good guys' and 'bad guys' (ibid.: 23). Although few people are unadulterated heroes or villains, historical dramas rarely acknowledge these 'grey zones' and instead offer moral absolutes.

Schindler's List imagines the Holocaust as a metaphysical struggle between good and evil through its black-and-white cinematography and its binary between the hero, Oskar Schindler, who saves over 1,000 Jews, and villain Amon Goeth, a sadistic camp commandant. Like many other historical dramas, it is rooted in the *Bildungsroman* genre, which seeks to arouse the audience's moral conscience in parallel with its hero's moral growth. When the *Bildungsroman* is adapted to films about distant conflicts, the protagonist's moral growth is situated against an oppressed people's struggle, dividing the plot into foreground and background material (Goldberg 2001: 248). In *Schindler's List*, the Holocaust forms the background for Schindler's moral transformation, as when he observes a Jewish ghetto being 'liquidated' from a hilltop. A girl in a red coat is singled out in red tint, signifying danger: an innocent child's life cruelly snatched away.

Schindler's conversion exemplifies the 'one good man' motif, where a man becomes 'good' through a 'change of heart', purifying the past of its ambiguities. Far from unique to genocide stories, this narrative of male heroism – needless to say, women never have the chance to be 'good men' – also underlies *The Lives of Others* (*Das Leben der Anderen*, 2006), a historical drama about the former East Germany, where a Stasi officer listens to 'The Sonata for a Good Man'. The audience is made to feel how he is moved through the music, how it works a change in him. Something similar occurs in *The Pianist* (2002), where a Nazi officer helps the Jewish protagonist, Władysław Szpilman, after hearing him play the piano. Western classical music – a symbol of European high culture – becomes the unqualified catalyst of a character's moral transformation into a 'good man'.

In his pale grey suit, Schindler comes as an emissary of light, striding onto the platform of Krakow station, and plucks his trusted accountant, Itzhak Stern, off the train that is about to send him to his death. The high-contrast lighting creates a halo of light around him, marking him out from the dark and drab surroundings. The light expresses Schindler's moral goodness and his saviour's hand, contrasting with the locomotive's darkness and, later, the Auschwitz death factory and its plumes of black smoke. In the film's present-day coda, real survivors, accompanied by the actors who played them, place stones at Schindler's Christian grave in Israel. The shift to colour indicates a present free of the past's sadness and gloom, while maudlin violins emphasise the Jews' deliverance through their saviour's act of goodness. The film cultivates admiration for its hero and appreciation that he is finally given his due, leaving us with those feel-good emotions. Through this vicarious identification, it grants audiences the wish-fulfilling moral gratification of acting like a hero. More concerned with whether someone is a 'good man' than with the world and its injustices, films of this ilk focus on exceptional people, offering consolatory fictions about the capacity to resist evil in ways that fail to do justice to the political complexities of genocide or indeed any other kind of oppression.

Historical dramas often represent the past 'as *separate* from the viewer in the present, as something over and done with, complete, achieved' (Higson 1993: 113, original emphasis). *Schindler's List*'s use of black-and-white for the past and colour for the present creates clear-cut boundaries between genocide and the normal social order, reinforcing the idea that the Holocaust is 'unique'. Conventional narrative structure urges the desire for order to be restored and justice to be delivered, a moral framework that imposes closure on events. It implies that the struggle has been won, affirming a teleological view of history as delivering us to a more benign present in which genocide no longer prevails.

Due to Hollywood's global circulation, *Schindler's List*'s version of the past reaches millions of people. Its unsubtle, Manichean thinking evades what Arendt called 'the banality of evil', a phrase coined in her report on the trial of Nazi war criminal Adolf Eichmann. It is customary to assume that perverted, sadistic dispositions are what motivate perpetrators of atrocity, setting them apart from 'us'. The word 'banality', for which Arendt was heavily criticised, stresses that many (though not all) perpetrators of genocide are ordinary, rather than malignant. This does not detract from the horror of what they did, but highlights a more unsettling, persuasive kind of evil that genocide throws into relief. In the Third Reich, Arendt noted, there was 'ubiquitous complicity' with the Jews' segregation and, later, their disappearance, which 'stretched far beyond the ranks of Party membership' (2006: 18).

The banality of evil offers a different perspective on what constitutes the 'horror' of events, which many Holocaust scholars are adamant that no dramatic film could ever represent. Most express a dislike of realism, or what would be more accurately described as verisimilitude. In film theory, realism is believed to rest upon a claim to transparency of representation, giving viewers the impression that they are looking through a window into reality rather than a constructed world (MacCabe 1974: 12). This ideological 'reality effect' is enhanced by the rhetoric of 'authenticity' in a film's marketing and textual construction, including claims of being 'based on a true story'. Instead, critics favour trauma as a narrative model. Since their central epistemological claim is that genocide cannot be represented, they judge films on whether they display sensitivity to this conundrum. Modernist techniques are valorised for their ability to render a 'post-traumatic' consciousness, emphasising disturbance and fragmentation of meaning (Hirsch 2004). Brechtian self-reflexivity is applauded for indicating and generating awareness that events have been mediated, not misguidedly attempting to show the past as it 'really' was.

Among film scholars, the most celebrated Holocaust film is *Shoah* (1985), which deals with the unrepresentability of extermination and creates an anti-representational aesthetic to this end, rejecting both archival footage and dramatic re-enactment. Its director, Claude Lanzmann, deemed that it would be 'a moral and artistic crime' to use a helicopter shot to film a village as that would betray the ideal of witness testimony and present a perspective unavailable to historical participants (Lanzmann et al. 1991: 94). Yet the film, in its entirety, selects, orders and juxtaposes, which controls how we relate to its content and offers value judgements. Constructed from images, sounds and words, it *is* representational. It is not only through devices such as tracking shots, panning and overhead shots (which *Shoah* uses extensively) that a film alters the past but through an array of technical and artistic choices at each instant of its running time. As a mechanical entity, moreover, film offers perceptions that are always going to be different from those of human participants.

Therefore, in reply to both the scholarly desire for an anti-representational aesthetic and mainstream filmmakers' rhetoric of authenticity, filmmaking unavoidably transforms its historical sources, whichever style is chosen. It cannot be 'truthful' in the sense suggested by either Lanzmann or the promotional tagline 'based on a true story'. Tendencies towards fabrication exist not merely 'to make the stories more commercial or palatable', but because the medium itself guarantees that 'such invention is ultimately involved in every moment on the screen' (Rosenstone 2006: 28).

Films cannot reproduce historical reality; rather, they construct their own historical story-world, organised by filmmakers. Notwithstanding their invented elements, they 'can make cogent observations on historical events' (ibid.: 25). Like pictorial compositions, they foreground certain aspects, while backgrounding others, enabling viewers 'to see certain things and to miss others' (Mboti 2010: 325). This approach differs from traditional demands for historical 'accuracy', yet, as Nyasha Mboti writes, 'the fact that films are constructs does not . . . free them to disfigure events'. Rather, their potential is to provide illuminating perspectives and speculations on history, generating new insights through their creative juxtapositions. This prompts different kinds of questions from the dominant trauma paradigm. What kind of historical story-world does a film create and what, within it, enables or prevents insights about how genocide happens? What do we gain, or lose, from the thinking within the forms a film adopts?

In the next section, Arendt's 'boomerang thesis' will be briefly elaborated and then the remainder of the chapter will bring together these perspectives in detailed film analyses.

THE 'BOOMERANG THESIS'

In *The Origins of Totalitarianism* (first published in 1951 as *The Burden of Our Time*, and revised thereafter in several editions), Hannah Arendt attempts to discover about the Nazi genocide '*What happened? How did it happen? How could it have happened?*' (1979: xxiv, original emphasis). In what has become known as her 'boomerang thesis', she claims that totalitarianism inherits its genocidal ideology from imperialism: Nazism became conceivable through a combination of race ideology and bureaucracy tested out in the imperialists' overseas territories, the violence of which returned to Europe in the form of the Holocaust. She thus distinguishes between traditional anti-Semitism and modern race thinking, which took root in the nineteenth-century West, gained respectability from pseudo-scientific theories and laid the basis for exterminatory practices. Imperialism separated humanity into greater humans and lesser humans, justifying conquest and elimination of entire groups of people under a moral imperative in the name of 'Progress'. Arendt cites the postscript from Kurtz's pamphlet in Joseph Conrad's novel *Heart of Darkness* (1899) – 'Exterminate all the brutes!' – which lays bare the disparity between the imperialist enterprise's moral claims and its harsh reality for subjugated people. This became the answer to the white man's encounter with Africa, leading to

> the most terrible massacres in recent history, the Boers' extermination of the Hottentot tribes, the wild murder by Carl Peters in German Southeast Africa, the decimation of the peaceful Congo population – from 20 to 40 million reduced to 8 million; and finally, perhaps worst of all, it resulted in the triumphant introduction of such means of pacification into ordinary, respectable foreign policies. (Arendt 1979: 185)

For Arendt, the African colonies provided

> the most fertile soil for the flowering of what later was to become the Nazi elite. Here they had seen with their own eyes how people could be converted into races and how simply by taking initiative in this process, one might push one's own people into the position of the master race (ibid.: 206).

The imperialist enterprise afforded both 'the gentlemen and the criminal' the opportunity to test their beliefs and methods and to commit outrages unencumbered by customary laws and restraints, far away from home where nobody knew the full extent of what they were doing (ibid.: 190). As Africans were '"natural" human beings', lacking the creation of a world that distinguishes humans from nature, Arendt claims, the Europeans massacring them '*somehow were not aware that they had committed murder*' (ibid.: 192, emphasis added). This displays extraordinary insight into the Europeans' impunity in their imperial adventures, yet Arendt's cultural positioning renders her oblivious to her own imperialist construction of Africans as uncivilised 'natural' beings. Some have criticised what they portray as her insufficient attention to German colonialism, responsible for the first twentieth-century genocide, of the Herero and Nama peoples in Namibia in 1904. But what she actually does is critique all European imperialism rather than focusing on Germany alone. As Marlow says in *Heart of Darkness*, 'all Europe contributed to the making of Kurtz' (Conrad 1973: 71).

Around the same time, though independently of Arendt, the Martiniquan writer Aimé Césaire also spoke of the 'boomerang effect' of Nazism upon Europe in his *Discourse on Colonialism* (first published in 1950).[2] However, writing from the perspective of the colonised, during France's mid-twentieth-century colonial wars, he articulates an explicit critique of Western habits of perception merely implied in Arendt's account. In a key passage, he claims that Hitler 'applied to Europe colonialist procedures which until then had been reserved exclusively for the Arabs of Algeria, the "coolies" of India, and the "niggers" of Africa' and hitherto 'tolerated' and 'legitimized' (Césaire 2000: 36). To justify enslavement, theft, rape, torture and murder, the colonised have habitually been excluded from notions of common humanity. This paves the way for atrocities, along with public consent to them: 'each time a head is cut off or an eye put out in Vietnam and in France they accept the fact, each time a little girl is raped and in France they accept the fact, each time a Madagascan is tortured and in France they accept the fact' (ibid.: 35).

In *The Wretched of the Earth* (1961), Frantz Fanon makes two further points that relate to this analysis: firstly, that Europe's wealth is founded on colonialism and slavery (a reminder that resource extraction and capital accumulation by means of enforced labour underpins colonial violence) and, secondly, that 'colonialism does not simply state the existence of tribes' or different 'races'; 'it also reinforces it and separates them' (Fanon 2001: 74). For Fanon, the boomerang effect occurs within the settler–native relationship in which the native inherits 'the settler's logic' and seeks to oust the settler by force (ibid.: 67).[3] This dynamic has played out in Rwanda, a German colony (1897–1918) before it came under Belgian rule (1918–62). Racial distinctions were instituted by colonists to set people apart in a divide-and-rule strategy and were again manipulated by elites in a power struggle during the 1994 genocide: Hutu extremists assumed the identity of 'natives' seeking to expel the Tutsis, deemed to be sidekicks of the former colonial masters (Mamdani 2001).

Linking the Holocaust to a broader history of European imperialism and going beyond customary interpretations of genocide as an 'exceptional' event, the 'boomerang thesis' offers a more frightening picture of genocide as a historical norm and colonial legacy that marks the present. One way that legacy is manifested today is in coercive actions that dehumanise civilian populations in terror campaigns (torture, aerial bombing, drone wars) and even during 'humanitarian' interventions. Race thinking persists in making such actions conceivable. I shall now consider how films deal with these issues.

REINVENTING THE HERITAGE GENRE: *THE BOY IN THE STRIPED PYJAMAS*

British heritage productions are, perhaps, the best-known contemporary cinematic 'genre' that corresponds to Empire. Typically, they are sumptuous period dramas that construct a nostalgic version of the imperial past. In his influential account of this production trend, Andrew Higson describes it as 'a packaging of the past that is designed to please, not disturb' (1993: 122). Although initially applied to British filmmaking, the term has been extended to period dramas with similarly high production values made elsewhere. Lutz Koepnick has argued that the heritage genre now provides the cinematic language for representing the Nazi past in German cinema. In such films viewers are treated to a sensory experience of the past that airbrushes out its most unpleasant aspects, through 'sweeping narratives, digitally improved set designs, meticulous attention to historical fashion, hairstyle as well as atmosphere, and galvanizing surround sounds' (Koepnick 2002: 77). Like Higson, Koepnick argues that heritage functions on behalf of ideological consensus, creating serviceable pasts from a present-day political perspective, in this case reunified Germany (whereas Higson's focus was Thatcherite Britain). For example, *Aimée & Jaguar* (1999), a story of a German-Jewish lesbian love affair, counterfactually retrieves a site of multicultural coexistence from 'a history of intolerance and persecution' (Koepnick 2002: 57). Another well-known film that would support Koepnick's argument is *Downfall* (*Der Untergang*, 2004), which portrays the final days in Hitler's bunker from the perspective of his secretary Traudl Junge, dividing its cast into 'good' and 'bad' Germans in a way that occludes wider complicity under the Third Reich (see Bathrick 2007; Cooke 2007). In Koepnick's view, heritage filmmaking not only 'aestheticize[s] the past', it tries 'to exorcize history's evil' (2002: 56, 76). In the following reading, it will be argued that *The Boy in the Striped Pyjamas* unsettles these principles, as the British heritage genre meets the Nazi past.

Based on the bestselling 2006 book by Irish writer John Boyne, the BBC–Miramax co-production *The Boy in the Striped Pyjamas* follows the story of eight-year-old Bruno, whose family leaves Berlin to live in 'the countryside', due to his father's 'work'. Out of his bedroom window he espies what looks like a distant farm, and he resolves to befriend the children who live there but is discouraged by his parents: his mother, Else, realises who the children are when Bruno describes them wearing 'pyjamas', and his father, Ralf, insists that 'they are not really people at all'. Disturbed by their house's proximity to the 'farm', which she knows is really a concentration camp (implicitly Auschwitz), Else has the window boarded up. Nonetheless, Bruno ventures out there and strikes up a friendship with Shmuel, a Polish Jewish boy, whom he finds sitting on the other side of the camp's electrified barbed-wire fence.

In the *New York Times*, Manohla Dargis gave the film a damning review: 'See the Holocaust trivialized, glossed over, kitsched up, commercially exploited and hijacked for a tragedy about a Nazi family. Better yet and in all sincerity: don't' (Dargis 2008). *Boy*'s poster pictures two children sitting on either side of a fence, evoking a narrative image of friendship across 'enemy lines' – a fantasy of reconciliation and childhood innocence. The story stands accused of misrepresenting concentration camp conditions by suggesting that a friendship between an eight-year-old son of a Nazi camp commandant and a Jewish inmate of the same age could take place when in fact Auschwitz's perimeter was heavily guarded and children, if deemed too young to work, were frequently killed upon arrival (though records show that some children did live and work there). In another negative account of the film, John Haynes criticises it for its dishonest aspiration to the authority of 'History' through its use of realism (2009: 96). But *Boy* does not make pretensions to historical fidelity. As its producer, David Heyman, states, 'such a friendship was not possible' (2008: 30). Its story premise is a deliberate invention. To judge the tale solely by the criterion of empirical veracity, as some critics have done, would be to ignore the way it utilises the possibilities of historical drama as a speculative evocation of the past. In so doing, it provides an unusual and powerful perspective on the Nazi genocide that stresses wider complicity. Some might object that this reading relies on subtle communication of themes lost on those who only find out about historical events by watching historical dramas; nonetheless, the themes exist within the film for whoever wishes to revisit them.

The device of storytelling through a child rests on the belief that its perspective is innocent, which risks occluding the socio-political processes behind genocide. However, *Boy* does not fall into this trap. It is instructive to compare it with *Life is Beautiful* (*La vita è bella*, 1997), a previous attempt to portray the Holocaust from a child's viewpoint. In *Life is Beautiful*, a father, Guido, tells his little boy, Giosuè, that the concentration camp in which they have been imprisoned and forced into brutal labour is a 'game', with a prize of a tank awaiting the winner, in order to shield him from its harsh realities. In *Boy* Bruno sees Shmuel's striped attire and the number on his shirt, and wonders whether the camp inmates are playing a 'game'. Shmuel emphatically tells him they're *not* wearing pyjamas, rather uniforms that they have to wear as their own clothes were taken away, that the numbers are prisoner numbers, and that the camp is *not* a game, a lesson that Bruno, in a bitter reply to *Life is Beautiful*, learns too late. *Life is Beautiful* largely uses the Holocaust as a background for its story: the 'lesson' it teaches us is not the historical annihilation of the Jews, but a father's love and sacrifice for his son. In contrast, *Boy* uses its story to bring aspects of the genocide into sharper focus.

Most of this is subtly implied rather than made explicit through its dual address as a crossover film, targeted at both children and adults. (The film had a 12A certificate in Britain and PG-13 in the USA, though elsewhere its rating was higher, including 16 in Argentina and 14 in Chile.) While the novel is a *Bildungsroman*, where events are filtered through the child's limited perspective and narrated as a stream of consciousness using child-like language and the five senses to evoke his idiosyncratic experience of the world, the film keeps the child's viewpoint central but simultaneously reveals its larger knowledge of the situation through sound, editing and camera movement or by aligning itself with adult characters, particularly the mother, whose role is much larger in the film; she forms a second protagonist, another 'bystander', who is not so innocent. The film inhabits both the boy's half-knowledge and his mother's, layering levels of 'knowledge' between characters. Since we are placed in the same position of knowledge regarding sights, sounds and smells, the audience enters a bond of complicity with the adult German characters, able to interpret the multisensory cues that Bruno can't, or that he misinterprets.

The film's treatment of complicity not only illuminates citizens under Nazism but other forms of public consent to extreme measures. It does this, firstly, by defamiliarising the Third Reich, shutting off our distancing mechanisms, and presenting the German characters as in many ways similar to its target audience, to remind us of similarities with our present moment. In the opening shot, credits are superimposed on a slightly rippling red background. As the camera ranges over its surface, we gradually realise that what we are looking at is a billowing Nazi flag, creating a proximity between us and the Nazi object before we know it. In the score, composed by James Horner, ominous piano chords give way to a more cheerful, melodious arrangement with strings as we glance at the public square below, where Bruno and his friends are playing aeroplanes. We follow them racing through the streets, oblivious to soldiers rounding up people. On the soundtrack, an oboe introduces a poignant note as the film hovers over an apartment block, where people are being forced out of their homes and onto trucks; it attends to what the characters fail to perceive, although it is right before them. The self-assured piano and string theme recurs when we enter Bruno's family home, full of servants cleaning glassware, laying out cutlery and polishing the floors for a party to celebrate his father's 'promotion'.

At the party, Bruno's father, dressed in his regalia, descends the staircase to a 'Heil Hitler' salute from the bourgeois gathering. The cast is almost all British and the dialogue is spoken in impeccable British accents, including by the Ukrainian-American actress Vera Farmiga, who plays Bruno's mother. Bruno himself is like a character from a boy's imperial adventure story. With their bustling servants, intricate period detail and piano accompaniment, these opening scenes have the 'textural reassurances' (Osmond 2008: 51) of a Merchant–Ivory film, unnervingly juxtaposed with Third Reich iconography.

Although shot in a realist style, *Boy* has the de-realising air of a dream, 'so strange to watch' (ibid.). Reviewers unanimously agree that one of the reasons it is 'unsettling' is because the 'thesps' body language and delivery [is] distinctively un-German' (Elley 2008a: 59). Even Dargis remarks on the oddness of the accents. On the surface, this stylistic decision seems pragmatic. The use of English marks its hegemony, a means of maximising profit in an international market, while the British accent is generic for internationally produced films with European settings. Yet standard practice in most English-language films about the Third Reich is for Nazi characters to speak German (or English with a German accent), while other characters speak English (for example, *The Pianist*, *The Reader* (2008), *Schindler's List*). This suggests that the film's purpose is to make the Germans like 'us' and question the exceptionality of the Holocaust.

British heritage films tend to characterise British rule as 'essentially benign' in contrast to the 'cruel and racist tyrannies of the Third Reich' (Richards 2001: 129). While Germany has, historically, served as the Other for Britain, this film explores a kinship: an antidote to the 'bad German' view of history. Although it would be wrong to equate the British Empire with the Third Reich, a belief in race hierarchy was central to both. Through its subversive use of the heritage genre, *Boy* underlines this family resemblance.

In its portrait of Bruno's family, the film traces a continuity between bourgeois culture and genocide. Their privileged background prevents them from seeing Jewish suffering and caring about their fate; the people being rounded up in the opening scenes have, in this sense, already disappeared before they have physically departed. At their Auschwitz mansion, a middle-aged Jewish prisoner, Pavel, is employed for household chores, acknowledged by the family only when they are giving him orders. The life-world of the bourgeois family is portrayed as facilitated by slave labour and production in the camps, but (at least initially) they remain completely blind to this. Evoking contemporary parallels with torture and the 'War on Terror', the film suggests that this 'structural nonseeing on the part of the bourgeois, metropolitan subject' (Rothberg 2009: 284) is a contributing factor to the occurrence and persistence of genocide and other forms of imperial violence.

Bruno's father is played by David Thewlis, whose extensive research for his part included reading the autobiography of Auschwitz commandant Rudolf Höss, who lived with his wife and children in a mansion only 150 yards away from Auschwitz, and employed prisoners to work in the house and gardens:

What I did most of all was try and go to the root sources rather than taking anything from movies I've seen . . . [Höss] was a father of five, a married man, and – in numerous passages relating to his extreme devotion to his family – talking about tucking his children into bed and his extreme love for his wife. And I did everything I could to make it plausible that such people existed: an idea of a monster, but an idea of a human being who was driven by the times and obviously – in my own belief – his anti-Semitism and his own racial attitudes to perform such atrocities. (Quoted in Margolies 2008: 10)

Unlike Goeth in *Schindler's List*, the commandant portrayed by Thewlis has the normality of a family man, a caring father and loving husband, largely seen in his domestic role with the accoutrements of outer respectability – but supervising genocide all the while. By acknowledging this continuity between the 'normal' and the monstrous person, the film avoids a simplistic 'good'/'evil' binary. The commandant's 'work' remains off stage, with oblique hints as to its nature. It is explained to Bruno as being 'for the good of the country' and 'trying to make the world a better place' – socialising him and others into the belief that what is being done is morally justified, necessary for the common good.

Carrying out his 'work' under a sense of duty, the father leads a double life. Pertinent to such a character, who straddles two worlds, the life of Auschwitz killing and his family life, is Robert Jay Lifton's notion of psychological doubling. For Lifton, doubling is key to genocide and the atrocity-producing situation more generally. It is 'a means of adaptation to extremity', which can be adopted by both victims and perpetrators, enabling an individual to function in a harsh environment, since it involves elements of disavowal: for perpetrators, a disavowal of the murderous nature of their actions (Lifton 1986: 422). Lifton describes the doubling between an 'Auschwitz self' and a 'prior self'. The prior self needs to see itself as a loving husband and father, a self expressed to family and friends outside the camp. Meanwhile, the Auschwitz self does the 'dirty work', 'violating his own prior moral standards' (ibid.: 420). To make this work, the Auschwitz self's requirements are translated into the terms of the prior self's conscience: duty and loyalty to the country. The two selves/worlds are kept separate, with ideology – beliefs about race hierarchy – forming a bridge between the two, linking the commandant to notions of the greater 'good' his work serves.

Hannah Arendt wrote about how totalitarian regimes set up bureaucratic 'protective walls' to hide the disparity between their aims and the 'norms' of reality, and to conceal them from the public, enabling them to act on their belief that 'everything is possible'. She believed that this, rather than their art of persuasion through propaganda, was the secret of their success (Arendt 1979: 361). Euphemisms for killing, such as 'resettlement' or 'deportation', served to conceal the actual nature of Nazi crimes from civilians. Lifton observes that Nazis also deployed code terms such as 'special treatment' that were 'specific enough . . . to maintain bureaucratic efficiency' but sufficiently vague to make murderous acts seem benign. This 'deamplification of language' helped to foster what he calls 'the mixture of part-secrecy and "middle knowledge"' surrounding the Nazi genocide (Lifton 1986: 495–6).

In *Boy*, such partial or 'middle knowledge' is enacted through both Bruno and his mother, with whose curiosity the audience is aligned. In several scenes, we are privy to what the mother knows and hears, but Bruno doesn't; the audience's co-audition with her lays the basis of our complicity. A key scene is when Else detects a bad smell in the front yard. One of Ralf's soldiers, Lieutenant Kotler, inadvertently exposes the secret: 'They smell even worse when they burn, don't they?' To emphasise her moment of realisation, the film frames Else alone, at first uncomprehending, then disbelieving, and finally aghast. Meanwhile, billowing smoke from the crematorium confirms the nature of Ralf's 'work'.

Although the 'Final Solution' was kept a state secret (its association with mass murder dampened by its pragmatic emphasis on problem-solving), the film, in its speculation about the past, raises questions about what people knew and how they responded. It imagines civilians like Else as being, to some extent, aware of what was happening to Jews and accepting of their victimisation. When Pavel bandages Bruno's injured knee after an accident on the garden swing, she can barely bring herself to look at him to thank him. She is not like the fictionalised Traudl in *Downfall*, whose expression of horror at Hitler's anti-Jewish rants airbrushes the past by suffusing it with present-day politically correct perspectives. The film thus avoids *Downfall*'s apologetic and retrospective identification with people who are presented as not 'really' Nazis at heart. Else is depicted as someone who, although personable, has internalised a mild anti-Semitic worldview. Previously, she was aware of the camp's existence, but not its true purpose, and was willing to turn a blind eye. Unlike the fictionalised Traudl, one could imagine Else agreeing with the sentiment with which the historian Ian Kershaw sums up mainstream attitudes to the 1938 pogrom *Kristallnacht*: 'Anti-Semitism, O.K., but not like that' (1983: 273). Indeed, when Else confronts Ralf about the extermination, he appeals to her shared beliefs about Jews and justifies it as a patriotic duty during a war.

Ralf's justification embodies the 'Nazi image of Auschwitz as the moral equivalent of war' (Lifton 1986: 431). Earlier, when asked how long his post will last in 'the countryside', Ralf answers: 'As long as it takes to win the war.' As Arendt and others have remarked, the atmosphere of war made the 'Final Solution' seem more acceptable (Arendt 2006:106). War provided a parallel to the Nazis' endeavour. During wartime, energies of hatred are channelled against the enemy whom 'one has to kill . . . in order to preserve – to "heal" one's people, one's military unit, oneself' (Lifton 1986: 431). Consequently, constructing victims as a threat to the nation facilitated Auschwitz killing:

Nothing helped the Nazis to wage a race war so much as the war itself. In wartime, when it was all too usual to exclude the enemy from the community of human obligation, it was all too easy to subsume the Jews into 'the image of the enemy'. (Browning 1998: 186)

By highlighting the use of war as justification, and the concentration camps as part of a battle against 'enemies', the film, moreover, evokes a present-day parallel: denial of rights, detention without charge, and torture of 'enemy combatants' in the 'War on Terror'.

In another scene, Bruno watches his father screen a propaganda film about the camp. With voiceover commentary similar to a British public education film, it presents the camp as a benign place for the Jews' 'resettlement', full of sporting activities, people relaxing at a café for 'a nutritious meal', and contented children playing on stepping stones. When it concludes, the audience congratulates Ralf for his good work. Bruno, at this point wracked with doubts from his conversations with Shmuel, feels reassured and hugs his father with renewed affection. But then the film's perspective shifts to the stairs, where Else, now withdrawn from company, is seen shaking her head. Undercutting the child's naivety, the film places us in complicity with both the soldiers at the viewing and Else, who know the 'documentary' is fictional.

The first Nazi death camps were established in late 1941. Previously a 'peasant farmstead', Auschwitz was one of six in Poland, chosen for its isolated location and transport links (Lifton 1986: 160). (Bruno's initial belief that it is a farm is one of several additions that the film makes to the novel, along with the propaganda film.) Auschwitz is what the occupying power called the Polish town of Oświęcim, the name change itself embodying 'colonial violence' (Rothberg 2000: 28). While all concentration camps were places beyond ordinary processes of law, where inmates were stripped of their rights, Auschwitz is described by SS staff who worked there as having a particular feeling of extraterritoriality – 'what happened there did not count' (Lifton 1986: 210). Cut off by distance from their own country, so few people back at home knew what they were doing, the behaviour of the death camps' SS staff is comparable both with imperial colonies, where power could be exercised without restraint, and with the present-day network of 'War on Terror' jails.

Boy elliptically evokes camp brutalities. Shmuel relates the random and unexplained prisoner disappearances, including his grandparents on arrival and later his father. He and the other prisoners are subjected to work, as a means of terrorising and humiliating them, and intentionally exhausting them (to the point of death). Kept in a state of starvation, he is always hungry. Nor does the film romanticise the prisoners. Shmuel says he prefers to come out onto the grounds, because of infighting among camp inmates.

However, it is the 'quiet cruelties' (Dean 2004: 100) that permeate relation-

Figure 2.1 *The Boy in the Striped Pyjamas* evokes the 'small cruelties' that permeate relationships between Jews and non-Jews, as when Bruno disowns Shmuel.

ships between Jews and non-Jews that the film describes best. When Bruno injures himself on the swing, Pavel is able to give him an authoritative diagnosis and professional first aid because, as he explains to Bruno, he was a doctor, though he no longer practises. Misunderstanding, Bruno quips that he can't have been a very good doctor if he was only 'practising'. The film allows us to feel the unknowingly brutal insensitivity of this remark when Pavel seems unable to respond verbally; instead, his face and demeanour convey his grief, producing dramatic irony, since *we* know why Pavel is no longer practising, even if Bruno doesn't.

At a dinner scene, where he is waiting upon the family and their guests, Pavel is brutally punished for a mishap by Lieutenant Kotler. He is dragged off screen and beaten, as the diners sit there without doing anything, most of them (apart from Else and Bruno) unresponsive to his cries. Afterwards, he is never seen again and only Bruno asks when he is coming back, the implication being that he has died, which the others take for granted. That Pavel is seen and heard without his presence (or absence) affecting others indicates that they no longer experience him in human terms – that he is, to borrow a term from Orlando Patterson's work on slavery, a 'socially dead person' (1982: 8). Patterson's concept of social death describes a process of radical ostracism, an injustice that was widely condoned by denying the slave's humanity. Similarly, under the Third Reich, 'semi-conscious erasure of the Jews' became so much part of everyday reality that it ceased to become noticeable, except to Jews themselves (Dean 2004: 94).

Small cruelties are present even in the relationship between Bruno and Shmuel, undercutting the fantasy of reconciliation. When Kotler finds Shmuel eating pastries in the house, where he has been summoned to polish glassware, Shmuel pleads that Bruno offered him the food, but Bruno disowns him, claiming that Shmuel was helping himself. Far from an innocent bystander, Bruno lies to protect himself, due to his fear of Kotler, whose brutality to Pavel he has witnessed. Next time Shmuel appears, he has a painfully bruised eye. However, it is not just physical punishment to which Bruno has exposed him, but also the psychological cruelty of disavowing his existence. While discourses of sentimental humanism claim children to be innocent, therefore exempt from moral responsibility, *Boy* suggests they can be morally ambivalent, implicated in events. In this respect, it differs from other films about wartime complicity such as *Au revoir les enfants* (1987) – where a boy witnesses a Jewish classmate's persecution yet preserves his image as a righteous moral subject – although it is not as extreme as *The White Ribbon* (*Das weiße Band*, 2009), where children are budding torturers.

In the film's climax, Bruno exchanges his clothes for the camp uniform and dives into a tunnel he has dug under the fence to help Schmuel find his missing father, a plot device enabling him to enter the camp and experience its brutal realities for himself. Together the boys stumble upon locations from the propaganda film: the exterior of the hut that formed the so-called 'café' and the stepping stones, grim and bare without any sign of playing children. The camp has a depressing and frightening aspect that Bruno never imagined. In a riposte to *Schindler's List*, the film breaks the moral taboo of representing a gas chamber, deemed a horror that cannot, indeed must not, be shown. In Spielberg's film, naked women are voyeuristically glimpsed in their abject terror through a spyhole. What they and we are led to believe is a gas chamber turns out to be a harmless shower, producing light relief for the audience, as the film plays with the boundaries of what is considered acceptable to show and draws back: the water, shimmering in the light, is an image of their salvation. In *Boy*, one of the prisoners reassures the others by saying 'It's just a shower' when they are ordered to undress. Inside the crowded chamber, among other naked male bodies, Bruno and Shmuel hold hands in the panic and confusion that ensues as the lights go out. Unlike *Schindler's List*, the film does not cut to the voyeuristic perspective of the spyhole but rather glances up at an aperture in the roof from which a masked soldier is seen from below, pouring crystals of Zyklon-B.

The finality of this hard-hitting ending is underlined with an exterior shot of the masked soldier putting away his equipment: he has finished his job. From the grief-stricken Else as she clasps Bruno's abandoned rain-soaked clothes, the film shifts to Ralf in its penultimate shot. As he stands drenched in the rain, it feels his sobering realisation, finally, that *he has committed murder*, just as, like a boomerang, the camp's colonial violence returns to his own family.

Bruno's untimely death embodies the 'too late!' characteristic of melodramatic temporality (Williams 1998: 69), but in case at any moment we are thinking 'He's not supposed to be there!', the film catches us out by returning to the gas chamber in its final shot, emphasising that *none* of them should have been there. Slowly gliding back, the film reveals the empty undressing area with hundreds of discarded uniforms draped on benches and hanging forlornly on pegs – gesturing to the huge scale of lives lost, not just the fictional tragedy of Bruno's family. As the camera comes to a rest, holding the scene in still contemplation, there is a faint reprise of the film's ominous opening chords.

HOTEL RWANDA AND *SOMETIMES IN APRIL*: THE INTERNATIONAL COMMUNITY AND THE 'SOCIAL DEATH' OF AFRICANS

While Else in *Boy* belongs to a silent majority who permitted the Holocaust to happen, the next two films, *Hotel Rwanda* and *Sometimes in April*, deal with a late twentieth-century entity, 'the international community', which is criticised for not acting when it should. These films are part of a subsequent surge in international interest in the Rwandan genocide, largely ignored at the time it occurred, which includes *Shooting Dogs* (2005), *Shake Hands with the Devil* (2007) and *Kinyarwanda* (2011). These films teem with motifs of salvation, redemption and reconciliation. For example, *Shooting Dogs* provides a story of a white hero's redemption in its fictional character of Father Christophe, while *Shake Hands with the Devil* is about Canadian general Roméo Dallaire, head of the UN peacekeeping mission in Rwanda, who managed to save thousands of Tutsis, despite orders not to intervene. The motifs of redemption and salvation serve ideological functions: to allay bad conscience for past actions. My analysis defends the films in so far as they emphasise the international community's complicity as part of an *ongoing* atrocity-producing situation. It argues that the international community's differential treatment of Rwandans belongs to a longer imperial history in which the 'social death' of Rwandan Tutsis was preceded by the 'social death' of Africans. Yet while highlighting the colonial violence underpinning the genocide and the international response, some films reproduce imperialistic attitudes by bolstering the West's role as a much-needed rescuer, as we will see in *Hotel Rwanda*.

   An English-language international co-production, helmed by Irish director Terry George and made with South African, British and Italian funding, *Hotel Rwanda* tells the story of Paul Rusesabagina, manager at the Hotel des Milles Collines in the Rwandan capital, Kigali, who saved the lives of 1,268 refugees by sheltering them in the hotel. Called an 'African *Schindler's List*', it focuses on the tale of one exceptional man while purporting to be a document of what really happened. On some of its posters was added the subtitle 'A TRUE STORY'. Rusesabagina, who was employed as a consultant on its production, accompanies George on *Hotel Rwanda*'s director's commentary, enabling us to hear, as we watch, the voice of the hero whose personal story it is. George explains that he did not wish to speak about where he placed the camera and other stylistic choices that usually fill director's commentaries – a strategy that deflects attention from the film's constructed nature, reinforcing the idea that what you see is what happened.

Nonetheless, through its sound-images, *Hotel Rwanda* offers a number of historical insights as well as ideological mystifications. In the beginning, we hear the tuning of a radio, creating a mélange of sounds over the corporate logos that open the film. There is a multiplicity of voices and languages, among them that of a broadcaster announcing US President Bill Clinton's concern about the deteriorating situation in Sarajevo. Eventually, these are cancelled out in favour of one station. State-run RTLM 'Hutu Power' radio rings out of the screen's darkness, calling attention to the international media blackout and RTLM's saturation of the airwaves, both regarded as facilitating the genocide: the former by fostering an oblivious international community (as well as a feeling of impunity among those joining in the killing) and the latter by inciting genocide through inflammatory propaganda. Called 'the soundtrack' of the genocide (Thompson 2007: 6), RTLM is a recurring audible presence, conveying the violent intrusion of anti-Tutsi hate speech into everyday life. Through this popular medium, the population is conditioned into the belief that genocide is morally acceptable.

Over the radio, we hear the Hutu Power narrative, clothed in patriotic sentiment, expressing the belief that only Hutus are true Rwandans and Tutsis are settlers, invaders and collaborators with the colonists. 'Now they have come back, these Tutsi rebels' – a derogatory reference to the Rwandan Patriotic Front (RPF), an army consisting of Tutsi refugees and other opponents of the then-ruling government, led by President Juvenal Habyarimana – 'let us go to work [and] cut the tall trees,' the radio commentator announces, 'tall trees' being a codename for the Tutsis. The rhetoric of 'going to work' builds on the function of the machete, a farming tool used for clearing the land. In this rhetoric, to kill Tutsis is to work for the country's good. In another metaphor, Tutsis are labelled 'cockroaches' to justify their extermination (similar to Nazis' characterisation of Jews as vermin). Based on a selective vision of history that excludes the colonists' handover of power to the Hutus and massacres of Tutsis in the intervening decades, the Hutu Power narrative of revenge against former colonial 'masters' follows an essentialist logic. The film does not, however, sufficiently interrogate this logic.

While the soundtrack prepares us for visuals of Hutu mobs amassing on the streets and reveals the political calculation of the genocide, the film offers a totalising view of perpetrators. Waving their machetes, the Interahamwe, the ruling party's youth militia, whose name literally means 'those who work together', are a menacing presence, cast as the evil, swarming natives of the colonial imagination, many of them wearing distinctive multicoloured shirts known as *kitenge*. Later, the film gestures to the historic killing of ten Belgian UN soldiers – an act calculated to prompt a reduction in UN troops, who were in Rwanda on a peacekeeping mission following the Civil War (1990–3). A lorry-load of Interahamwe arrive and threaten Colonel Oliver (a fictional version of Dallaire), tossing him a blood-stained UN helmet. Through its emphasis on mob violence, the film attenuates our perception of state-sanctioned violence, both that of the Presidential Guard, who were historically responsible for the Belgian soldiers' deaths, and that of outside governments, who did not *fail* to act so much as acted to support their own interests. Calculating that the risks of military action outweighed its poten-tial economic advantages, given Rwanda's strategic unimportance, the US and UK governments deliberately reduced the UN force in Rwanda from 2,500 – which, according to Dallaire, would have been sufficient to stop the killing – to a mere 270 (Curtis 2003: 358; Rwafa 2010: 401). In addition, they were among the UN Security Council members who voted for a resolution to discard the word 'genocide' for the conflict precisely so that the UN would *not* act. It so happened that Rwanda was then one of the Security Council's ten non-permanent members. The UN's decision-making was therefore swiftly communicated to the genocide's masterminds, indirectly contributing to the increased scale of slaughter.

An important expository scene occurs at the hotel bar, where an American cameraman, Jack Daglish, is curious about the 'difference' between Hutu and Tutsi. A Kigali journalist, Benedict, informs him about the European colonists' construction of Tutsis as 'taller and more elegant'. During colonial-ism, divisions between Hutu and Tutsi were 'politically enforced' (Mamdani 2001: 221) through the population's classification into three 'races' – including 'Twa' along with 'Hutu' and 'Tutsi', although this is not mentioned in the film, which favours binaries. With the introduction of identity cards under Belgian rule in the 1930s, a child's identity was identified through the father, meaning that, officially, there were no hybrid identities, despite generations of intermarriage and cohabitation between communities.

Benedict's dialogue exposes how discourses about differences between Hutu and Tutsi are based on racial stereotypes inherited from colonialism. Jack's subsequent conversation with two women seated at the bar confirms the impossibility of distinguishing solely on grounds of physical appearance – 'They could be twins!' he exclaims when they reveal they are Tutsi and Hutu respectively. But, despite trying to transcend racial stereotypes, *Hotel Rwanda* maintains an essentialist outlook. 'So what are you, Paul?' Jack asks Rusesabagina. 'I am Hutu,' he replies. The real-life Paul Rusesabagina had a Hutu father and a Tutsi mother, and is therefore *constructed* as Hutu within the patrilineal system; the film, however, has him straightforwardly Hutu.

This makes him more morally appealing, since 'he seems to have, at his own personal risk, bridged a "tribal" chasm', which aids the conflict's presentation as a split between two sides: good and evil, Tutsi and Hutu (Mboti 2010: 323).

With his Western attire and affluent, middle-class lifestyle, Paul is clearly presented as being like 'us' (that is, the film's target audiences in the West). While importance, agency and status are heaped upon him, other Rwandans are sidelined to the position of mere backdrop. Through the film's 'one good man' motif and its focus on him as saviour, Paul bears Oskar Schindler's torch. The *Bildungsroman* format charts his moral growth from passive bystander to concerned citizen, framing him close up in key scenes, highlighting his concerned or aghast expressions through dramatic lighting, while his Tutsi wife Tatiana is positioned behind him or cowering on the floor in abject terror.

At the same time, the film does not shirk from showing Paul as someone who bribes, lies and flatters – using corrupt means to save lives, similar to Schindler. General Bizimungu, the army's chief of staff and one of the genocide's masterminds, is seen relaxing in the hotel while Paul plies him with drinks. Paul also presents Georges Rutaganda, the Interahamwe's vice-president, with an expensive cigar. Rutaganda keeps the hotel supplied with beer, which, in turn, is used to pacify Bizimungu's soldiers. At one point, a crate of machetes drops from the loader that is meant to be carrying Rutaganda's beer. They are from China, Rutaganda informs the astonished Paul – an allusion to international trade, where machetes and other weapons, like beer, are bought and sold as profitable commodities. As well as implicating China as an exporter of machetes, the scene reminds us that Rutaganda, Paul's 'friend', is a leading *génocidaire*.

Despite these shady dealings, Paul is put on a pedestal as a unique hero, portrayed unequivocally as a 'good man', which is problematic for the same reasons as it is for Schindler. Some have tried to discredit the film, alleging that Paul is not a hero at all but someone who fraternised with killers (Ndahiro and Rutazibwa 2008). But, like the film, this just offers another binary perspective, whereby people are viewed as either heroes or villains. As Nyasha Mboti comments, 'the attempt to reduce Paul to a villain is as naïve as the accounts that seek to make him a hero' (2010: 326).

The presence of cameraman Jack is indicative of the international news crews who were in Rwanda at the time to cover the peace accords. Despite this presence, there is only one known film of killing captured by a journalist, that by Nick Hughes, which was shown on international news in April 1994 (Thompson 2007: 1). Using a long lens characteristic of news media images, *Hotel Rwanda* recreates this historic footage in Jack's video. Paul applauds Jack for the footage, believing that, when they witness the atrocities, people around the world will intervene. More worldly wise, Jack replies: 'If people see this footage, they'll say "Oh my god, that's terrible", and then go on eating their dinners.'

Captured in the genocide's early days, Hughes's footage of kneeling and praying women being hacked to death 'should have been one of the iconic media images of our time', similar to Nick Ut's 1972 photo of Phan Thị Kim Phúc, the napalm-burned girl fleeing naked from an attack in Vietnam (Thompson 2009). Instead, it was broadcast around the world to an overwhelming lack of response. Jack's memorable lines in *Hotel Rwanda* point to the limited function of such atrocity images, which provoke short-term protest and numbing. As I argued in this book's Introduction, this has to do with the way TV news footage is constructed. Decontextualised through clichés like 'tribal rivalry' and Third World disaster, and submitted to news agenda priorities, it often muffles the reality it purports to show.

A key aspect of this news media construction is the social death of Africans, a colonial legacy which *Hotel Rwanda* expresses in its scene of the evacuation of foreign nationals – highlighting a historical event when Rwandans were abandoned through the inaction (or, rather, action) of Western governments. In the driving rain, foreigners are escorted from the hotel onto a bus by hotel workers obediently holding umbrellas over their heads like colonial subjects, whose 'continued service' is demanded even as they are consigned to their likely deaths (Torchin 2005: 48). In the belief that the UN convoys are there to ferry them to safety, a priest and nuns escort orphans to the hotel only to be told: 'No Rwandans. Foreign nationals only.' With their upraised hands, the orphans are reminiscent of the boy in the Warsaw Ghetto photograph, creating a parallel with the imminent execution and doomed youth depicted in this famous Holocaust image. As UN soldiers wrench the tearful nuns away from the children, the film lets us feel their pain through the rain, while the African children's chorus from the theme song, 'A Million Voices', floods into the soundtrack, adding to the scene's pathos.

The international community's hypocrisy and racism is criticised. Colonel Oliver tells Paul slightly earlier: 'You're black. You're not even a nigger. You're an African.' Oliver's troops could have stopped the genocide, yet, like the real-life Dallaire, he is ordered not to intervene by the UN; instead, he must help evacuate foreigners. His words emphasise 'the unequal value of life and the global construction of the African nonsubject' (Härting 2008: 72). That is, the 'social death' of the African.

Many of the passengers boarding the bus are blonde white women, a racial coding that sets them apart from Africans. A black journalist who is momentarily stopped by a UN soldier further highlights the rescue's racism – the assumption being that he has no right to be evacuated until he produces his UK passport. Towards the end of the sequence, the film scans the bus windows, where passengers are seen looking out, and comes to rest at a blonde woman, accompanied by her dog – an image that suggests not only Western class and race privilege, but also that a dog is considered more worthy of rescue than an African. Alongside her is a man taking a photograph with his pocket camera, an allusion to disaster tourism. The next shot reveals the composition of his photo: the abandoned Rwandans lined up in front of the hotel.

In its retrospective exploration of the genocide, the film invites us to look, hoping to rectify the faults of the historical event, when the world stood by and did nothing – to turn passive watching into active witnessing. It thus appeals to the viewer's moral conscience, retrospectively teaching us a lesson supposedly to make sure it doesn't happen again. It seeks to make us feel uncomfortable, creating an allegiance with the shamefaced foreigners who are leaving as well as pity for the abandoned Rwandans. Jack underscores the awkward situation by offering money to the Tutsi woman he questioned at the bar in order to assuage his guilt. As he walks out into the rain, he declines the umbrella that a hotel worker obligingly holds over him and mutters, lowering his face: 'Christ, it's so shameful.'

Shame is a recognition of the wrongfulness of the past. As such, it would seem better than the sentiment that 'the past hasn't anything to do with us'. But, as Sara Ahmed remarks, shame can also be a detachment of responsibility. Shame works to 'conceal how such wrongdoings shape lives in the present' by displacing them into the past, so that events seem merely regrettable, cut off from the present – a way of circumventing responsibility for injustice in the past and present. Paradoxically, by enabling us to feel bad, shame enables us '*to feel better*' (Ahmed 2004: 102, original emphasis). By hanging our heads in shame, we assume that we have done our 'bit' and can resume our business, without taking responsibility for what has occurred. It doesn't do anything to change the state of affairs in which we just carry on with our TV dinners; rather, it perpetuates it.

That shame is a politically harmful emotion is also borne out by Western governments' attitudes to the RPF regime led by Paul Kagame, in power in post-genocide Rwanda since 1994. Because Kagame and his people have been victims of genocide, they have garnered the West's sympathy and desire for the regime to have 'moral legitimacy' (Pottier 2002: 55). Due to their shame at their 'inaction' during the genocide, Western governments have been ready, firstly, to give credence to the RPF narrative that the Hutu refugees who fled to Congo in the aftermath were all *génocidaires* and, secondly, to overlook the regime's own human rights abuses (see Umutesi 2004; Hintjens 2008). Striking similarities exist with Western interactions with Israel following the Holocaust (see Chapter 5).

In its cinematic structures, *Hotel Rwanda* repeats standard motifs of Third World crisis and reproduces the 'social death' of Africans – something it purports to criticise. A pivotal moment is when Paul's van grinds to a halt in the mist-enveloped countryside where, due to the bumpy ride, he and his driver think they have driven off the road. Climbing out of the vehicle, Paul stumbles upon bodies littering the road and stretching to the horizon. When the van restarts, our knowledge of the obstacles in its path activates haptic sensations and lends the scene 'a grisly viscerality' (Torchin 2005: 47). While the spectacular image of bodies strewn on the ground serves as testimony to atrocities, it dwells on the genocide's physical horror rather than the socio-political processes behind it.

With the lack of strategic or economic incentives to justify intervention, the Rwandan genocide represents a crisis for the West's humanitarian projects – modern-day civilising missions that form part of its military-industrial complex. The legacy of imperialistic ways of seeing can be seen in *Hotel Rwanda*'s glorification of the West and UN as much-needed saviours. The UN convoy, exclusively manned by white European soldiers (although the UN is an international body), arrives to cheers and jubilation. Through the UN's association with promised salvation, the narrative demonstrates the consequences of what happens when 'we' turn away – positioning Rwanda as a Third World nation stuck in a state of dependency on the West and diminishing the RPF's and the African Union's role in halting the genocide. In this way, *Hotel Rwanda* justifies interventionist politics, reaffirming the West's superiority and the 'white man's burden'.

As in *Schindler's List*, the representation of history through a celebratory narrative of salvation turns survivors into 'winners', triumphing over adversity. Finally, at a camp for displaced children, Paul and Tatiana are reunited with their nieces Anaïs and Carine, previously feared lost. The children's chorus from 'A Million Voices' is repeated as the film commemorates in its closing freeze-frame the extended family walking towards safety, accompanied by the benevolent (white) Red Cross worker who facilitated their reunion and without whom this happy picture would not be complete.

Despite being a US studio production, *Sometimes in April* displays a more sophisticated portrayal of genocide than *Hotel Rwanda* and avoids the paternalism towards Africa that mars the other film. Shifting between three settings – the International Criminal Tribunal for Rwanda (ICTR) in present-day Tanzania, Rwanda in 1994 and the present, and the USA in 1994 – it has a spatio-temporal complexity in which past and present, near and far, merge into critical images. For instance, the soundtrack over early scenes in Washington announces singer Kurt Cobain's suicide, implying that an obsession with celebrity helps bury news of genocide. At a US government press conference, a journalist asks if the 'rebels' are 'Tutu or Hutsi' and 'which ones are the good guys'. His gaffe draws attention to the moral binaries that form our customary framework for understanding conflict, reflected in narratives such as *Hotel Rwanda*. Moreover, of the films discussed, *Sometimes* is the only one to emphasise how the categories of 'Tutsi' and 'Hutu' are discursively produced.

The film's opening titles roll up over successive maps from the colonial era to the present. Colonial space literally carves up the continent along grids that supplant the spatial experience of the indigenous cultures it conquers (Noyes 1992: 129). In this series of superimpositions, the film visually conveys the German and Belgian colonists' imposition of their power over the land and its people – the Hutu, Tutsi and Twa, who had shared the same language and culture for centuries, now classified into three different 'races'. An excerpt from *Son of Imana* (*Fils d'Imana*, 1959), a Belgian missionary film made for 'the benefit of the native people' (Mosley 2001: 91), follows, showing a condescending handshake between a white official and a Tutsi king. Another piece of colonial-era footage documents the colonists' racial measurements of the 'natives' – all of which situates the conflict in a complex history, highlighting continuities between the colonial manipulation of racial identities and the genocide, the latter firmly rooted in elites' lust for power, not tribal rivalry.

Sometimes utilises documentary conventions, though it is a fictional story. Concerned to avoid imperialistic structures of perception that underlie films like *Hotel Rwanda* as well as *Son of Imana*, its Haitian writer/director, Raoul Peck, incorporated survivors' testimonies into his script, which he envisaged as a form of participatory storytelling, 'telling [the Rwandans'] story *with* them', his own cultural positioning making him particularly attuned to these issues (Peck 2006). Peck grounds the film's authenticity in its use of testimony and location shooting: each historical event is purportedly shot in the 'real location' 'where it happened and exactly how it happened', including the Kayumba swamps, where survivors hid for long periods among decomposing bodies. Effort was made to obtain 'authentic' props (UN vehicles, ID cards, and roadblocks constructed to specification), costumes and characters' mannerisms. Wanting to avoid the generic African accent used by Hollywood, Peck encouraged his actors to find 'authentic' accents for English-speaking or French-speaking Africans.

Along with extensive news and archival footage, titles are inserted to announce locations and estimates of people killed to emphasise the genocide's rapidity and scale. Scenes are filmed in an unadorned realist style, often from the shoulder like news footage, with, Peck claims, no attempt to aestheticise, so people can say 'Yes, that's how it was' (Peck 2006). Yet, the film does – inevitably – aestheticise and fictionalise its material, including through the decision to shoot in English.[4] Therefore, my analysis does not claim that *Sometimes* is 'more realistic' than *Hotel Rwanda* but that, through a different set of stylistic choices, it offers an alternative interpretation and a more complex viewing experience.

The fictional protagonist, Augustin, played by the British actor Idris Elba, is neither a saviour nor a 'winner' triumphing over adversity. Like Paul, he is married to a Tutsi wife but, unlike *Hotel Rwanda*, the film emphasises his contradictory position. As a soldier involved in training the army and the

Interahamwe, which kills Tutsis, including his entire family, Augustin is complicit in the atrocities – a collaborator as well as a victim and survivor. At first, he denies that the genocide is happening, disregarding its signs as rumours. When the film alternates between Colonel Bagosora (one of the genocide's chief architects), purposefully marching with his men through the proverbial corridors of power, and the preparations for genocide, it makes connections that Augustin cannot, or will not, make at this point. *Sometimes* also indicts France's role in providing military support to the Rwandan government in order to maintain influence in the region; again, Peck's cultural location as a Haitian helps in providing this critical perspective. The presence of French soldiers accompanying Bagosora in the military compound and his inventory of foreign-supplied weapons (Albanian Kalashnikovs, Czech grenades and American M16 rifles as well as Chinese machetes) further subverts the idea of the genocide as an outburst of tribal rivalry and suggests, instead, that it is an all-too-routine outcome of the global arms trade and balance-of-power politics.

Sometimes further displays complex historical thinking by portraying perpetrators as ordinary people 'coordinating' themselves to the violence. 'I'm going to work', a rural man matter-of-factly tells his wife as he leaves home, picking up his club. The Interahamwe are imagined as mostly casually dressed youths hanging out at roadblocks, not the evil swarming masses of *Hotel Rwanda*. During the film, the radio is heard 'directing' the genocide, informing killers of names on execution lists. In the first flashback to 1994, we are taken into the RTLM studios, where Augustin's brother Honoré is a presenter, renowned for his 'history lessons' interspersed between popular hits such as Billy Ocean's 'Caribbean Queen', establishing RTLM's appeal to the younger generation. Instead of demonising the genocide's perpetrators as evil, this makes us question the distance between 'them' and 'us'. Honoré is a complex individual: prosecuted for his role in inciting genocide at the ICTR in the film's present day, he also tries to save Augustin's wife Jeanne. Crucially, the film does not convert him into a 'good man' after this one good act. Neither are the RPF presented as unqualified 'good guys'; they are shown carrying out reprisal killings after the genocide.

Partly due to its avoidance of the 'one good man' motif, *Sometimes* gives greater narrative agency to women, though it tends to essentialise them as victims and martyrs. Jeanne, whose rape and death are represented in flashback with Honoré's voiceover, becomes a martyr through his narrative, killing herself and her rapists with a grenade. When killers burst into an all-girls school, the headmaster sees it as his 'duty' to hand over the Tutsi children, while Martine (later Augustin's partner) protects the schoolgirls and ensures they understand the implications of their choice to stand together in solidarity. For this heroic act of resistance, the schoolgirls are uniformly shot, among them Augustin's daughter Anne-Marie.

While the school massacre is filmed in a conventional way (a soldier strikes Martine in the stomach with a rifle butt before the shooting squad guns them all down), it is unnervingly juxtaposed with scenes of bureaucracy in Washington, where US officials are examining satellite pictures showing evidence of mass graves, yet still refusing to put soldiers on the ground: it has 'Somalia written all over it', declares one official, referring to the humiliating retreat from Mogadishu in 1993 after eighteen US soldiers died in a failed mission, an incident often cited to explain the USA's reluctance to intervene in Rwanda. The scene's banality in contrast to what is happening on the ground serves to expose the US government as out of touch. This is further underscored when Prudence Bushnell (deputy assistant Secretary of State for African Affairs), portrayed by Debra Winger as the film's only sympathetic Westerner, watches in quiet exasperation a TV interview with US State Department spokesperson Christine Shelly, while 'Day 65, 620,000 people killed' flashes up on our screen. With her insistence on the official phrase 'acts of genocide', which, under the UN Convention on the Prevention and Punishment of the Crime of Genocide (1948, the 'Genocide Convention'), has to be coupled with 'intent' in order to be legally recognised as the crime of genocide, Shelly reduces the situation to mere wordplay in order to avoid the responsibility to act.

In its evacuation scene, *Sometimes* does not glorify the UN as a saviour. At the Saint-Exupéry French School, foreigners push their way past a crowd of Rwandans and are lifted onto a UN truck. There are no abandoned orphans and no melodramatic score to arouse sentimental emotions; instead, the air is filled with screeches of protest, a chaotic atmosphere, unlike the gracefully choreographed evacuation in *Hotel Rwanda*. That is not to say that the evacuation in *Sometimes* is not choreographed; it is choreographed differently. Once all the foreigners are aboard, a UN soldier fires bullets into the air to disperse the crowd. As the truck drives off, the film closes in on its UN lettering, lending a sinister association to this logo. At a bend in a nearby road, the Interahamwe start to appear, one by one, individuated from each other by their different clothes, yet banded together, as conveyed by their machetes scraping on the gravel and feet tramping in unison. In their car, Augustin and his friend Xavier follow the UN truck to a roadblock where Xavier pretends to the Interahamwe that they are part of the UN convoy. Here, the UN force has no charismatic leader like Colonel Oliver. Instead, the stony-faced UN soldier to whom Xavier appeals to support his stratagem rigidly adheres to his administrative orders and refuses to play along. As a result, Xavier is left to the Interahamwe's mercy, singled out as a Tutsi and executed. Like the US government, the UN is portrayed as a bureaucratic organisation, more associated with the banality of evil than benevolent rescue.

Rape and sexual violence have been a particular focus of discourses and representations of the Rwandan genocide, including in *Sometimes*, where we are introduced to a rape survivor testifying at the ICTR. Previously silenced or merely thought a 'byproduct' of war, the crime of wartime rape has now achieved belated international recognition as a result of the ICTR and the International Criminal Tribunal for the Former Yugoslavia (ICTY), where witnesses revealed mass rapes. Rape has now been certified a war crime, a crime against humanity, and an aspect of genocide under the Genocide Convention, deemed to fall under its category of 'serious bodily or mental harm' if committed as part of an 'intent' to destroy a population group. The ICTR itself marks the first time rape was upheld and charged as a part of genocide, yet it has a poor record on actual rape convictions; many defendants were acquitted or released on appeal (Nowrojee 2008; Buss 2010).

These developments in international law are the culmination of feminist struggles to ensure that rape be recognised as a 'weapon of war', starting with Susan Brownmiller's *Against Our Will* (1975), which argues that rape is an assertion of male power, although this generalised framing of rape can be criticised for eliding the histories of colonial domination and racism that also underpin rape. In the Rwandan genocide, rape is inseparable from race ideology. As revealed in the ICTR media trial, sexual violence against Tutsi women was incited by radio hate propaganda, making rape an integral part of the onslaught. Tutsi women were raped because of their perceived role as reproducers of their race and unattainable objects of desire, and suffered horrific mutilation of their wombs and vaginas, as well as being deliberately infected with HIV.

In cinema, rape is often represented through stereotypical conventions that hold up the woman's 'victimized body' for the male gaze and turn it into 'the body of cinema' (Lebeau 1995: 139; Horeck 2004: 92). *Sometimes* avoids sensationalising rape in its portrait of the rape survivor, a secret witness initially heard as a disembodied voice through a wall and resounding around the courtroom before she is seen. Her testimony against a municipal leader echoes some of the ICTR's real-life trials, where political, administrative and military leaders were charged with rapes carried out by those under their authority, even if they did not directly participate; as rapes were so widespread, the defendants were deemed to have known about them and to have either permitted or encouraged them.

Another indirect perpetrator is the priest at the church where Jeanne takes refuge. He accompanies soldiers who infiltrate the refugee-filled church to rape and murder. The film subverts the traditional narrative role of the church and other public institutions as redeemers and illuminates that, during the genocide, churches and other places of shelter and sanctuary, including schools, became killing stations. It resonates with Hannah Arendt's observations of the Third Reich, as well as those of researchers into the Rwandan genocide –

that ordinary people, including members of 'respectable' professions usually regarded as a bulwark against violence, such as doctors, nurses, priests, teachers and human rights activists, collaborated (Mamdani 2001; Dumas 2013).

THE NIGHT OF TRUTH: AFTERIMAGES OF VIOLENCE

While historical dramas frequently adopt a retrospective standpoint, implying that the past is 'over and done with', those that deal with the conflict's aftermath can counter those perceptions. The mass participation and intimacy of the Rwandan genocide destroyed not only bonds between family members, but also those relating to 'the entire spectrum' of social activities: 'cultivation, sharing of drinks, cows, weddings, football, etc.' (Dumas 2013: 63). This has posed problems for reconciliation, since victims and perpetrators were often well known to each other. *Sometimes* contrasts the ICTR – held in Tanzania under UN auspices to prosecute the genocide's high-level leaders – with a local conflict resolution system, *gacaca*, which focuses on grassroots perpetrators, overseen by local judges and conducted in the local language, Kinyarwanda. *Gacaca* has been promoted as a path to national reconciliation, a way of healing past wounds, comparable to the Truth and Reconciliation Commission (TRC) in South Africa. Like the TRC, dramatised in films such as *In My Country* and *Red Dust* (both 2004), its theme of reconciliation between former victims and perpetrators has enticed the film industry; *Kinyarwanda*'s tagline, for example, is 'forgiveness is freedom'.

A film that emphasises the *difficulties* of reconciliation is *The Night of Truth*, set in a fictional African country in the aftermath of a genocidal war between ruling Nayaks and 'rebel' Bonandés, who have risen up against the repressive regime. Following a truce between the two warring parties, the Bonandés' leader, Colonel Théo Bogwanda, holds a celebratory feast and invites the Nayak President Miossoune, his wife Edna and their troops. The result is an exceptionally fraught evening and, finally, a hard-won reconciliation. The director, Fanta Régina Nacro, hailed as the first female fiction film director in Burkina Faso, regards her film as the third in a series with *Hotel Rwanda* and *Sometimes in April*: 'My film could not exist without those two going beforehand; it is the completion' (Amadiegwu 2005: 20). However, unlike the other two films, it is not a conventional historical drama.

As a film from another African country (located in west Africa whereas Rwanda is in central Africa), *Night* is significant for how it deals with the genocide – not directly, but 'through fictionalized, somewhat delocalized tales that take on universal weight' (Dovey 2009: 255). Nacro conceived her script with both Yugoslavia and Rwanda in mind. Her initial impulse for making the film came from seeing reports and documentaries about the Yugoslav war, where 'the fact that women were raped, and some even had acid poured into their vaginas, made me think about the question of atrocity' (Amadiegwu 2005: 20). The Rwandan genocide began shortly thereafter, while the Bosnian War was ongoing. At the heart of *Night* stands the attempt to understand 'how it was that people who might have shared a coffee one day would the next day be killing each other' (ibid.). Events in Yugoslavia affirmed to her that such atrocities were not limited to Africa – that the potential for extreme violence resides in every society and within each individual.

While *Night* could be accused of reinforcing stereotypes of warring African 'tribes', its imaginary setting enables it to explore common processes behind genocide and, indeed, the atrocity-producing situation in general. Shot with a mixture of amateur and professional actors (including real soldiers) together with a handheld camera, it has a raw, home-movie feel. However, its formal inspiration is Shakespearean drama. The play it most closely resembles is *Titus Andronicus* (c. 1592), whose motifs of rape, mutilation and murder resonate with the Rwandan genocide's horrors. In the play, Empress Tamora incites her sons Demetrius and Chiron to rape and mutilate Titus's daughter Lavinia, in revenge for his killing of her other son, Alarbus; in his own gruesome revenge, Titus bakes 'two pasties' out of Demetrius's and Chiron's heads and serves them up to her and the Emperor at a feast. However, whereas the play is driven by the motor of revenge and endows it with moral justification, *Night* exposes revenge as a catalyst in a cycle of violence in which each side believes itself to be morally vindicated. The violent dynamics of score-settling come to be seen as another 'boomerang effect'.

Night has no benevolent hero to reassure the audience. Colonel Théo, who emerges as a potential hero, is himself a perpetrator of horrific crimes, and is roasted alive in an equally horrific revenge attack. The atrocities alluded to in the film are reminiscent of those during the Rwandan genocide, when 'people were quartered, impaled or roasted to death' (cited in Mamdani 2001: 6). As *Night* is not constrained by the taste considerations of conventional historical drama, it can deal more frankly with the violent past, including by utilising body horror to imagine open physical and psychological wounds. Its use of graphic violence, however, does not adhere to the conventions of spectacular screen violence and does not make factual claims: as Nacro says: 'What I am showing is not the exact violence as it happens, but the mental image of vio-lence which persists' (Amadiegwu 2005: 20).

In graphic flashbacks which impart a dream that Théo had, we see muti-lated body parts floating in a blood-tinted river. A boy's head lies in a puddle. Because the images are fleeting and almost subliminal – the dampened ambient sound inducing a surreal atmosphere – they are not channelled into senti-mental, humanitarian affect as they are in the sea-of-corpses scene in *Hotel Rwanda*. As overt reminders of carnage, they are also different from sanitised

Figure 2.2 Women paint murals telling stories of the violent conflict that forms the backdrop to their lives in *The Night of Truth*.

snippets of violence on TV news. The flashback is turned against its conventional usage, which 'consume[s] the past through action images' (Landy 1996: 21). Instead, it figures the continual intrusion of past violence on the present, like retinal afterimages. These strategies should not be regarded as a reiteration of the trauma paradigm, as *Night* deploys them to explore the causes and contexts of violence rather than to 'work through' a particular past.

The film's visceral use of mise-en-scène compels us to experience its characters' history as a perpetual overlay of the past on the present. Murals, painted by women, tell stories of rape, mutilation and killing through expressionistic forms and colours, like a storyboard containing components of the film. Among the contorted limbs and faces is an Edvard Munch-like scream. With their angular forms, expressionistic compositions have unsettling effects: 'every distortion agitates the viewer's cognitive patterns' (Powell 2005: 27). The brown background emphasises vivid splashes of blood-red and white figure outlines, which have a sensational force in themselves. As the film glides along these communal paintings, some of them still being painted, it invites us to reflect on the violent past that forms the background to the artists' lives, a metaphor made concrete by the fact they literally *are* the background, adorning the Bonandé compound's walls, while life casually passes before them: a motorbike, followed by donkey carts, go past.

When the President insists on coming to the feast with his men armed, Soumari, Théo's wife, declares: 'Men make peace, men make war. It's nothing to do with me or the children.' Yet the film's portrayal of women and children is more complex than this statement allows. Sat on the floor, children light-heartedly tease each other about their amputated fingers and legs, the low-level camerawork enhancing this portrait of everyday intimacy with violence. Too young to have known anything else, their childhood is cut short by their routine experience of atrocity. In this non-sentimental way, the film imparts the violent history etched upon them.

In the figures of Edna and Soumari, the film explores women's roles as both instigators of violence and peacemakers. As in Abu Ghraib, women's participation in atrocities in Rwanda, either killing with machetes, or offering support roles to the killing squads, generated debate, particularly around Pauline Nyiramasuhuko, the first woman to be convicted of genocide and incitement to rape at the ICTR. In *Night*, Edna is not 'evil' personified but a complex character, consumed by grief. The film opens with her at her son Michel's grave, insistent that his spirit will not rest until he is avenged; ghosts of the dead, crying out for revenge, similarly haunt other characters. How Michel was killed, during a massacre of Nayaks by Bonandés at the town of Govinda, is extremely meaningful to her, as she relates to Soumari during the feast: 'They cut off his testicles and crammed them in his mouth.' At Soumari's pained expression, Edna enjoins her to drink to reconciliation, with bitter sarcasm reminiscent of Titus at his banquet after he reveals his daughter's barbaric treatment.

Another character who bears *ressentiment* about the past is the film's 'jester' figure, Tomota. He first appears on a country road, swinging a machete and shouting 'murderers' and 'cockroaches' at the President's convoy. When he recognises Fatou, a character introduced in the next scene, who is returning traumatised to the Bogwanda household after being raped and witnessing her family's deaths, as someone who married a Nayak, he instantly wants to kill her as a Nayak spy. Tomota articulates the undercurrent of fear, hatred and distrust between the two groups. In the kitchen, he joins the cooks assembling the feast and spins racist stories: 'The Nayaks are not men like us. If you catch one you'll see he'll have scales on his skin. Like a snake!' The women scream with disgust and applaud him. Some join in with equally implausible tales, while Fatou is isolated in the corner, preparing a braised snake, a Nayak dish she has been asked to cook as a goodwill gesture to their guests.

Night brings into sharp focus the formation of a shared intersubjective reality around stereotypes of 'the enemy'. In Rwanda, where Tutsis were called by the dehumanising term 'cockroaches', a killer later reported: 'We no longer saw a human being when we turned up a Tutsi in the swamps' (cited in Zimbardo 2007: 16). As a way of degrading victims so as to carry out murder with an easy conscience, dehumanisation sets the conditions for 'normal, morally upright, and even usually idealistic people to perform acts of destructive cruelty' (ibid.: 307). But perceptions of others as less than human may not even be conscious, as the previous discussion of imperialism, slavery and genocide from Arendt through Césaire to Patterson has attempted to highlight.

The feast's tense atmosphere exhibits the conflict between, on the one hand, the African justice of *ubuntu* and idea of 'truth and reconciliation', which work through forgiveness, and, on the other, desire for retribution. At first, both sides are reluctant to lay down their arms, which they have brought to the feast. The film emphasises the awkwardness of reconciliation, as each side is invited to eat the other's culinary delicacies – braised snakes and roasted caterpillars. On either side, the dignitaries oblige with equal measures of politeness and distaste. Food is used as a visceral encounter with cultural difference. The colonial past is present in the formal language of state – French – with which the two sides address each other while speaking their own language among themselves; the Bonandés and Nayaks are thus distinguished from each other linguistically and culturally, in contrast to the Hutu, Tutsi and Twa in Rwanda, who share the same language and culture.

The thoughtful and resourceful Soumari bans the playing of drums at the festivities, anticipating that they may reignite the violence. She pours drink on the soil to placate the dead's restless spirits and urges the President to help her persuade the soldiers to disarm. In return, she receives with good grace the news that the man who tortured and killed her father is jailed but will not be executed, recognising that 'the vengeful cycle of blood-letting' must eventually stop (Kemp 2005: 46). Nevertheless, as the evening wears on, it fills with characters' memories of acts of victimisation and perpetration. When the drums finally beat, they awaken memories of Govinda, sending Théo into a traumatised stupor by which Edna recognises him as Michel's killer. Although Théo confesses his guilt, she refuses to forgive and has him surrounded by Nayak soldiers and roasted alive on a spit as a form of retributive justice – an agonising death whose sensory horror the film does not fail to impart. Edna herself is shot point blank by her husband in retribution for this act when he and others appear on the scene.

By *Night*'s reckoning, there can be no easy reconciliation. Yet, somehow, life goes on and it does suggest an escape route from the manipulation and hatred that underpin genocide. Edna and Théo are buried in the same grave. Towards the film's conclusion, Tomota visits the grave to salute his former colonel and provides an update on the situation, including that the colonel's brother N'Gove is now defence minister: 'And the Bonandés and the Nayaks? There aren't any Bonandés and Nayaks anymore. Now we're all Bonandayaks.' Revenge is not the answer; it is the system that needs changing. The community creates a new political identity beyond binary identities that encompasses both groups. The binary is dissolved in a larger identity, configured in the common grave. Importantly, this new political identity is created on a power-sharing basis, in contrast to the post-genocide politics of identity in Rwanda where, despite the new, apparently more inclusive 'Rwandan' identity, only a Tutsi is given the prerogative to represent the nation.

Night underlines that more is at stake in learning the lessons of genocidal events than account-settling with perpetrators, commemoration of the dead, or even healing traumatised survivors. Unlike many genocide films, it offers hope without illusions about human goodness or triumph over adversity. Rather than 'reforming' its characters through moral conversion, it emphasises human plurality as the basis for establishing agreements and new covenants as the only safeguard. Here we might invoke Arendt again: 'No moral conversion of man [*sic*] . . . is needed, required, or hoped for in order to bring about political change for the better' (1992: 18). As the final credits roll, *Night* takes us into a classroom, where Fatou is teaching schoolchildren a text by Théo whose message is of common humanity ('We're from the same clay. We've lived through the same nightmares, endured the same sufferings'). As she teaches the future generation, the film tracks across the rows of desks, taking in the children's young, concentrating faces. The schoolroom scene proposes that the future resides in these children. For genocide and atrocity are not just about the past but hold implications for present-day society, with the need to find ways of breaking deadly repetitions of violence. Films contribute to this debate by exploring how people give their consent to atrocities or become part of systems of violence, rather than when they seek moral solutions to political problems – the one 'good man' to set everything aright.

NOTES

1. Although Jews were singled out for total destruction, the Nazi genocide included a number of other victim groups, among them the Sinti and Roma (commonly known as gypsies), who are still persecuted in Europe today (Lewy 2000).
2. For further comparison of Arendt and Césaire, see Rothberg (2009: 33–107).
3. Jean-Paul Sartre describes Fanon's rhetorical moves as 'moment[s] of the boomerang' in his preface to *The Wretched of the Earth* (Fanon 2001: 17).
4. *Sometimes in April* was planned to be made in French; this was changed to English for commercial reasons.

CHAPTER 3

The Art of Disappearance: Remembering Political Violence in Argentina and Chile

Out of an aeroplane hatch, paper cutout people tumble into the sky and crash to the ground. During their fall, their names, ages and dates of disappearance appear in titles. This scene is from the documentary short *Abuelas* (2011), which blends animation with real-life testimonies in its tale about family life during the 1976–83 military dictatorship in Argentina, when an estimated 30,000 people disappeared into secret detention centres, many of them tortured and finally killed, their bodies buried in unmarked graves, or secretly dispatched, drugged but still alive, from planes out at sea. At a panel discussion, its Iranian-born director, Afarin Eghbal, and British screenwriter Francesca Gardiner explained that that their reason for making the film was that these atrocities had taken place in their lifetime and, yet, like many of their generation or younger, they had previously known nothing about them (Eghbal and Gardiner 2011).

This chapter focuses on the art of imagining and remembering the disappearances in Chile and Argentina in films made by filmmakers from those countries and from abroad. Each of these films responds to the political 'art' of disappearance with a particular kind of cinematic experience, ranging from thrillers (*Imagining Argentina* and *Chronicle of an Escape*), through poetic, performative and animated documentaries (*Nostalgia for the Light*, *The Blonds* and *Abuelas*), to surreal narrative (*Post Mortem*). Critics who have written about these (or similar) films in the context of national cinema studies have noted that they are concerned with memory (Page 2009; Sorensen 2009). But, as these films are made at least in part for transnational audiences, how do they encourage those audiences to identify with memories they have never had?

A frequent criticism of films aimed at global markets is that they 'minimize specific referential markers' and 'gloss over' the complexities of the past so as not to alienate audiences from 'elsewhere' (Podalsky 2011: 60). In this chapter, I argue that these films about the disappearances construct 'memory-worlds' and 'dream-worlds', containing both general and specific referents, that act as mnemonic triggers, capable of interfering with, and disturbing, our own personal and cultural memories. Moreover, I argue that their endeavour to reach beyond the limits of national communities enriches, rather than weakens, their ethical and political potential by fostering what Michael Rothberg has called 'multidirectional memory', capable of evoking and articulating other histories of the disappeared.[1]

Used by repressive regimes to crush their political opponents, enforced disappearance is a widespread historical phenomenon that has given the verb 'to disappear' a chilling transitive meaning. A disturbing addition to the history of modern atrocity, yet with roots in previous colonial practices, enforced disappearance was officially adopted as a state policy by the Nazis in their 'Night and Fog' campaigns; it was also used in Franco's Spain and in the Soviet Union under Stalin. During the Cold War, it was practised by Latin American militaries and deployed against the militant left inspired by the Cuban Revolution (1959). Trained at the US Army School of the Americas as part of US foreign policy, those militaries themselves had a longer history of involvement in brutal practices that goes back to colonialism. The Argentine military described their opponents' guerrilla tactics as a 'dirty war', though the phrase equally applies to their own and other regimes' operations during the 1960s–80s, when 'dirty wars', using enforced disappearance and torture as instruments of repression, proliferated across much of Latin America.[2] The military juntas gave moral justification to their tactics as a necessary defence against subversive elements. Enforced disappearance remains a technique of state terror in many parts of the world. And in the 'War on Terror', waged by the USA with the complicity of many other countries (including the UK), using 'extraordinary rendition' and targeted killings, we have witnessed its return on a global scale.

As defined in the International Convention for the Protection of All Persons from Enforced Disappearance, enforced disappearance is carried out by states, or with their acquiescence, and conceals the whereabouts of arrested or abducted individuals in order to place them 'outside the protection of the law', at risk of torture and murder (UN 2006).[3] As a political crime, it may be understood as the art of making people disappear imperceptibly and effacing the evidence. Diana Taylor suggests that it is a trick or spectacle that manipulates appearances to promote the illusion of normality, while striking terror into the population, especially relatives of the disappeared, who are left paralysed with uncertainty regarding their loved ones' fate. She deploys the term 'percepticide' to describe the 'self-blinding of the general population' in Argentina:

> People had to deny what they saw and, by turning away, collude with the violence around them. They knew people were 'disappearing.' Men in

military attire, trucks, and helicopters surrounded the area, closed in on the hunted individuals and 'sucked' them off the street, out of a movie theater, from a classroom or workplace. And those in the vicinity were forced to notice, however much they pretended not to. (Taylor 1997: 123)

Although denial, as Stanley Cohen (2001) has pointed out, is a common feature of responses to atrocity, it is intrinsic to the strategy of disappearance, which entails the collusion of the national and also often the international community. While the US role in the 1973 Chilean military coup to overthrow Salvador Allende's democratically elected socialist government is well known (the first film to reveal this was *Missing*, discussed below), British authorities also colluded with Augusto Pinochet's regime. They were fully aware of the atrocities soon after they began, yet determined to maintain good relations with Chile because of economic or strategic advantages. A Foreign Office brief from the time stated: 'We have a major interest in Chile regaining stability, regardless of politics.' As Mark Curtis glosses, for the latter read 'regardless of the people of Chile' (2004: 271). In addition, Britain supplied the aircraft (Hawker Hunters) used to bomb Allende's presidential palace on 11 September 1973, and continued to supply arms thereafter. During the Falklands War with Argentina (1982), Britain sought cooperation from Chile for military intelligence in exchange for undermining UN investigations into human rights abuses (ibid.: 275). And Britain's Prime Minister, Margaret Thatcher, was a stalwart defender of Pinochet.

On the regimes' part, denials range from claims that there are no kidnappings, no secret detention facilities, and no torture and murder of political opponents, to deliberate hoaxes staged for the international media and community of human rights monitors. This is what happened when Argentina hosted the 1978 World Cup: the basement of the Navy Mechanics School (known by its Spanish acronym, ESMA), which served as a notorious extermination centre and a departure point for death flights over the sea, was turned into a players' relaxation area (Feitlowitz 1998: 172). Concealment of dead bodies in secret mass graves or other unmarked deposition sites also forms an act of denial, contrasting with the ways in which death is usually publicly acknowledged.

Disappearance is an interdiction of thought. It is calculated to stop us thinking about it, to relegate these uncomfortable thoughts to the edges of our awareness. Over time, such a strategy is compounded by amnesia or, rather, selective memory and unconscious forgetting. When the dictatorships in Argentina and Chile ended, truth commissions were set up. In Argentina, the National Commission on Disappeared People (CONADEP) published its report *Nunca más* ('Never Again') in 1984, leading to the trials of military juntas in 1985, in which army commanders were convicted of their crimes against humanity. In Chile, the National Commission for Truth and Reconciliation, focusing on victims of disappearances and killings, made its findings public in the Retting Report (1991). Collecting survivor testimonies and other evidence of secret detention, torture and mass killings, the value of such reports lies not simply in their revelation of 'the truth' after years of cover-up and denial, but public acknowledgement of what had been kept alive in the private memories and nightmares of the disappeared and their relatives.

Since disappearance is a sensitive topic in the places where it is happening or has happened, it is subject to state censorship and self-censorship, and film-makers face considerable risk if they tackle it, including the risk of disappearing themselves. My decision to focus on films about the Argentine and Chilean disappearances is due to the fact that they now form a considerable body of work, with a number of factors stimulating a resurgence of these themes in contemporary cinema.[4] Pinochet's 1998 arrest in London and then his death in 2006, together with the lifting of former Chilean censorship laws in 2002, have given that country's filmmakers greater liberty to tackle the topic, while the abolition of amnesty laws in Argentina in 2005 has also enabled a renewed attention to the past there. In her study of Argentine national cinema, Joanna Page links this resurgent interest to 'the social context of its expression', namely the 2001 financial crisis, the result of neo-liberal economic policies introduced under the dictatorship (2009: 152). However, I am keen to see these films not merely as negotiating a particular national past, but in terms of the work of memory that they provoke in transnational audiences: how films make memories of the disappearances available to a wider public, and enable us to engage with this past. The next section therefore elaborates the theories of memory that underpin my argument before analysing the films.

FILM AS A MEMORY-WORLD

In the previous chapter, I dwelt on how film creates its own historical story-world, in productive tension with our own world. Just as film cannot reproduce historical reality, so it cannot reproduce thought functions like memory or dreams (Frampton 2006: 203). Film is not a repository of memory content, providing us with other people's memories; it constructs its own memory-world, which acts on and mediates our memories. Rather than a 'prosthetic memory', as Alison Landsberg has contended (2004: 2), film is a prosthesis *for* memory, capable of extending our sensory perceptions into our memories and shaping them in particular ways.

The roots of this thinking lie in Henri Bergson's philosophy, where each moment of our existence bears two aspects, the actual (perception) and the virtual (recollection): 'Perception is never a mere contact of the mind with the object present; it is impregnated with memory-images which complete it as they interpret it' (Bergson 1988: 133). According to this view, all our sense-perceptions are informed by memory, and vice versa. This forms the basis of Gilles Deleuze's theory of the time-image in cinema, which he claims was created after the crisis of the 'action-image', giving rise to purely audio-visual situations that, rather than extending into action, invite viewers to complete the image by rummaging through their own memory circuits (Deleuze 1989: 47). Following Bergson, Deleuze distinguishes between 'habitual recognition', a functional response to an object, resulting in a spatially confined action or reaction ('the cow recognizes grass, I recognize my friend Peter'), and 'attentive recognition', where perception does not extend into action; instead, the object evokes recollection-images: 'it is the man I met last week at such and such a place. . .' (ibid.: 44). Deleuze links habitual recognition with conventional action-oriented cinema, where images are determined by story development and characters' actions and reactions. However, if, as Bergson suggests, the splitting between perception and recollection occurs at each moment of our existence, then the dynamic that Deleuze ascribes to the time-image is a potential locked in every image.

As Laura Marks reminds us, the Bergsonian model of perception upon which Deleuze draws is multisensory. Like the taste of the madeleine cake in Proust's *Remembrance of Things Past*, the senses are 'vehicles for memory' (Marks 2000: 201). Memories are activated by the senses and 'all sense percep-tions allow for, and indeed require, the mediation of memory' (ibid.: 202). According to Marks, film images arouse their viewers' memories by registering meanings at a sensory/bodily level. Sensations are produced through mimesis on viewers' bodies as they identify both with the sensory activities of on-screen characters and with the film's own sights and textures, which synaesthetically or haptically evoke the other senses. In this way, 'each audiovisual image meets a rush of other sensory associations' (ibid.: 222).

Filmmakers often deliberately summon up sensory memories 'in order to intensify the experiences [they] represent' (ibid.: 223). As Marks observes, this becomes more crucial 'when official histories cannot comprehend certain realms of experience, or when they actively deny them'. Drawing upon her work, I would argue that those who are familiar with the places and histories evoked in a film may have a fuller sensory experience of it, and therefore a deeper engagement with the memories it directly evokes; on the other hand, they may feel that its constructed memory-world fails to correspond to their memories. The experience of film spectatorship thus calls attention to the body as 'a political witness', full of remembered knowledge (ibid.: 200). Yet, although the sensory textures of the place and time being depicted may be unfamiliar to us, the cinematic image invites us to engage with them, and our own sensory memories and embodied histories will affect our response.

By triggering our own sensory memories, films bring histories that we did not directly experience to bear on our bodies, placing us in relation to them. Deleuze proposes that when we search for a recollection in response to a perception, we place ourselves in 'the past in general', then choose among the various 'sheets' of our past (1989: 99). In memory, we bring together the near and far – all the 'sheets of the past' are in contact with each other and related to the present, offering a model of non-chronological time that Deleuze sees mirrored in the cinematic time-image.

Cinematic images have an ability to reorder experiences in a similar way to memory and make that reordering evident to our senses. Sheets of the past are capable of being placed alongside each other in a single image, provoking viewers to search for corresponding 'sheets' in their own memories (ibid.: 116). Although the films in this chapter deal with the collective memories of particular societies separated by geographical and/or generational distance from their transnational audiences, their construction of the past may include 'us' in indirect or indeterminate ways. Through their multisensory images, the films lure us onto sheets of the past to which we did not think we belonged. They plunge us into their memory-worlds, where memory becomes shared and multiple.

Michael Rothberg uses the concept of 'multidirectional memory' to challenge common beliefs about the nature of collective memory and its ties to group identity. Rather than the idea of memory as unique and exclusive to particular groups, and fundamentally separate and opposed to the memory of other groups, he proposes an alternative vision of memory 'as subject to ongoing negotiation, cross-referencing, and borrowing; as productive and not privative' (Rothberg 2009: 3). Here, the remembrance of one history does not erase but evokes others, and 'has the potential to create new forms of solidarity and new visions of justice' (ibid.: 5). Hence, one of the contentions of this chapter is that representation of memories of the disappeared in Argentina and Chile may enable the articulation of similar histories of victimisation and terror.

Although more commonly understood in terms of one memory blocking out another, Sigmund Freud's theory of 'screen memories' is also relevant here. 'Screen memories' are those everyday, comforting images which can be recalled with sensory vividness when one thinks back, say, to one's childhood. For Freud, their value resides in their relationship with other, more disturbing memories that have been suppressed (Freud 1962: 320). The temporal relationship between the screen memory and the content it has screened out can vary: it can be retrospective, anticipatory or 'contemporary' (Freud 1989: 63–4). Freud's theory emphasises the extent to which memories are *juxtaposed*, as well as their unreliable and contingent character, although screen memories are not exactly false, as they are formed in the present from residues of memories relating to our childhood or later life. It shows how memories undergo similar processes to dreams: condensation (for example, several people or objects merged into one), displacement (the replacement of one image by another) and secondary revision (the transformation that inevitably arises when we try to remember and narrate a dream) (Freud 1991: 651). The similarity between dreams and memory should not surprise us, as dreams are composed of fragments of memories; and memories, as Bergson noted, trigger a virtual experience of past events comparable to dreams.

Let me first demonstrate my argument about memory with *Missing* (1982), which follows the story of a US citizen who goes missing during a military coup in an unnamed South American country (implicitly Chile) and his wife's and father's attempts to trace him. For Haile Gerima, *Missing*'s focus on Western protagonists, played by Western stars, is scandalous and typical of Western media devaluation of Third World lives: 'Throughout the film, we witness a graphic depiction of masses of faceless, nameless Third World people in the background, while in the foreground we are skilfully manipulated and emotionally tormented by one American character who is missing' (Gerima 1989: 75). Although the problems that he highlights about Western cultural domination are significant and real, Third World and Western stories are not separate but inextricably linked, as shown in *Missing*'s plotline, which strongly implicates the USA in the coup, revealing the US business interests at stake in the overthrow of Allende's socialist government.

Missing's foreground–background dynamics juxtapose two stories/memories within the same image: that of the missing American and that of countless others who went missing under US-trained and -backed military dictatorships across Latin America. Of course, *Missing* is not the only film with such a dual narrative focus; as noted earlier in the book, there is an established genre of films about distant conflicts in which a white/Western protagonist's adventures take place against the backdrop of an oppressed people. However, it is especially significant in *Missing* because, as Catherine Grant (2008) points out, it would have been impossible due to censorship to make a film on the topic at the time in Chile – or indeed in many other Latin American countries. *Missing*'s aesthetic approach encourages us to read it as evoking the disappearances across Latin America that could not then otherwise be cinematically represented, as signalled in its opening credit sequence, where children playing in the background are reflected in the car window from which the protagonist, Charlie Horman, looks out. Reflections create a doubleness in the visual field, a relay between the actual and the virtual image, as well as implying potentially multiple virtualities. *Missing*'s story of a lost American and his relatives' search to find him becomes the actual image that triggers multiple virtual images of others who disappeared. This is reinforced by the fact that it was released in Argentina in 1982 under the Spanish title *Desaparecido*

('Disappeared') and also later (under the same title) in other Latin American countries.[5]

Cinema performs a similar function to memory-work and dream-work in imagining the past. Watching films that relate to other people's memories can be disruptive of the memories that we have as individuals and as communities. The notion of 'screen memories', with its emphasis on the mutability of memory, also prompts a shift from questions of 'historical accuracy' to questions of *how* we remember the past, including the many different ways of remembering it – questions that are suffused with ethical and political implications, since memory is always, inevitably, an alteration and forgetting of aspects of the past.

DISAPPEARANCE AS A THRILLER PLOT

The words 'sinister' and 'uncanny' frequently recur in witness recollections of disappearances, attesting to 'the disorientating, even incapacitating, fear' that engulfed people at the time and that lingers in the present (Feitlowitz 1998: 73). With its portrayal of sinister, violent happenings, power corruption, and death as a punishment for those who know too much, the thriller genre shares a certain affinity with events of political disappearance and is capable of evoking powerful memories. Indeed, as Slavoj Žižek has pointed out, referring to the thriller in general, 'the theme of the "disappearance that everyone denies"' is a thriller plot, with a 'conspiratorial Other' using deception to stage the impression that the missing person never went missing nor ever existed (1992: 79).

As defined by Fredric Jameson, the 'conspiratorial thriller' usually features protagonists who are detective-like figures through whom the hidden, deeper workings of society are revealed (1992: 33). *Missing* is a classic example and aspects of the genre are reflected in the two films discussed next, *Imagining Argentina* (2003) and *Chronicle of an Escape* (*Crónica de una fuga*, 2006). Under the pretext of accessible entertainment, these thrillers impress upon us multiresonant images that can summon memories of similar patterns of disappearance across national borders, or trouble memories of complicit societies. Although regarded as one of the most 'obvious' genres and, as such, largely beneath scholarly investigation, the thriller lends itself particularly well to this kind of remembrance due to the bodily and sensorial triggers it unleashes. But in the following analyses, I argue that *Imagining Argentina*'s multidirectional memory potential is limited, partly due to its reliance on an ocular regime, whereas *Chronicle of an Escape* utilises a range of the genre's haptic sensibilities, producing more compelling memory-images.

A US–Spanish co-production, *Imagining Argentina* features an international cast, drawn from around Latin America (Mexico, Panama, Costa Rica),

Spain, the USA and the UK. In its fictional story, Emma Thompson plays a journalist, Cecilia Rueda, who is targeted by the military after she publishes an article about the kidnapping of schoolchildren who had protested about bus fares (an actual event in Argentina known as 'Night of the Pencils', documented in the 1986 film of that title). When she disappears, her husband, theatre director Carlos Rueda (Antonio Banderas), acquires second sight, enabling him to share the experiences of the disappeared – a device through which the film creates a visual memory of the horrors of the past and invites the audience to identify with its victims. Yet, although supported by human rights organisations such as Amnesty International and defended by Thompson, it met a hostile critical response (Dawtrey 2003: 16). According to a *Screen International* review, 'this story conveys neither the horror of the deeds nor the terror of those who lived through them' (Fainaru 2003: 27).

But despite attacks on the film for its 'uncomfortable blend of graphic brutality with . . . magic realism' (Dawtrey 2003: 16), there is an established tradition of magical realism to represent violent histories (think of Salman Rushdie's *Midnight's Children* (1981), whose narrator has psychic powers). Although criticised for failing to evoke the 'horrors' of the disappearances, it catalogues them with considerable attention to circumstantial detail, including: the raids by plain-clothes death squads in green Ford Falcons; the network of clandestine detention centres; the use of the cattle prod (*picana*) to apply electric shocks to sensitive body parts, a common method of torture in both Argentina and Chile; rape as a torture tool; the form of water torture known as the *submarino*; executions; and the dropping of the disappeared out of aircraft. Therefore, I contend, the problem with *Imagining Argentina* is not *what* it depicts, but *how* the visions invite us to remember this past.

When the military regime ended, Carlos tells us in the opening voiceover laid over period archival footage, the generals urged people not to look back. Having altered the meaning of the word 'disappear', they now exhibited the wish 'to disappear the past'. 'But we must look back,' Carlos insists and, as he does so, the film arrests and pauses the images, seguing into black-and-white film of the Mothers of Plaza de Mayo, the mothers of the disappeared who, with their distinctive white headscarves and placards bearing photographs of their missing children, keep their memory alive in weekly marches before the presidential palace in Plaza de Mayo, Buenos Aires's main public square.

The notion of 'disappearing the past' reveals the ideological power of memory to emphasise certain aspects of the past while leaving others unstated. That *Imagining Argentina* itself is susceptible to this process is evident from its closing statistics on disappearances in Argentina and references to numbers of 'disappeared' in other countries, listing Bosnia-Herzegovina, Chile, Colombia, Congo, El Salvador, Guatemala, India, Indonesia, Iraq, Mexico, Peru, Sri Lanka, 'and thousands more in Libya, Cuba, Morocco, Russia and Turkey', with Amnesty International named as the informational source. The titles conclude with the statement, 'Somewhere in the world today, someone is "disappearing!"' While this reminds us that disappearances have not just occurred in a distant past, but continue in numerous places, it is ironic that the country list excludes the USA, as in 2003, when the film was released, it was embarking on its own disappearing acts. *Imagining Argentina* easily lends itself to an imagination of bad things happening to other people in other places, and this lessens its capacity to unsettle Western audiences, who are let off the hook regarding Western complicity. This goes hand in hand with its touristic gaze at the disappearances through Carlos's second sight.

Carlos compares his second sight to a hallucination or remembering a scene in a movie. Able to see into the past and the future, he is endowed with cinematic powers: to flashforward and flashback. Flashbacks are like 'sudden uprushes of memory' (Frampton 2006: 17) and conventionally function as signals for memory, indicated by a marker separating them from the body of the narrative. As Gilles Deleuze writes, the clearly signalled flashback 'is like a sign with the words: "Watch out! Recollection"' (1989: 48). In *Imagining Argentina*, Carlos's flashbacks are marked by a look off screen, grounding the subsequent images in his point of view through eyeline-matching conventions, so that we know that what we are seeing is a version of what he is seeing. In much of the film, memory is reduced to this standard use of flashback.

Through Carlos's privileged viewpoint, the film provides audiences with superior knowledge that elides the very quality that makes disappearances so disturbing – which lies, precisely, in *not* knowing the fate of loved ones, an absence that for many relatives persists to this day. This is evident in scenes involving the character Gustavo, a reference to the young naval officer Alfredo Astiz, who helped to run ESMA and infiltrated the Mothers of Plaza de Mayo under the assumed name of Gustavo Niño; he attended their meetings and demonstrations while posing as the brother of one of the disappeared. Astiz was known as 'the Blond Angel of Death'; a nickname that is translated into Gustavo's disarmingly innocent appearance when he is first encountered at the Mothers' meeting at Santa Cruz Church, a scene that recreates an actual incident, Astiz's 'sting' of December 1977 (see CONADEP 1986: 128). The film generates suspense by alternating between the church interior and aerial views of the road outside, where an army of green Ford Falcons is sinisterly gathering. In the ensuing scuffle, Gustavo is himself attacked and nine women, including two nuns, are hooded and kidnapped. But while, in *Imagining Argentina*, Gustavo is later exposed as a traitor through Carlos's psychic powers, Astiz's real identity in their midst remained unknown to the Mothers, who did not have that reassurance of knowing.

Mostly pictured in clear and brightly lit compositions, Carlos's visions visually objectify memories of the disappeared and their reliability is never questioned. For example, in response to one relative of the disappeared to whom he offers his services as a clairvoyant, the film generates Carlos's vision of her daughter's body lying in a ditch, transparently rendered in a long shot. Through Carlos's second sight, we are also able to pierce ESMA's gleaming white exterior and enter its far less salubrious basement: from overhead, Carlos's colleague Silvio is seen, hooded and pacing about in his cell. The film reproduces the privileged role of vision, and its connotations of objectivity and distance, in Western regimes of knowledge. Distance vision is affiliated with what Laura Marks calls optical visuality, which depends on 'a separation between the viewing subject and the object' (Marks 2000: 162). Through Carlos's second sight, *Imagining Argentina* largely offers distanced perspectives on the disappeared, a clinical gaze removed from their experiences, not near enough for us to feel or identify with them closely; its spatial distance amounts to emotional distance. This reinforces my point that what is problematic about the film is not its combination of psychic visions and historical brutalities, but this tourist-like surveying of tragedies.

As this gaze is bestowed upon a male character, it has a gendered aspect, associated with the 'male gaze'. However, its mastery is qualified in Carlos's visions pertaining to Cecilia, which, unlike his other visions, are ambiguous and enigmatic, hinting at rather than attempting to transparently render the hidden world of the disappeared. At a deserted warehouse at night, the sound of a foghorn is heard, suggesting Cecilia's whereabouts may be near the harbour. An owl perches on a gatepost, a mascot from an aviary close to a rural detention centre. Carlos sees shadows cast on the wall: images of Cecilia struggling with her captors. Here, the film stages the failure of the realist illusion, as Carlos cannot relive Cecilia's ordeal except in the mediated shape of his own imagination, figured through shadow play, a proto-cinematic image that links together the mediation of cinema and memory. At this point, it suggests that the memories of relatives of the disappeared are haunted by numinous figures, not the lucidly drawn images of Carlos's other visions.

For Marks, haptic visuality can be more revelatory of a situation than what is merely seen, as it has the capacity to evoke more associations: 'rather than making the object fully available to view, haptic cinema puts the object into question, calling upon the viewer to engage in its imaginative construction' (Marks 2002: 16). Imagination in *Imagining Argentina* shifts from the mode 'I see it' to 'I feel it' in a sequence that begins when Gustavo, now transformed in a uniform with slicked-back hair, cruelly invites Cecilia to 'choose' who will be the next rapist of her daughter Teresa, who has also been kidnapped. 'Let them take me,' Cecilia utters with deadened eyes and a drained, expressionless face. Nonetheless, the choice is made for her, from the line of military men awaiting their 'turn', and Teresa is dragged away. The film shifts to Cecilia sitting alone in her cell, forced to hear her daughter's shrieks. Covering her ears, Cecilia bends over in pain and emits a silent cry, her mouth agape like the tortured figures in the paintings of Francis Bacon or Edvard Munch. The silent scream, whose sound cannot reach anyone, conveys the solitude of disappearance as well as haptically evoking the sense modality of sound.

When she is observed staring fixedly, Cecilia explains to the guard: 'I'm remembering.' It is not her past upon which she is dwelling, but her present experiences in detention, which she seeks to store in her memory, so that she can testify about them. Her gaze at her cell wall, where the paint is flaking away in Rorschach-like patterns, lends a haptic texturing to the film's representation of her remembering. It also activates our sense of touch, rather than merely sight, in order to evoke the horrors of this past.

Chronicle of an Escape, also known as *Buenos Aires 1977*, gives importance to the role of non-visual senses in constructing its memory-world and nightmare-world of disappearance. Its story of four men who were imprisoned in the Mansión Seré detention centre and managed to escape is based on the testimonies of Claudio Tamburrini, who wrote the memoir *Pase Libre*, and Guillermo Fernández, who acted as a production consultant. It draws on the Latin American tradition of *testimonio*, which often revolves around 'a significant life experience' recounted by direct participants (Beverley 1996: 24). Yet, as Elzbieta Sklodowska has noted, such witness testimony 'cannot be a direct reflection of his or her experience, but rather a refraction determined by the vicissitudes of memory, intention, ideology'. In addition, the mediation of the interlocutor, in this case the film producer, who selects and edits the material in accordance with film conventions, 'further superimposes the original text, creating more ambiguities, silences, and absences' (cited ibid.: 34).

Going beyond a merely factual account of what happened, *Chronicle* utilises the sensory apparatus of the horror and thriller genres to portray the disorientating phenomenological experience of disappearance. Set in Buenos Aires in 1977 and 1978, the film, moreover, intentionally evokes memories of the 1978 World Cup, which was held in Argentina and won by the home team: firstly through the protagonist Claudio, who, like the real-life Tamburrini, is an amateur footballer, and secondly through a scene of a failed escape attempt, where a TV broadcast of a match from the World Cup plays in the background. In this scene, the film takes the artistic licence of making the characters' detention coincide with the World Cup (which happened in June whereas the men escaped in March). When the Argentine side scores a goal, hope of escape is momentarily shattered, as both guards and prisoners shout 'Argentina! Argentina!', reminding us that football nationalism was co-opted into tacit support for the regime. Moreover, through its reference to the World Cup as a shared memory of the time, when Argentina was celebrated as the champion although disappearances were happening, *Chronicle* provokes the memories of those who were not directly involved. Its nightmarish revisiting of that era through heightened sensory effects solicits our identification with experiences that might normally be considered distant from our own.

Right from the outset, *Chronicle* offers a far more intimate portrayal of the disappearances than *Imagining Argentina*. It imagines the terror of the raid on Claudio's family home at ground level; his mother pleads with plain-clothes men from the death squad seeking to arrest him as a 'terrorist' suspect. Testimony of the death squads and their methods is elaborated in terms of the thriller genre, as a detainee is forced to cruise the streets with the squad to identify other suspects and Claudio's abduction takes place in full view of neighbours and passers-by, displaying his abductors' impunity and instilling such fear in the public that nobody dares to stop them. The nervous, low-level handheld camerawork, combined with the soundtrack's repeated chimes and bass piano chords, instantly generates a sense of unease, an auditory mirroring of our heartbeat. *Chronicle*'s minimalist but expressive soundtrack by itself tells the story and communicates its blindfolded characters' own reliance on auditory and other non-visual perceptions.

Chronicle has a diary format – with titles in the form Day 1, Day 3, Day 31 – but rather than covering every day, they are intermittent, suggesting gaps in the film's representation of events. This underlines the fragmentary, incomplete nature of memory as well the sensory disorientation produced by detention, where victims are kept blindfolded in order to deplete their spatio-temporal awareness, so that it is hardly even relevant to speak of days. Mansión Seré, a former aristocratic home in a suburb of Buenos Aires, was destroyed by the military to erase the evidence before the regime ended, so the film does not use the actual location but one we assume is like it. Soldiers nick-named it 'Attila', while neighbours called it 'The House of Terror', as screams and shootings could be heard at night (Feitlowitz 1998: 167). Goings-on were to some extent paraded to the public to generate local fear. Accordingly, *Chronicle* depicts Mansión Seré in the gothic iconography of the 'terrible house'. Low-angle exterior shots reveal it as a decaying colonial mansion; on the night of the escape, lightning flashes over it. As Anna Powell writes of the haunted house in *The Haunting* (1963), 'it is at once a shadowy memory-image and a solid bricks-and-mortar building with a power of its own' (2005: 168). Drawing upon this horror convention, *Chronicle* emphasises how the house stands in its own reality, apparently separate from normal space-time coordinates, yet also bearing down upon the neighbourhood. Claudio's screaming as he is tortured is laid over previous images of his entry into the house, so that his screams seem to resound around its environs.

Inside, the house is a disorientating space. Here, the film's visual style harks back to German expressionist cinema, with its oblique angles and prominent shadows transforming the appearance of external reality to express inner landscapes of fear, anxiety and estrangement. It also deploys a thriller characteristic, namely the creation of unsafe space, filled with a sense of menace (Maltby 2003: 354). The mobile, handheld camera points up the staircase, hinting at and generating the sense of horror in that place, and reveals the faded grandeur of its hallways and rooms, heavy with shadows, to the accompaniment again of ominous piano chords. In an expressionistic play of light and shadow, doorways open, revealing the elongated shadows of the torturers. Light itself becomes a vehicle in the story, as prisoners are kept in inner rooms that are windowless or have blacked-out windows, shutting out daylight to distort their sense of time.

The prisoners are blindfolded, so most of the time they don't see the faces of their captors, yet they contrive ways of seeing by peering around the edges of their blindfolds or nudging them up with their knees. Scenes are framed to reflect their distorted perspectives, as in a shot of a doorway turned 90 degrees to express a prisoner's sideways vision while lying on the floor. These distorted visuals convey the nightmarish quality of these memories of the past. Since their vision is compromised, they rely on other senses, including sound and smell, which become heightened. Sounds of the outside environment become a means by which they make sense of where they are, establishing the house's location in a quiet but reasonably well-populated neighbourhood. Trains clattering past and sounding their horns suggest a nearby level crossing. In destabilising vision to place emphasis on bodily knowledge – auditory, tactile and proprioceptive perceptions – the film invites viewers to participate in a similar altered state and piece together clues.

A domestic environment usually provides a container for the body, catering to its functions and needs (Scarry 1985: 38). When a person is detained and tortured, this is inverted: the room is turned into a weapon, common domestic objects are turned into torture tools, and the body is imprisoned, sealed off from all proper contact from the world. In the film, the main torture scenes take place in the bathroom and bedroom, each stripped to their basics; their furnishings, designed for comfort or convenience, are turned into apparatuses and palimpsests of pain. The bathtub is utilised for 'submarine'-style water torture, in which the prisoners are immersed in dirty water. In the bare rooms where the prisoners are kept, the only pieces of furniture are mattresses, caked in blood and dirt. In the attic, where four prisoners (Claudio, Guillermo, Gallego and Vasco) are confined, a bare light bulb hangs from the ceiling, casting strange shadows. Prisoners are forced to strip naked, to eat without cutlery, and to betray each other to ensure their own survival. Their captors show them their malnourished reflections in a mirror in order to demonstrate how unrecognisable they have become to themselves and to others: to persuade them that, if their bodies are falling to pieces, so are their whole beings.

According to the report *Nunca más*, the detention centres were designed to strip victims of all human attributes and break down their identities, not just to physically eliminate them; to enter a detention centre effectively meant 'to cease to exist' (CONADEP 1986: 52). In the regime's official discourse, 'a *desaparecido* was neither living nor dead, neither here nor there' (Feitlowitz 1998: 49). The film encapsulates this form of enforced non-existence, a mode of being 'in the world but not part of it, alive in the realm of death' (ibid.: 166). From within, the prisoners at times perceive signs of ordinary life going on as 'normal' – the outside world for whom their ordeal does not appear to exist. To disappear is also to leave the world, as we realise is the fate of prisoners who are 'released'. When one of them, Tano, is told he is to be sent home, he is injected with a drug, marched in single file with other prisoners and driven away in a truck that disappears into darkness, implying they are to be killed.

Although it encourages us to identify with victims of disappearance, *Chronicle* displays a non-partisan attitude to leftist guerrillas, hinting at violence on both sides. Guerrilla tactics included kidnapping, bombing and assassinations, but the military regime vastly exaggerated the scale of the insurgency, which was by no means equal to the repressive response.[6] In Argentina, there were two major guerrilla groups, the Peronist Montoneros and the Maoist ERP (People's Revolutionary Group). While some prisoners are depicted as politically active (namely Guillermo) or relatives of leftists (Vasco is the brother of a Montonero), *Chronicle* focuses on innocent victims swept up in the whirlwind. Tano informs on Claudio after his name is plucked at random from his address book, while other suspects are identified just as arbitrarily from people's photo collections. While this highlights how ordinary people become 'collateral damage' of such repressive measures, it elides the real Tamburrini's political activism in order to make him a more sympathetic character.

But state-sanctioned disappearance and torture are injustices whomever they befall. The film underlines this when Guillermo is taken to the office of a judge. The squad orders him to walk to the door and ring the doorbell, but they blindfold him just as he enters, revealing that they are in league with the judge. In an open-plan office, in plain view of his employees, the refined, well-dressed judge does nothing to stop abuses of secret detention and even authorises Guillermo's sentence without trial. During the regime, the military controlled the justice system and gained the collusion of the judiciary, corrupting the entire legal process and allowing crimes of disappearance to be carried out with impunity. Some detainees were brought before military tribunals, a sham justice that showed the military's desire to make itself judge and jury. In a felicitous role reversal, the real Guillermo Fernández plays the judge in this scene, embodying the perpetrator who passed a death sentence on his younger self to expose this grotesque perversion of justice. The purpose of the visit is to humiliate Guillermo, intensifying his sense of helplessness before 'justice'. It paves the way for the next scene, which begins with a close-up of his bloodied face as he lies on the floor, having been tortured. Here, the thriller format gains political edge by showing that the state and its accomplices behave just like lawless gangsters.

It is Guillermo's idea to escape – it is, he realises, the only way prisoners can survive, not by aspiring to be heroes or martyrs, refusing to give up names, as that would simply lead to their deaths and the annihilation of all traces of their existence. In a pivotal scene, a screw comes loose from his bedframe, while one of the guards, Lucas, is busily mopping him with disinfectant. Canting up from a floor-level camera, the film captures the screw falling to the floor with a small thud; a detail that otherwise only Claudio notices. This small but significant screw helps the four men escape through the window and puts an end to the ordeals in Mansión Seré, which was subsequently closed down and the prisoners sent to 'regular' jails. 'We are going to disappear,' Guillermo announces to the others, telling them his planned 'rope trick' of using blankets joined end to end to descend from the window. On the stormy night of their escape, he is the last to leave. Scanning the empty room, the film reveals his scrawled message on the wall, 'Gracias Lucas' ('Thank you, Lucas'), declaring his own act of disappearance as a just reward to his captors.

As the four escapees run naked and handcuffed along the deserted, night-time suburban street, a passer-by sees them. He averts his gaze. His figure goes out of focus for an instant, before he briefly acknowledges the men and hastily turns away. 'Percepticide blinds, maims, kills through the senses', Diana Taylor writes (1997: 124). Through the cinematic technique of pulling focus, the film aptly captures this deliberate self-blinding.

The ending is powerful but understated. The escaped prisoners go back, not to a hero's welcome, but to a climate of fear. Gallego is reunited with his father, who, upon discovering that he is an escapee, is instantly fearful for his family. In the very final scene, Claudio encounters a mother and her baby – the same woman, then pregnant, to whom he had offered a seat on a bus near the film's start. A marker of time passing in the outside world, this ends the film on a bright and hopeful note full of the possibility of rejoining 'normal' life, yet it also suggests the outside world's utter oblivion to the fate of the disappeared.

THE BLACK HOLE OF ABSENCE

In its evocation of the nightmare underworld of the detention centre, *Chronicle of an Escape* blends testimony with fictional conventions. The following section discusses three documentaries whose impetus is not so much to impart factual knowledge, but to 'deliver the same emotional and aesthetic impact as fiction' (Wolf 2010: 17). Between them, they adopt strategies such as self-reflexive performativity, dream-like fantasy and poetic images to address issues of memory and loss.

Nostalgia for the Light (*Nostalgia de la luz*, 2010) is directed by Patricio Guzmán, who was detained in Santiago's National Stadium during the Pinochet dictatorship and forced into exile. His most famous film is *The Battle of Chile* (*La batalla de Chile*), released in three parts in 1975, 1976 and 1979 respectively. It charts the rise of Allende's Popular Unity Party and the coup. Smuggled out of the country and edited in Cuba, it remained censored in Chile until after the fall of the dictatorship. Guzmán's documentaries are preoccupied with dictatorship memory, but *Nostalgia for the Light* has a more elliptical, poetic approach. Set in the Atacama Desert in northern Chile, it draws parallels between the searches of astronomers and archaeologists looking for clues to the past and the searches of relatives for the disappeared, whose remains were secretly scattered in the desert.

The film starts with Guzmán's meditative voiceover, which lays open his own involvement in the leftist struggle and anchors the subject in his personal past, his boyhood in Chile. From images of the old German telescope in Santiago, which awakened his passion for astronomy, we are transported to a homely interior. The film offers us a portrait of a slumbering world as yet untouched by the tumultuous events of the 1970s. It conjures up an embroidered napkin, a lacework tablecloth, an old-fashioned radio, a crimson-cushioned stool and an antique sewing machine, enveloped in peaceful ambient sounds – domestic objects that remind Guzmán of his childhood home. It is a constructed memory-world that invokes the cinematic image's ability to summon up one's memories involuntarily through the sensuous impact of colours, forms and textures – evoking not the past as it was, but images that appeal to viewers' memories. These homely memory-images then cede to memory-images of violent histories that are more difficult to confront.

Otherworldly in its appearance, the Atacama Desert has been compared to a Martian landscape. With low-level camerawork brushing almost directly against the parched land, the film assimilates its deep red colours and cracked textures and magnifies the sound of shoes crunching on the salty ground. This sensory evocation of the landscape imparts awareness of the dry atmosphere and soaring temperatures. What attracts both astronomers and archaeologists to the desert is its high altitude and dry climate, which make the sky clear enough to peer into the edges of the universe, while human remains and other artefacts are preserved on the ground. Although an apparently empty, dead space without signs of life, the desert is teeming with hidden presence, holding pre-Columbian rock carvings and mummified human remains as well as Pinochet-era mass graves. It is, Guzmán's voiceover intones, 'a vast open book of memory'.

However, the desert does not belong to what Pierre Nora has called *lieux de mémoire* since it lacks the intentionality (a 'will to remember') that he ascribes to such sites (1989: 21). Rather, it is an archaeological site, which manifests accumulated layers of time. It is a space where different levels of the past coexist and coincide with each other. *Nostalgia* juxtaposes its highly sensuous images of this extraordinary landscape with relics of what previously happened there, thereby bringing that past closer to viewers. The desert itself is a memory-world, or even a 'world-memory' (Deleuze 1989: 98), in which we are invited to roam: to remember what has passed, in the place where it happened.

Latin America's colonial legacy persists in the sands of the desert in the form of the graves of miners, who were from poor, indigenous communities and died working under conditions of slave labour in the salt mines. Their belongings are also preserved nearby. An archaeologist whom Guzmán interviews, Lautaro Núñez, asserts that this is a legacy that Chile has wished to leave behind and deny; how it marginalised its indigenous people is 'practically a state secret', a history about which very little is known. By juxtaposing these memories, *Nostalgia* invites comparisons between brutalities against indigenous people and those against the more recently disappeared.

Remote and inhospitable, the desert was a prime location for atrocities. Pinochet's largest detention centre, Chacabuco, was built there in a disused salt mine, where indigenous miners had worked. Conveniently, there was no need to build anything; the miners' cramped quarters were converted into prison cells and 'all the military had to do was add barbed wire,' asserts Guzmán. The film combines black-and-white archival footage with present-day colour cinematography of the derelict detention centre, which further underlines continuities between these histories. It also brings the past to life through survivors' memories. A former inmate, Luís Henriques, remembers the watchtowers and electric cables, traces that were erased when the military dismantled the camp. He shows us a wall where prisoners etched their names; it remains there, despite the military's efforts at cover-up and the pressure of time and the elements, which also threaten to make the past disappear.

Survivors' moving stories are a testament to 'the agency that can be involved in suffering', showing the creativity and resourcefulness that enabled them to survive and continue life in the present (Traverso 2010: 185). One survivor is Miguel, an architect who was imprisoned in five detention centres and made drawings of each. Counting his paces across a room, he demonstrates how he measured dimensions and remembered them. By night, he drew and afterwards shredded his sketches into the latrines in order to escape detection. Yet once they had been drawn they could be recalled and drawn again. In exile, he was able to recreate his experiences in detailed, expressionistic pen-and-ink drawings of prisoners huddled in confined spaces and menacing guards, a feat that astonished the military. In *Nunca más*, Argentine witnesses are described as having a 'corporeal memory' as they could provide meticulous illustrations of their prison layouts that exactly matched official plans (CONADEP 1986: 58). By tracing Miguel's navigation through space, as he tallies up the steps and turnings, *Nostalgia* pays tribute to his embodied knowledge, testifying to a heightening of bodily senses under imprisonment as one of memory's phenomenal resources.

Nostalgia's main emotional focus is on women from Calama, a town near the Atacama Desert, searching for their disappeared loved ones, who were killed by the notorious Caravan of Death in October 1973, when Pinochet authorised General Sergio Arellano Stark to speedily execute prisoners during lightning visits to provincial camps. The film refers to these events through archival footage from *La verdadera historia de Johnny Good* ('The True Story of Johnny Good', 1990), a documentary made just months after the dictatorship ended, which shows the unearthing of mass graves in Pisagua, a coastal town in the far north. The image of suffering women has gained powerful currency in the context of disappearances, owing to groups such as the Mothers of Plaza de Mayo and the Calama women, who have been searching the desert for more than twenty years. The film emphasises their resilience and determination by juxtaposing black-and-white photographs of the earlier days of their search with present-day footage. Its most enduring images include those of the women shovelling with tiny spades, their figures dwarfed by the vast desert. Sifting the sand with their hands, they literally *feel* the grains for their loved ones' remains. But, the film reminds us, their search is not in vain. Even during its production, the body of a disappeared female prisoner was found, her mangled limbs jutting out from the sand, preserved in a similar way to pre-Columbian remains.

One of the women, Vicky Saavedra, found her brother's remains: a single foot in a shoe and fragments of his skull. Only then was she able to absorb the fact that he had died. Not knowing whether their disappeared loved ones are dead gives relatives hope that they may eventually return, while the fact that bodily remains are scattered makes identification very difficult and drags out uncertainty about their fate. On the verge of tears, the fragile but resolute seventy-year-old Violeta Berrios repeatedly expresses her desire for her husband's bones. The disappeared must be found in order to be properly mourned. The ongoing nature of that process is underlined by images of the found remains of the disappeared who have not yet been identified, stacked up in anonymous cardboard boxes, unlike the preserved remains of indigenous people, now carefully wrapped and housed in a museum.

Nostalgia gains much of its power from its astronomical metaphors. As the astronomer Gaspar Galaz explains, light takes time to travel from objects so that, for example, light from the sun reaches us after a time lapse of eight minutes. The past is therefore the filter through which everything is perceived. When we look at the night sky through a naked eye or telescope, we are looking at the past. While archaeologists excavate the desert to find out about the past, astronomers explore deep space to discover the history of the universe. The film alternates between the vast expanses of the desert and the vistas of space. With its hypnotic movement through CGI galaxies, it invites us to imagine losing someone in space and trying to find them, as a way of imagining the formidable task of finding people lost and missing in the desert.

These images deploy depth of field, which, according to Deleuze, shows time for itself, in a way that is not subordinated to movement, generating 'a certain type of direct time-image that can be defined by memory' (1989: 109). Deleuze is referring to use of deep focus cinematography to figure temporal relations through the composition of foreground, middle-ground and back-ground. However, in deep-space photography, spatial distance is literally temporal distance, as light from the furthest stars takes the longest to reach us; in the film's digital imagery, the tracking movement into the recesses of space is a journey through time. Deleuze argues that the time-image created by depth of field is not a recollection-image or flashback, but 'an invitation to recollect' (ibid.). It embodies 'the actual effort of evocation . . . and the exploration of virtual zones of the past, to find, choose, and bring it back' (ibid.: 110). *Nostalgia*'s deep-space cinematography likewise invites us to remember the numerous disappeared who haunt the regions of the past.

The word 'nostalgia' derives from the Greek *nostó* ('I return') and *alghó* ('I feel pain') (Seremetakis 1996: 4). In its beautifully evocative images, *Nostalgia for the Light* projects that longing onto the stars. Its montage works by free association, interrelating memory and dream, and suggesting links that otherwise might be perceived as outlandish. For example, a graphic match between a heavenly body's pitted surface and mottled human remains reminds us that our bones are made of the same material – calcium – as the stars. The connections between the film's disparate images are also suggested through the digitally superimposed luminous 'dust' that drifts across some of its frames. These dancing grains prefigure both the constitution of bodies from cosmic dust and cinema itself, composed of movement and light.

At the same time, the film is aware of the shortcomings of its parallels. Asked if there is a similarity between his own pursuit and that of relatives searching for their loved ones' remains, Galaz agrees there is a certain likeness but also a crucial difference: when he and other astronomers finish their daily searches, they can sleep peacefully at night, unlike the relatives who scour the desert for human remains that may never be found and who may never find peace until they do. The irreconcilability between the film's astronomical metaphors and the relatives' search for the disappeared is made poignant when Violeta exclaims: 'I wish the telescopes didn't just look into the sky, but could also see through the earth so that we could find them.'

Nostalgia might be seen as an attempt to console, to work through the losses of the past with images and metaphors that place the trauma in a cosmic perspective. However, I would claim that it uses its imagery and metaphors to juxtapose otherwise disparate regions of the past: to summon us to remember and make connections between different violent histories. This is the cosmic perspective that it offers.

Abuelas ('Grandmothers') is named after the Argentine Grandmothers of Plaza de Mayo, who joined the Mothers in their weekly march. As a group, their aim is to recover their grandchildren, kidnapped with their parents or born in captivity in detention centres, where many were adopted by military families. The film is based on interviews with four grandmothers, gathering their memories into a single narrative around one character. It deploys an animation method known as pixilation, 'the filming of live actors and real-life sets using stop-action photography' (Greenberg 2011: 8). The director, Afarin Eghbal, chose animation because she believes it 'offers a universal language instantly recognisable by everyone – for almost everyone worldwide has grown up watching and having some experience of animation from an early age' (NFTS 2011: 5). Motivated by a desire to reach a broader audience, Eghbal used animation here as a technique to draw in viewers, to 'create an emotional connection' to the subject rather than 'a polemic from the outset' (Eghbal and Gardiner 2011), yet it also creates distinctive memory-images for the disappearances that leave enduring traces on viewers' own memories.

Like *Nostalgia*, *Abuelas* starts by lingering in a homely apartment, which exudes a sense of being the Grandmother's lived-in space. We are introduced to her through a close-up of her fragile, gnarled hands, which are knitting. The film evokes our own tactile memories, maybe of our own grandmothers, and 'recruits' them (Barker 2009: 44) into its story. An English actress's voice is layered over the Spanish-speaking voices of the Argentine grandmothers. This multiplicity in the voiceover is sustained throughout, suggestive of the multiple testimonies upon which the Grandmother's character is based. As she reminisces about her hopes and expectations of becoming a grandmother, the film follows a ball of wool rolling towards a set of doors that open of their own accord into a room that magically transforms into a nursery. Pieces of furniture – a chest of drawers, a rocking horse, a cot – slide into the frame, and toys spin around the set, transporting us into a magical childhood world. This is violently undercut when the Grandmother relates her pregnant daughter's abduction. Again the door opens of its own accord. This time, miniature Ford cars skid into the apartment to amplified sounds of revving engines. Ford Falcons were a 'reigning symbol' and instrument of the Argentine state terror: 'They were seen everywhere – always without license plates, cruising the streets or quietly parked and waiting' (Feitlowitz 1998: 172). Not only do the animated cars express this sinister symbolism; their sudden encroachment imparts the intrusion of political violence into family life.

Views of the city dissolve into figures stencilled on wrinkled paper, reminiscent of outlines of the disappeared posted on the walls of Buenos Aires build-

Figure 3.1 Paper cutout people are cast out of an aeroplane and fall to the ground, the background changing to the brown hues of the character's apartment in *Abuelas*. Reproduced by kind permission of the director, Afarin Eghbal.

Figure 3.2 The slow, painful reconciliation between grandmother and granddaughter in *Abuelas*. Reproduced by kind permission of the director, Afarin Eghbal.

ings in 1983 (see Feitlowitz 1998: 168–9). In the film's signature sequence, the figure outlines became paper cutouts which are cast out from a military plane. During each fall, the background changes colour from a chalk-drawn blue sky to the brown hues of the apartment, dramatically offsetting the gliding figures, until they finally crash against the ground, whereupon the paper figures scrunch themselves up into balls and roll out of sight. With its stop-action technique, animation can create 'the sudden appearance or disappearance of a person or object, or the sudden replacement of one thing by another' (Ezra 2000: 28). This makes animation an aesthetic counterpart to the military's use of disappearance as a technique of state terror, capable of exposing the latter as a cheap magic trick. The death flights were the regime's most notorious method of disposing bodies, part of its attempt to make people disappear without a trace, although some bodies washed up on the shore (CONADEP 1986: 233). In 1995, navy captain Adolfo Scilingo publicly confessed that he had participated in death flights, confirming rumours and reports of their existence by witnesses (Robben 2005: 120). Unhindered by physical laws, animation can extend the boundaries of what can be conceived and imagined. As they tumble through the air, the cutouts vividly convey the disappearing tricks of state-sponsored terror: minimalist imagery that has maximum suggestiveness.

Abuelas emphasises the emotional difficulty of a reunion with a lost grandchild, who is forced 'to recognise that her parents were not her parents and that her real parents had been killed'. The Grandmother reveals it took five years for her and her granddaughter to say they loved each other. This slow, painful reconciliation is figured by a wall-mounted family photo, upon which is superimposed a girl's ghostly figure whose palm gradually touches her grandmother's hand. As Roland Barthes has illuminated, a photograph is suspended between life and death (1993: 79), similar to the situation of the disappeared. Photographs embody loss and absence, as well as an attempt to bring the subject back to life, a desire that *Abuelas* evokes in its animated photograph of the protagonist's daughter. Marianne Hirsch argues that family photographs invite an identification that transcends national/ethnic identities, since such photographs are highly conventional in nature (1997: 252). *Abuelas* uses the convention of family photographs to create a bridge between viewers from different backgrounds and connect them to each other. Its aesthetic approach is based on these 'identifications forged by familial looking' (ibid.: 267), which it uses to nurture and shape our relationship to memories of the disappeared.

In contrast, the disparity between conventional images like family photographs and the fate of the disappeared is pivotal to *The Blonds* (*Los rubios*, 2003), where Argentine filmmaker Albertina Carri attempts to discover what happened to her parents, Roberto Carri and Ana María Caruso, guerrilla activists who disappeared in 1977. Albertina was then just three years old, the youngest of three sisters. The film consists of interviews with neighbours and fellow revolutionaries, behind-the-scenes footage, and stop-action animated 'reconstructions' with a children's toy set. Carri explains her motivation for making the film as her inability to relate to other films on the topic, which have tended to focus on history and politics rather than personal loss; in her view, 'no one has reached into that deep black hole that is absence' (cited in Page 2009: 175–6).

The Blonds avoids standard use of documentary evidence (letters, testimonies, photos) so that audiences do not go away thinking, as Carri puts it, '"Okay, fine, now I know Roberto and Ana María, let's go home" . . . They're inapprehensible because they aren't here' (cited in Andermann 2012: 116). Indeed, when the film scans family photographs, it takes care not to show the parents, cutting their faces out of the frame. It questions its ability to recover what is absent, and exposes the pitfalls of recreating dimly remembered and partially understood childhood scenes.

In order to highlight the mediated nature of her own memories, Carri casts an actress, Analía Couceyro, to portray herself in the film. Analía announces herself as such to the camera, and is seen carrying out interviews, occasionally accompanied by the 'real' Carri. *The Blonds'* playful self-reflexivity has led some critics to read it as Brechtian, laying emphasis on how it 'inhibit[s] emotional engagement with the film's story' (Page 2009: 172). However, as might be expected from a film about a person haunted by her parents' loss and searching for clues about what happened to them, it is far from unemotional. But it takes the emotional nature of its subject for granted; rather than seeking to enhance emotions, it transmutes them. One way that it does this is through humour, an aspect often overlooked in the film's critical appraisals. It has many instances of humour, as when Analía visits the Centre for Forensic Anthropology, and has her blood taken for a DNA test although she has no biological link to the disappeared! By inventing such situations, the film plays around with the myth of generational 'authenticity'. Much of the humour in *The Blonds* comes from a perception of incongruity, which draws attention to the need to recall an irrecoverable past and the simultaneous absurdity of this endeavour when little or no traces of the disappeared remain.

The film's comic touches, which can be construed as frivolous, have drawn hostility from some critics who have alleged that Carri has depoliticised state violence (see Page 2009: 168–9). But, as John Morreall has argued, 'the comic is 'not "time out" from the world; rather, it provides another perspective on that world' (2009: 119). Comedy can have a critical and political purpose. That this playful attitude to the past marks a generational shift is a point that the film makes through a letter from the national film funding commission, which Analía reads out. The letter acknowledges Carri's proposal to make *The Blonds* as 'worthy', but rejects it, expressing a preference for a different type of film, made in a 'more rigorous documentary fashion', which would be a testimonial to her parents as important 1970s intellectuals. Carri acknowledges that her parents' generation needs such a film, but that is not the kind of film she wants to make. While the previous generation was concerned with the 'truth claims' of testimony and tended to portray the revolutionaries as heroes and victims, the approach taken by *The Blonds* (and subsequent films about the Argentine disappearances, including *Chronicle of an Escape*) is to highlight the mediations of memory: the past as a kind of fiction, and reconstruction as imagination – a performative re-enactment. This goes hand in hand with a more critical and revisionist stance towards the revolutionaries.

Friends and comrades of Carri's parents speak of them in idealised terms, as 'exceptional beings, beautiful, intelligent', turning their memories into 'political analysis'. These interviews are often replayed on video in the background, obstructed by Analía's actions, undermining the assumed truth-value of their testimony. She writes the following words in a notepad, highlighting the selective nature of memory: 'TO REVEAL THE MECHANISM OF MEMORY. OMITTING, ONE REMEMBERS'.

Standing in front of Carri's former family home, Analía recounts how two men bundled her into a car to make her identify people in family photos, while her sister Paula managed to resist and escape into the house: 'I think it was a red Ford, but maybe I imagined that. I don't know if some memories are real or if they're my sisters'.' The film briefly switches to black-and-white behind-the-scenes footage, with a crew member performing a clapperboard action, before Analía is shown repeating the anecdote slightly differently. The scene reinforces the sense that memory is mutable, giving rise to many different versions of the past, as she explains: 'All I have are vague memories, contaminated by so many versions. Whatever I do to get to the truth will probably take me further away.'

Carri manages to locate and interview Paula L., sole survivor of the detention centre, nicknamed 'The Sheraton', where her parents were held. However, as Paula L. declines to talk on camera, Analía relays her account. During the interview, she produced a drawing of the detention centre. But, as she refused to allow it to be shown in the film, Analía draws it for us, from her memory: 'Well, this is what I recall from what she remembered.' She holds up a basic drawing, several times removed from its so-called 'original': triply mediated by the memories of the survivor, Carri and her stand-in, Analía. Nothing could be further from Miguel, the architect with prodigious memory in *Nostalgia* and the witnesses of *Nunca más*, who drew similarly detailed illustrations of their prisons. *The Blonds* does not promise to deliver us an uncontaminated record of the past, or 'the real thing', a phrase associated with the Latin American genre of *testimonio* (Gugelberger 1996: 5). Instead, the 'evidence' it produces consists of images that are duplicated beyond recognition, altered and replaced by others.

In one of several stop-action animation sequences, the film imagines the parents' kidnapping as an alien abduction. To the tremulous melody of a theremin, the leitmotif of alien presence in 1950s science fiction films, a flying saucer whisks away two toy figures travelling on a highway. This abduction is a 'reconstruction' of a scene that happened when Carri was so young she is unable to remember, except through the dream-like displacement of animated fantasy. It fills in the missing gaps of a past that can never be straightforwardly remembered, highlighting the indirect and mediated character of her memories. Yet the scene also has the capacity to summon up viewers' own childhood memories through its use of Playmobil figures for, if they grew up under the same transnational urban consumer culture, they may remember the look and feel of those (or similar) plastic toys with their artificial, manufactured textures and primary colours. Childhood memories, as Jennifer Barker writes, 'reside at the surface of [our] skins' (2009: 45). This strange and sinister abduction fantasy disturbs and defamiliarises such memories.

The film also takes us back to the parents' abduction through interviews with neighbours. The first interview is with a next-door neighbour. Fearful and suspicious, she speaks to the film crew from across her front yard. She wants to know who will see the film, and never invites the crew inside. The filmmakers have more success over the road with another neighbour, who, it transpires, informed the authorities. Segments of this interview are interspersed in the non-linear narrative, so that its revelations are communicated in slices. The neighbour admits she was terrified when soldiers came into her house, but when she told them that Carri's family were 'blonds', 'they realized their mistake, and went straight over'. The film takes its title from this claim, which, in a literal sense, is entirely fictional, as none of the family are blond! However, 'blond' assumes a different meaning in this context – marking out a person as a stranger, like saying, 'white, blond, foreigner'. In accordance with the authorities' calls to denounce any 'suspicious' people, it identified the family as perceived strangers in the neighbourhood. Later on, Analía and the film crew don blond wigs, satirically acting out the incriminating accusation that landed both parents in the detention centre, resulting in their torture and murder.[7]

Another location to which the film repeatedly returns is the former detention centre where Carri's parents were held, now a fully functioning police station. When the crew go inside, they are accompanied by Carri's aunt, whose face shows palpable fear and apprehension. Close-ups of gun holsters carried by armed police suggest a persistent violence, capable of erupting at any moment. With her handheld camera, Carri explores the police station's interior, which, although shabby, does not really evoke the atmosphere in which the disappeared were confined and tortured. Unlike *Nostalgia*, *The Blonds* expresses scepticism about the extent to which the past can be retrieved from the places where it happened. Yet, in the participants' nervous body language and their reluctance to speak on camera, it nonetheless transmits enduring memories of the disappearances.

When the daughters lost touch with their parents, who managed to send letters during their first year of detention, they moved to the countryside to live with their uncle. There, 'cruel-eyed' kindergarten children taunted Carri, demanding to know where her parents were. Most of the Playmobil animations refer to her uncle's farm, where she would imagine her parents arriving by car or bus or on horseback, cherishing the hope they would return. In one scene, Analía is shown yelling in the woods, expressing Carri's anger and incomprehension at the decisions taken by her parents as revolutionaries, leaving their daughters to grow up and build their lives without them, accompanied only by 'horrible memories'. It is a controlled outburst of emotion, reinforcing my point that the film does not withhold but rather transmutes emotion. In a final rehearsal scene, Carri directs Analía to recite a list of her pet hates. The list concludes with birthday wishes, because she spent years wishing her parents would come back, and still cannot help doing so whenever she blows out birthday candles. The scene is repeated in a series of takes, which serves not, as Joanna Page claims, to 'detract from [the] emotive value of what is recounted onscreen' (2009: 172) but to insist upon it. At the scene's end, a close up on Analía's face is held for a few seconds, underlining the film's emotional impetus.

THE OTHER 11 SEPTEMBER

Though a filmmaker of similar age to Carri, Pablo Larraín does not return to his childhood in *Post Mortem* (2010), but approaches the enigmas of the past from a dream-like perspective that tries to evoke the mood of the era, tapping the irrational, subjective forces at work. *Post Mortem* is the second film in his trilogy about the Chilean dictatorship. The first, *Tony Manero* (2008), follows Raúl, a dancer obsessed with John Travolta in *Saturday Night Fever* (1977), who carries out murderous acts to achieve his ambitions; it evokes parallels between him and the regime, as state murders happen in the background. The third film, *No* (2012), is about the advertising executive behind the 'No' campaign for the 1988 referendum that finally ousted the dictatorship.

Post Mortem's protagonist is loosely based on a real historical figure, Mario Cornejo, one of three people who signed President Allende's autopsy report. Like his historical counterpart, he is employed as a coroner's assistant at a hospital in Santiago. The film imagines the everyday rituals of this marginal figure, who is confronted with the disappearances. It is reliant on physical, often wordless performances, especially from Alfredo Castro as Mario. Early on, political events literally brush past Mario and Nancy, his neighbour and sometime lover. Unwillingly, Nancy is taken to join a demonstration in support of Allende's government by a long-haired radical, Victor. The daughter of a communist, she has taken a different path as a cabaret dancer. Mario

and Nancy are both presented as 'blank' characters, detached from their surroundings, especially Mario with his impassive demeanour. Because we are not
invited to identify with them in conventional ways, what Gilles Deleuze calls
the sensory–motor link (between our perception and our reaction) is broken,
opening up more elliptical implications. As Marguerite Feitlowitz asks, in the
context of the Argentine disappearances, 'if the missing were eerily present by
virtue of their absence, in what sense were those present really *there?*' (1998:
151). She could be speaking of the somnambulistic behaviour of *Post Mortem*'s
protagonists, which reinforces its dream-like quality. Unpleasant dreams
represent aspects of ourselves 'that we wish to disown' (Rutan and Rice 2002:
41). As in a dream, Mario embodies those unappealing elements, particularly
the emotional coldness characteristic of wider society's attitude to the coup.
Through him, *Post Mortem* portrays the public's unexamined attitudes, calling
upon its audience to identify with this evacuated dream content and dream it
itself.

The narrative style at times has the bizarre illogic of a dream. The film
opens to a juddering, scraping sound. An elaborate camera movement frames
a tank from underneath as it rolls across a litter-strewn street. Then, the
film becomes quiet and still, as we are introduced to Mario, staring out at
his neighbourhood from behind a curtained window, waiting for Nancy to
return home. The suburban setting is defamiliarised by the previous shot – a
flashforward to the coup, hinting at the violence lurking beneath the façade
of normality. It imparts a surrealistic quality: 'the banal made strange with
intent' (Alexander 1993: 13). The surrealists understood film's ability to
evoke random memories and dreams, the similarity of cinematography to
dreamwork, and editing's ability to produce shocking, unexpected juxtapositions, blurring distinctions between reality and dream. Stylistically, *Post
Mortem* invokes this tradition.

Another segment that occurs out of sequence is Nancy's autopsy. Placed
after Nancy and Mario's encounter with the demonstration but before their
affair commences, it disrupts the story's linear flow. Imaged lying on the
autopsy table, Nancy's pale, emaciated body is foreshortened, creating another
disturbing premonition, this time of her disappearance and murder. A post-
mortem report is dictated and Mario takes notes. Cause of death: malnutrition
and dehydration. In the next scene, a boy (later revealed as Nancy's brother,
who disappears during the coup and is never seen alive afterwards) dictates
the report. These are what Deleuze calls 'irrational cuts', which 'not only
tear us away from a classical mode of construction', but also provoke us to
question their relationality, calling forth 'the unthought within thought'
(Frampton 2006: 138, 190). To see the film as having dream-like qualities is
not to attribute story events to the protagonist's dreaming mind. Rather, the
film uses its dream-like properties to disturb and defamiliarise the audience's

knowledge of historical events: to dredge up certain elements and bring them into consciousness.

'The other 11 September', as the Chilean coup is sometimes called, shares some of the same visual iconography as 9/11, an event that has come to eclipse it: 'both involve the spectacular destruction of a symbolic building as well as featuring "smoke" and "planes"' (Ortuzar 2013: 180). When the coup finally happens in *Post Mortem*, however, the film does not give us its visual image. The Chilean air force jets flying overhead on their way to bomb the presidential palace are heard, not seen, while Mario is in the shower. Also off screen, signalled by shattering glass, is the violent raid on his neighbour's house, already marked out as a place of left-wing activity. While Mario at least reacts with a quizzical look to the sounds of the fighter jets, he does not register the raid until he emerges onto the empty street to find Nancy's house trashed and nobody there apart from her injured dog. Nancy's family's disappearance takes place under his nose, without him noticing it. While memory of the Chilean event has been influenced by 9/11, as attested by the film *Machuca* (2004), where visual imagery of the presidential palace's destruction is replayed on TV, previously the coup's main memory supports were emblematic figures, especially Allende. *Post Mortem* returns to this emblem of the other 11 September.

Since Allende died when he was surrounded and bombed, his autopsy report's suicide verdict has been shrouded in controversy.[8] In the film, the autopsy takes place under military supervision. With the President abjectly reduced to meat and blood on the table, the dissectionist, Sandra, is unable to continue, so the coroner, Mr Castillo, is forced to finish it himself. Just as the autopsy opens up Allende's cranium to see what lies beneath, the film tries to 'filmically fracture and force open' the surface of society 'to reveal what is hidden' (Frampton 2006: 144). Ultimately, it performs an autopsy on its audience, forcing us to confront uncomfortable realities.

When the military take over the hospital and the tortured bodies of the disappeared surreally pile up in the foyer, it is like a return of the repressed, reversing the tricks of denial and amnesia. The absurdist scenario of the proliferating bodies is provocative in itself, permeating the mise-en-scène with visual idiosyncrasies as characters are forced to pick their way over corpses. Among them, Mario finds Nancy's missing father. *Post Mortem* takes us backstage in the state spectacle of disappearance, where disappearance may be understood not simply as an absence, but as an overlooked reality.

The army gives the disappearances a legalistic air by declaring a state of war, informing Castillo's staff that they should expect many 'casualties'. Although seen earlier in the film expressing sympathy with communists, Castillo readily adapts to his new role – a characterisation that indicts doctors' complicity. Sandra and Mario become part of a bureaucratic operation, noting the number and location of bullet holes on the unidentified bodies, assigning them numbers and 'moving them out'. Mario adapts like the rest, except for one uncharacteristically heroic act in which he attempts to save a victim with Sandra's help. Under the military's noses, they wheel the wounded man along corridors connecting the mortuary with the hospital and pass him into a nurse's care.

Sandra is the only one who openly protests. When she finds the corpses of the victim and the nurse, whom she had only recently seen alive, she is distraught. Her cry, 'Why are they here?', has the affective charge of a nightmare in which objects and people are uncannily displaced from one location to another in a bizarre shuffling of identities and existential states: from living to dead. When she admits she tried to save them, the soldier in charge intimidates her and everyone present by firing bullets.

That Mario himself is affected and transformed by the atrocities is underscored in the film's final sequence. While the earlier flashforward to Nancy's corpse might suggest that she is one of the disappeared, for whose death he is not personally culpable, this sequence dissolves his apparent ethical distance from what is happening around him once and for all. Unlike her father, Nancy returns and hides from the military in a shed, where Mario looks after her. Betrayed and humiliated when he finds Victor is also hiding there, he blocks the entrance to the shed with furniture, entering and exiting the frame to bring one item after another. Filmed in a relentlessly long (six-minute) take, the scene unfurls almost in silence apart from the clattering of furniture and Nancy and Victor's banging on the door when they realise they are being incarcerated. Larraín has declared that this ending is a metaphor for Chile's dark past, which it has 'swept under the carpet' (Matheou 2011). Like the film itself, it is a memory-image that confronts us with complicity, denial and political violence through an unfaltering image.

The act of remembering is not merely about commemorating the past but how we make use of those memories in the present, making it a political and ethical endeavour. Film makes this act possible by its ability to create evocative sensory images that trigger and disturb our own recollections and thoughts about the past. While dealing with the specificities of the Argentine and Chilean disappearances, it has been my intention in this chapter to show how these cinematic representations evoke memories of other disappearances. In 2006, the International Convention for the Protection of All Persons from Enforced Disappearance inscribed into international human rights law the right of any person not to be subjected to disappearance (UN 2010). Although Argentina and Chile, along with a number of other countries, have both signed and ratified the Convention, to date the USA and UK have not.

NOTES

1. For an earlier attempt to go beyond the typical aversion to transnationally produced and distributed films on this topic, see Grant (1997). By drawing on queer theory, Cecilia Sosa's work also explores the transmission of memories of the disappeared to those who have no direct relation to that past, yet it remains within the trauma paradigm (see Sosa 2011; Sosa 2012).
2. Countries affected include Brazil (1964–85), Bolivia (1971–81), Uruguay (1973–85), Guatemala (1978–86 especially) and El Salvador (1980–92), as well as Chile (1973–90) and Argentina (1976–83).
3. According to Brian Finucane (2010), the history of criminal prohibition against enforced disappearance goes further back than human rights declarations and instruments, and has roots in international humanitarian law. Enforced disappearance is also defined as a crime against humanity in the Rome Statute of the International Criminal Court (2002).
4. Another growing body of cinematic work on disappearance is to be found in Turkey (see Suner 2010: 55–66).
5. Information about *Missing*'s release dates and alternative titles is available on IMDb.
6. Feitlowitz reports: 'At their height in 1974–5, these leftist groups totaled no more than 2,000 individuals, of whom only 400 had access to arms' (1998: 6). Over the 1970s, they assassinated '400 policemen, 143 members of the military, and 54 civilians, mostly industrialists'.
7. In her interpretation of *The Blonds*, which emphasises its reworking of conventional family images and structures, Cecilia Sosa argues that the blond wigs are not just ironic, but an extension of kinship across those not directly affected by the violent history (2011: 78).
8. Another autopsy on Allende's body in May 2011 confirmed suicide.

CHAPTER 4

Uninvited Visitors: Immigration, Detention and Deportation in Science Fiction

In our contemporary world, asylum and immigration have become politically charged issues, questionably linked to terrorism in a post-9/11 climate of fear where those who are noticeably 'foreign' are deemed suspects. Despite globalising trends, marked by migratory movements and border crossings, barriers are going up along the frontiers of the rich world, restricting entry to asylum seekers and other disadvantaged migrants, who are held up at borders, kept in internment camps and detention centres, and subject to deportation. Those fleeing war, poverty and other forms of violence find themselves in new spaces of confinement and exclusion, although the unwanted migrants are often the fallout from the military interventions and colonial histories of the wealthy states reinforcing their borders against them. The terrorist threat following 9/11 is one of the reasons offered for the new 'deportation regime', which comprises elements of mobility control and detention, as well as actual deportation (Peutz and De Genova 2010: 4).

This chapter deals with science fiction films that have dramatised these issues in their dystopian worlds set in an alternative present or future. In the scenario that unfolds in *Children of Men* (2006), set in 2027, Britain has closed its borders and declared all foreigners 'illegal'. Immigrants are locked up in cages and mistreated in ways reminiscent of 'War on Terror' prisons and Nazi concentration camps. In *Monsters* (2010), the USA has constructed a wall along its border with Mexico to keep out the aliens that inhabit the extraterrestrial 'Infected Zone' south of the border. A spacecraft hovers above Johannesburg in *District 9* (2009), discharging an alien refugee population who are placed in a temporary camp that becomes a security zone.

Despite common assumptions that it deals with the future, science fiction (henceforth SF) is a historiographic mode: 'it relates to us stories about our present, and more importantly about the past that has led to this present' (Roberts 2006: 28). It has a number of elements in common with the historical dramas discussed in Chapter 2 and shares some of their pitfalls. Similar to those films, which present their own historical story-worlds through their imaginative creation of the past, and the memory-worlds in Chapter 3, SF designs and dwells in its own world, which is in constitutive tension with this world. As I argue in this chapter, the most powerful critical tool utilised in *Children of Men*, *Monsters* and *District 9* is their mise-en-scène, through which they explore the causes and contexts of this state violence against migrants that is an everyday part of wealthy societies. Their SF worlds are constructed to invoke historical memories of past atrocities, which enable us to locate attitudes to refugees and other disadvantaged migrants in a longer history of violence in which socially vulnerable people have been reduced to expendable non-persons. The films take us on a journey through their worlds, littered with signposts making links between past and present, enabling us to perceive present-day policies in a different way.

Although they are set in different geographical zones, the films share the special feature of combining location shooting with CGI. While digital effects are a staple of the SF genre, these films use them expressively to create a recognisable world that is a slightly altered version of our own in order to invite us to carry out ethical scrutiny of an oppressive geopolitical order. I am interested in how the films work within commercial constraints and harness SF genre pleasures to critical goals, but my claim for the genre's critical potential is qualified in a coda on *Elysium* (2013), a SF blockbuster in which the global poor seek to escape a ruined planet for a luxury space station inhabited by Earth's wealthiest citizens, only to be shot down and deported by 'Homeland Security' when they enter its airspace.

While previous chapters have been concerned with multisensory perceptions evoked by cinema, this chapter and the next dwell on the spatial configurations of power that affect how bodies inhabit space, and how cinema illuminates those spaces of violence. As Sara Ahmed remarks, while 'bodies that pass as white move easily' (2006: 132), other bodies are constructed as 'out of place' and held up. The terrorist threat generates fear, which 'shrinks bodily space' (Ahmed 2004: 64). However, it is not the fearful whose space shrinks but those marked as objects of fear, who are subject to bodily containment and detention, including those who literally arrive in containers.

There are stark inequalities at the heart of migration, which has traditionally been from poorer to richer parts of world, a divide that has to do with histories of colonialism and slavery. Migrants 'make a bid for the rich world to escape the other' (Harding 2012: 56). The socio-economic inequalities between rich and poor are more prevalent than racial inequalities in debates about migration, although the two are clearly interlinked. Referring to EU plans to create an all-European border police, Slavoj Žižek declares that the underlying purpose of these new walls is 'safeguarding prosperous Europe from the immigrant flood' (2009: 87). He highlights segregation as a reality of globalisation, a new, more brutal form of racism than previous ones, no longer based, like imperialism, on a claim to 'natural' superiority, but rather 'unabashed egotism'. Here, 'the fundamental divide is one between those included in the sphere of (relative) economic prosperity and those excluded from it' (ibid.). Indeed, wealthy countries prefer immigrants from other wealthy countries over those from poorer countries. This applies to both asylum (for example, in the UK, applications show higher refusal rates from applicants from poorer parts of the world) and 'regular' migration, where a paramount concern is to attract the 'right' migrants (defined by skills and salary levels) and discourage the 'wrong' sort (Harding 2012: 40).

The 1951 UN Refugee Convention (with its 1967 Protocol) obliges signatory nations to confer refugee status to anyone who has fled their country 'owing to a well-founded fear of being persecuted' and to protect them from being returned to states where they face persecution (UNHCR 2010: 14). By defining refugees in this way, the Convention distinguishes them from other migrants, including economic migrants, who can, theoretically, benefit from the protection of their governments if they return home. While many would argue this distinction is important to preserve, Jeremy Harding raises the point that, although economic migrants lack a legal basis on which to claim asylum, 'the hardships they face in their own countries' may be 'as severe as the political persecution from which refugees are fleeing' (2000: 6). Moreover, wealthy signatory states are known to give the Convention their formal assent, while introducing measures to deter would-be entrants, claiming the right to refuse or bestow asylum as they wish (Harding 2012: 54).

Desiring not to be perceived as a 'soft touch', governments of wealthy states implement forms of detention and deportation to reduce immigrant numbers and demonstrate their power and efficacy. At detention centres – effectively high-security prisons – 'illegal' immigrants are locked up, pending deportation. A British Home Office report defines 'illegal' immigrants as those who have: entered the country illegally (through forged documents or clandestine means); overstayed the period allowed by their residence permit; or been rejected for an asylum claim (Woodbridge 2005: 1). In his book *Deportation is Freedom! The Orwellian World of Immigration Controls*, Steve Cohen points out that, in other aspects of law, only acts are illegal; however, in immigration law, people are called illegal (Cohen 2006: 57). The adjective 'illegal' is turned into a noun, dehumanising those people. The label is particularly worrying for asylum seekers, many of whom are forced by their circumstances to break the law to enter their host country. In British Home Office terminology, an 'asylum seeker' is someone whose claim to refugee status has not yet been recognised, depriving them of a legal basis for their stay. Such 'official re-labeling' is part of the process of 'deciding who is worthy of humanitarian assistance'

(Trinh 2011: 47). It also serves to bolster the arguments of right-wing media commentators and policy makers, who stigmatise asylum seekers and other disadvantaged migrants as a threat and burden to society, helping themselves to healthcare, jobs and housing. The repeated combination of 'bogus' with 'asylum seeker' 'inflames the culture of suspicion, which sooner or later extends to all applicants' (Harding 2012: 41).

To counteract the dehumanisation of refugees in government rhetoric and mainstream media, humanitarian agencies try to give refugees a 'human face' in their campaign materials, by utilising close-ups and first-person testimonies that invite recognition and compassion; such strategies offer reassurance that they are 'just like us' and make it harder to endorse harsh policies (Tyler 2006: 194). Realist films and documentaries that elicit sympathy for migrants undertaking dangerous journeys adopt a similar strategy. For example, the docudrama *In This World* (2002) follows two young Afghans, Jamal and Enayat, on their harsh journey from a refugee camp in Pakistan across land and sea to the UK. It emphasises the dangers they face: narrowly escaping being shot by Turkish border police; travelling by freight container to Trieste; and facing the threat of deportation either on arrival in the UK or when Jamal turns eighteen, as part of British Home Office policy on child asylum seekers.

This kind of aesthetic strategy tends to revolve around a conventional iconography of victimisation consisting of endangered women and children. As I argued in this book's Introduction, compassion is based on a power relation, a fantasy of benevolence; it is a moral, rather than an ethical, attitude. Since children are ideologically associated with innocence, they are deemed to be the best ambassadors for a moral cause and the most deserving of our benevolence. According to Susan Moeller, images of endangered children are intended to elicit audience sympathy on an 'apolitical or suprapolitical' level (2002: 48). Constructed to enable First World audiences to feel for subaltern people, such images interpellate viewers as rescuers whose intervention will give victims a wished-for salvation; a kind of imperial rescue narrative that does not unsettle the dominant world picture.

Moreover, by promoting identification with people 'like us', these sorts of representation are likely to stress certain physical or behavioural traits shared with the target audience. It is a strategy that follows the discourse of assimilation in which, Trinh Minh-ha comments, immigrants and refugees are encouraged to 'be like *us*', but never to be us (Trinh 1989: 52, original emphasis). In most cases, refugees do not represent themselves; they are represented by others, endowing the privileged with the power to grant recognition and confer 'humanity' to others. Even when forms of self-representation exist, they are usually expected to follow similar conventions, in order to gain wide circulation, resulting in selective visibility and thus differential allocation of 'humanity'.

The SF films discussed in this chapter are not entirely free of these problems and may be thought an odd choice of alternative, since most SF producers and consumers belong to the dominant class (i.e. white, rich, male, heterosexual).[1] The genre has been shaped by colonial and imperial projects, the legacy of which is evident in films like *Star Wars* (1977), where colonial expansion occurs in outer space. Yet, though SF often endorses the ideologies of dominant culture, it also has a history of alliance and allegiance with the marginalised – a tradition including, for example, *Planet of the Apes* (1968), *Blade Runner* (1982), *Alien Nation* (1988) and *Code 46* (2003), which the films in this chapter draw upon and extend. In addition, SF has a number of additional critical tools that lend it ethical and political potential beyond the moral sentimentalism of victims' stories – tools that map the structures of violence linking 'us' with 'them'.

Unlike realist fiction, SF does not attempt to render the world transparently, but always to defamiliarise it. Thereby it raises questions about our world that challenge familiar understandings. SF is a kind of thought experiment, a game of 'what if' (Roberts 2006: 9). It extrapolates from the laws and trends of our world to create another world with a new set of norms. In Darko Suvin's definition, SF is the genre of 'cognitive estrangement' (1979: 4). By mapping an alternative possible world, in which the reality of our own world is made strange, a process that Suvin likens to both the Russian formalists' concept of *ostranenie* ('defamiliarisation') and Brecht's notion of 'alienation', SF allows us to recognise our own world from a new, critical perspective. In this way, it offers us 'a diagnosis, a call to understanding and action' (ibid.: 12).

The dynamics of most SF, particularly in the dystopian mode, are moral rather than ethical – sounding 'warnings' about the future. Yet the genre does not simply deliver cautionary tales and moral prescriptions; it can also confront us with images that interrogate and provoke. A dystopia imagines a society apparently worse than the one in which viewers currently live – 'nightmarish visions of future or alternative worlds' which may appeal to some 'as a way of making their own worlds, however troubled, seem comparatively benign' (King and Krzywinska 2000: 17). However, by displacing immigration detention and deportation into their SF scenarios, the films considered here create alternative worlds that closely resemble our *own* societies, thereby unsettling complacencies about the present. Their worlds play out the consequences of present-day policies, while creating parallels with past colonial practices, enabling us to perceive how the unwanted are treated as an outcome of these histories.

Adam Roberts proposes that SF is a symbolist rather than an allegorical genre: 'Symbolism opens itself up to a richness of possible interpretation, where allegory maps significance from one thing to another' (2006: 14). This distinction helps illuminate how films in this chapter produce images that are both context specific and evocative of other histories. Suvin uses the term 'nova' for points of difference between our world and the SF world yet which retain symbolic links to our world. One of the most potent SF symbols is that of the alien, often used to designate another 'race' or, unsurprisingly, given the interchangeability of the term with 'immigrant' in immigration control discourse, an 'illegal alien'.

SF typically imagines the encounter with 'alien' cultures from the dominant culture's perspective; similarly, critical discussions tend to treat alien encounters as encounters with difference and alterity, often in a way that tends to reify race and otherness. In contrast, my argument in this book is more about how otherness is *produced* through particular forms of power and *endorsed* for politically expedient purposes. Since the category 'alien' is only meaningful 'within a given community of citizens' (Ahmed 2000: 3), it is important to recognise it, like the attribution of 'illegality' to immigrants, as a discursive production. The alien designates that which is outside the human community – it encapsulates the *processes* of racial othering and dehumanisation that people undergo. Hannah Arendt understood this clearly when she observed that refugees have lost their access to supposedly universal human rights. Thrown out of the family of nations, as homeless and stateless aliens, refugees are simultaneously thrown out from the human community of rights-bearing citizens (Arendt 1979: 294). Once humanity is divided up into citizens with full rights and others who are deprived of those rights and legal status, the latter are inevitably classified as lesser beings.

SF has long been preoccupied with the boundaries between the human and non-human, often thinking about the theme conservatively, as in numerous alien invasion narratives, where the subjugation of aliens is justified on the basis that they are not (fully) human. But it also has the potential to illuminate how these boundaries are constructed in racist and colonialist discourse, denying humanity to certain groups. This kind of SF, of which *Blade Runner* is a clear precursor, is capable of bringing to our attention 'ideological constructions of otherness' (Roberts 2006: 19) and displaying the power strategies that *produce* otherness. It thus becomes a symbolic means of articulating the experience of a marginalised group of people.

In *Cinematic Geopolitics*, Michael Shapiro claims that a film's mise-en-scène can be 'more telling than its storyline' (2009: 9). For him, 'a critical film articulates a world rather than merely a specific drama within it' (ibid.: 11). Through landscape shots, using long takes, wide angle, deep focus and location shooting, a film is able to 'usher in' historical time and space, and map the violent cartography of contemporary politics. The spectator is guided by the question 'What is there to see in the image?', not merely 'What are we going to see in the next image?' (Deleuze 1989: 272).

This argument has interesting implications for the SF films discussed in this chapter, which combine these realist filmmaking methods with CGI. Moreover, whereas Shapiro confines his discussion to realist cinema, SF has an established tradition of mise-en-scène for the purposes of socio-political commentary. This goes back at least as far as *Metropolis* (1927), famous for its contrasting shots of its futuristic city of skyscrapers inhabited by the rich and the underground caverns and factories where the poor work and live, all created with studio sets and the special effects of the day. The city's spatial organisation, including its binaries of high/low and inside/outside, evoke contemporary social divisions, resulting in a '*politicized production design*' (Desser 1999: 84; original italics). It is also in the dystopian cinematic tradition heralded by *Metropolis* that we find a generic precedent for contemporary SF's imprisoning and confining structures and environments.

In critical discourses and film reviews, special effects (especially CGI) are often aligned with distracting or 'excessive' spectacle, assumed to have a negative impact on narrative and characterisation. But one of the imports of the discussion so far is that, far from being 'mutually exclusive', spectacle and narrative work together (Purse 2013: 21). Although digital imaging has distinctive properties (immateriality, non-indexicality, infinite capacity for transformation), as Lisa Purse argues, it shares the same expressive goals as cinema's other representational tools such as narrative structure, characterisation, performance, mise-en-scène and cinematography, extending and enhancing the latter's meanings. Digital effects conjure up 'carefully designed spaces and actions', capable of vividly 'dramatis[ing] power relations' (ibid.: 22). They create their own mise-en-scène, or add to an existing one. Technically, the term 'mise-en-scène' is as much of a misnomer for digital elements as the term 'camera', but Purse suggests that both retain their usefulness, as these filmic conventions leave their mark in the look of the finished film. While the digital has been heralded as instituting a 'break' with cinema's indexical link to its profilmic reality (the person, object or scene placed before the camera to be filmed), Purse claims that this is not straightforwardly the case, since digital imaging often aims to imitate the indexicality of photochemically based cinema, even though no camera and no profilmic subject is necessary to generate its images. Digital imaging is therefore typically used to achieve a seamless illusion of reality, or verisimilitude. However, Purse suggests that not all films are interested in this aspect, and some even override it in the goal of generating particular meanings; *Children of Men* is one of the films she cites in support of this claim.

While many films are now hybrids of recorded reality and digital elements, the ones discussed in this chapter combine these elements in innovative ways. The digital is a manipulation of the image, which, of course, has ethical implications. It adds to the already malleable character of the film medium – the finished film that we get to see is always the result of reality-altering decisions made by filmmakers that affect how we perceive a given scene or character. But 'in the new digital image, everything is manipulable', and thus 'everything is re-thinkable' (Frampton 2006: 205). These possibilities were anticipated by the Soviet filmmaker Dziga Vertov, whose *Man with a Movie Camera* (*Chelovek s kinoapparatom*, 1929) contained an image of a man inside a beer glass, and, later, by Gilles Deleuze, for whom cinema frees us from natural perception, creating its own space and time, and is therefore capable of showing us new things which we are unlikely to perceive in reality. For Daniel Frampton, 'the mix of traditional recorded cinema with digital effects announces a new kind of fluid film-thinking'. Here it is 'not so much a question of creating "completely" new worlds, but of refreshing our image of (our way of *seeing*) the real world' (Frampton 2006: 205, original emphasis). The mix of recorded and digital generates a form of digitally mediated perception that shows us new ways of apprehending our reality. Digital imaging includes the compositing of foreground and background elements; since the digital is capable of juxtaposing anything, it can produce unexpected and thought-provoking combinations. As will be shown in the following film analyses, 'special effects' can be used to defamiliarise our perspectives of our own world, creating hybrid spaces where different historical moments coexist, in order to provoke us to rethink policies and practices of the present, including how they are haunted by the colonial past.

CHILDREN OF MEN: THE POLITICS OF IMMIGRATION CONTROLS AND CONTEMPORARY BRITAIN

A UK–US–Japanese co-production released by Universal Studios, *Children of Men*, based on a novel by P. D. James, was co-scripted and directed by the Mexican filmmaker Alfonso Cuarón. Its themes resonate with the US–Mexico border, although it is firmly set in Britain and vividly captures its contemporary politics. Set in a future world where no babies have been born for eighteen years, its story follows Theo Faron, who reluctantly gets involved with the Fishes, a resistance movement campaigning for immigrants' rights. He agrees to help a miraculously pregnant black refugee, Kee, across the border to the Human Project, a secret organisation seeking a cure for infertility. According to Slavoj Žižek (2007), 'the true focus of the film' lies 'in the background'. Instead of making a direct political parable, *Children of Men*, he says, refers to oppressive social reality through the 'paradox of anamorphosis', similar to Hans Holbein's painting *The Ambassadors*, in which a skull is anamorphotically distorted and can only be properly seen when one looks at the picture obliquely: 'If you look at [the oppressive social dimension] too directly . . . you don't see it.'

In order for this technique to work, Žižek maintains, the oppressive social reality must remain in the background. However, as Zahid Chaudhary points out, the camera continually refocuses its attentions so that background objects become part of the foreground (2009: 82). In this analysis, I emphasise the continual reframings and intrusions into hitherto off-screen space through which the film brings to our attention the dehumanising implications of immigration control rhetoric: camera movements that trace and provoke thoughts largely independently of the fast-paced, thrilling plot. As *Children of Men*'s cinematographer, Emmanuel Lubezki, remarks, 'The camera is inviting you to see something external to the plot and saying that it is also important. The camera is inviting you to see the context in another way' (2006: 74). At the same time, the foreground/background dynamics highlighted by Žižek are crucial as a way of getting audiences to confront realities that they might be less likely to accept if they were at the film's forefront.

This attention to background and margins also subverts the principles of *Children of Men*'s *Bildungsroman* plot, which follows Theo's path from apathy to activism. As mentioned in Chapter 2, this kind of plotline typically gives the privileged (rich, white, male, heterosexual) protagonist 'the lion's share of time, resolution, safety, and closure' (Goldberg 2007: 44). According to those conventions, the white protagonist has the ability to act and move freely in the world, and to appropriate the power to speak and act for others. We are made to care for and identify with him, while the vulnerable and often-disposable bodies of racialised Others are placed in the background, their suffering 'absorb[ing] the threat of such pain from (white) western bodies' (ibid.: 59). In *Children of Men*, by contrast, there is one storyline privileging the

Figure 4.1 In *Children of Men*, the London of 2027 is only slightly defamiliarised through CGI to present a future that looks much like our present.

main characters, and another in the margins to which the camera is constantly drawn and provokes us to reflect upon. The stereotypical implications of the central story in which the white male hero rescues a black woman are undercut by the fact that the white protagonists, played by star performers, are denied conventional resolution, dying one by one in the course of narrative: first Theo's ex-wife and leader of the Fishes, Julian (played by Julianne Moore), then his friend Jasper (Michael Caine), and finally Theo himself (Clive Owen). Moreover, through thoughtful camera movements that attend to what is happening in the background, it is not so much Theo but the viewer who is urged to undertake a journey from apathy to activism.

Children of Men opens with a recognisably grubby and derelict London setting. Well-known streets are slightly altered with digitally added video displays on the façades of buildings and double-decker buses. This not only renders the environment more futuristic, but also emphasises the contemporary conflation of terrorists with 'illegal' immigrants. The ubiquitous video screens appeal to the public to 'report any suspicious activity' and identify 'illegal immigrants', bombarding them with the government and media's xenophobic rhetoric. The film's sonic architecture is full of sounds of alarm, proclaiming security threats and alerts.

This is a future world not so dissimilar from now. Among the near-contemporary references embedded in the mise-en-scène are the 2001 foot-and-mouth epidemic, the 2003 Stop the War campaign, and the 7 July 2005 terrorist bombings in the capital. These anchor the film in the recent past and suggest that all these events are interlinked and have led to this present. The outpouring of grief for the death of the world's youngest person, the eighteen-year-old 'Baby Diego', which opens the film, echoes the public mourning of Princess Diana's death and establishes the perverse dichotomies of apathy and compassion in contemporary life. People are able to mourn a distant 'celebrity' yet become blasé to the suffering all around them. The pseudo-documentary style, using long takes, whip pans and other frenetic movements into off-screen space, rather than frequent cutting, makes it seem as if the camera is a chance witness to events, unaware of the next centre of dramatic interest. This, together with an accumulation of details from our own past and present, works in the service of verisimilitude, rendering this 'future' world more credible. More importantly, the camera's darting movements display an inquisitive form of thought, eager to explore this world and ensure that we notice the signs, including roadside shrines of cards and flowers and pyres of burning cattle, to inform our inquiry into the history of the politics of the present.

In the film, refugees are called 'fugees', a contraction that subtly changes meaning by eliminating the original word's compassionate associations, similar to the semantic devaluation undergone by the term 'asylum seeker'. News headlines declare that 'all foreigners are now illegal', an extrapolation from present-day headlines calling for tighter immigration controls and blaming immigrants for national and social breakdown. Expressing fears of being 'swamped', contemporary UK tabloids are filled with imagery of 'floods' and invasions by undesirable people, 'welfare scroungers', 'health tourists' and 'bogus asylum seekers'. Current rhetoric is particularly targeted at disadvantaged migrants from eastern Europe, including Roma, who are not regarded as deserving of the same rights of free movement and work as other EU citizens. All the major British political parties now see keeping foreigners out as a vote winner. In July 2013, Home Office vans drove around London with signs encouraging illegal immigrants to turn themselves in and 'go home', while sweeps of immigrants were conducted at railway stations. *Children of Men*'s SF vision of Britain extrapolates from policies on border control, detention and deportation which threaten to turn not just Britain but all of western Europe into 'a federation of police states' (Harding 2012: 64). Its images are as resonant today as they were when the film was released. The security screens on buildings form an extension of the Foucauldian model of surveillance based on Jeremy Bentham's panopticon: a prison structure where prisoners can be watched at all times, although they do not know when, so they discipline themselves and monitor their own behaviour. In the heightened security state of the film and our own reality, citizens are encouraged to police themselves, to become the state's eyes and ears.

In one scene, we follow Theo as he walks past a line of police in riot gear and cages of immigrants. Theo's ability to negotiate his way past immigrants without noticing them is a sign that they have become worthless and apparently non-existent to him, therefore non-human. When he exits the frame, the film hurtles into the depths of the scene, past a queue of people about to be placed into cages, some of them desperately holding up their passports. As screams are heard overhead, the camera angles up to frame possessions being thrown out of a high-rise block of flats. Evicted and dispossessed, immigrants are robbed of their identities as they are herded into cages and moved around like freight. The scene carries echoes of the Holocaust as well as referring to the British Home Office's depersonalising terminology of 'removals'. British detention centres were renamed 'removal centres' in the 2002 Asylum and Immigration Act. Carrying out the deportation of refused asylum seekers and other immigrants by force and 'in secret, well away from public scrutiny' (Ware 2010: 105), the Home Office is also known to use airport cargo terminals for this purpose. *Children of Men*'s vivid imagery gives concrete form to this dehumanising treatment that characterises immigrants as cargo goods – delivering a visceral impact lacking in the everyday utterance and normalisation of such terms and practices.

Armed with helmets and shields, the police act as instruments of the state, administering its repressive measures. The scene's overwhelming impression is of brutality and force, emphasised by the imagery of garbage removal as a bulldozer clears and crushes belongings, classifying the immigrants and their livelihoods, by implication, as human waste. Through camera movements that observe what is happening in the background and peripheries of the frame, the film challenges social consensus about measures maintained by a willing or apathetic public allowing violence against 'categories of rubbish people' (Scheper-Hughes and Bourgois 2004: 21). It portrays the *result* of policies that reduce people to the status of 'unworthy life', regarded as less than human, a category into which the elderly, the disabled and various racial, religious and sexual out-groups have fallen. 'Unworthy life' links together the film's disparate themes, from refugees through the government-promoted form of euthanasia, Quietus, to the slaughtered livestock.

When Theo disembarks on a railway platform lined with cages of immigrants destined for deportation, the film lingers on this image, reminiscent of the Nazi deportation of the Jews, who were also stripped of their citizenship and legal status. As political scientist William Walters observes, due to 'its proximity to the wider field of expulsions . . . deportation is always susceptible to, and associable with, these other practices. These other forms of expulsion lurk in its shadows; their invocation always threatens to destabilize its legitimacy' (2010: 82). This describes the film's tactics precisely – invoking the past to unsettle our acceptance of deportation as a normalised part of our present. When a German-speaking woman complains about being locked in a cage with a black man, the scene juxtaposes racial persecution past and present, asserting similarities between Europe's treatment of Jews during the Second World War and its present-day treatment of immigrants. About the refugees, Theo's friend Jasper comments: 'After escaping the worst atrocities and finally making it to England, our government hunts them down like cockroaches.' His words echo Hannah Arendt's observation about the chain of contempt involving both persecuting and receiving states: 'Those whom the persecutor had singled out as the scum of the earth – Jews, Trotskyists etc. – actually were received as scum of the earth everywhere' (1979: 269).

Allowed to travel due to his status as a privileged white citizen, with a cousin who has influence with the government, Theo extends himself with ease through the world, unlike others caught up at barriers and coerced into stasis. This changes when he escorts Kee and her midwife, Miriam, into a refugee camp at Bexhill, on the south coast. They enter this camp, with the connivance of a security guard, in order to access the Human Project, whose ship is due to meet them there. Here, Theo is forced to undergo the experience of the Other.

Bexhill refugee camp powerfully revives the dark associations of detention and deportation, evoking memories of Nazi concentration camps and the Soviet gulag as well as the 'War on Terror'. At the entrance, the sign

'Homeland Security. Bexhill Refugee Camp. Restricted Access' arches over-head on a metal support, recalling photographs of Auschwitz. The use of US nomenclature, 'Homeland Security', reminds us of the USA's domestic front on the 'War on Terror' – namely border controls with Mexico – as well as the British tendency to adopt measures and terminology of security from across the Atlantic. Simultaneously a detention centre for refugees and suspected terrorists, Bexhill enfolds into itself multiple spaces – Nazi death camps and ghettoes, Guantánamo Bay and other global 'War on Terror' prisons, and recent war zones – inviting us to join up the dots between past atrocities and present-day practices. Bexhill reveals the concentration camp not as a thing of the past, a mere 'historical fact' or 'anomaly', but rather, as Giorgio Agamben points out, 'in some way . . . the hidden matrix and *nomos* of the political space in which we are still living' (1998: 166). It is what Michel Foucault (1997) calls a 'heterotopia', a place where otherness is policed and enforced but at the same time holds alternative possibilities (a platform of escape for the main characters, Bexhill is also transformed by the refugees who live there).

Those cast out of the pale of humanity are imprisoned in Bexhill, their legal status suspended, subject to mistreatment and torture. From the characters' bus, driving into the camp, we are shown lines of men in poses reminiscent of Iraqi prisoners in the Abu Ghraib photographs, some of them placed in cages. One caged prisoner is a hooded and cloaked figure standing on a box, shaking as if he is being electrocuted – an image referring to one of the most notorious photographs from the Abu Ghraib prison scandal. The windows of the bus act as frames within the frame, alluding to the still frames of the photographs but putting them in motion by means of the camera's journey past these *tableaux vivants* of torture. Although they are held at a distance, in the background or at the edges of the frame, this is not a typical Brechtian distanciation; rather, in this sequence, foreground and background merge with powerful affect.

When the bus comes to a standstill, immigration guards with dogs come on board to shift the passengers. Miriam, a character from the foreground, is forcefully removed and taken outside to join the anonymous crowds in the background. As this happens, the lights on the bus are switched off, throwing the main characters and other passengers into silhouette. This rather theatri-cal staging makes the foreground narrative drama recede momentarily so that figures and events in the background can be witnessed more prominently. Aligned with Kee's distraught gaze, we watch Miriam being forcibly hooded. The blaring of the siren yields to a non-diegetic choral track that lends a melancholy tone, amplifying the affective charge of this sequence, which ends by revealing the grim aftermath of torture or execution procedures in the form of bodies laid out on the ground. With this merging of foreground and background, the film swerves away from a narrative strategy that centres on the safety and resolution of white heroes and instead emphasises a more pluralistic identification with those whose rights are traded for the benefits of 'our' security.

It is from the immigrant community that the characters get some of their best support, as exemplified by Marichka, a Romani refugee, and the Georgian family who help Kee and Theo during their stay in Bexhill and provide them with a rowing boat to meet the Human Project. The positive valence that the film gives to immigration is apparent most of all in the appropriately named Kee herself as the key to the future, although her characterisation is not without stereotypical associations (see Chaudhary 2009: 94). For Barbara Korte, the film's utopian perspective resides in Kee as a black mother: 'In very explicit terms, the film makes the point that a black woman, and a refugee woman, for that matter, might guarantee a future for Britain and the whole world' (2008: 322). In the face of calls for more restrictions, the film favours immigration as a hope and solution for a world where there is a shortage of young people, due to demographic trends towards an ageing population, which it projects in its SF infertility scenario.

After Theo rows Kee and her baby out to the buoy where the Human Project's ship, *Tomorrow*, is due to collect them, he dies from fatal wounds sustained during a shoot-out between the Fishes and the British military. He dies for Kee in what would be a conventional heroic sacrifice were it not for the fact that it is on behalf of a black woman and, presumably, a black future for humanity. In her reading of the film, Lisa Purse draws attention to a supposed mismatch in the final shots of the *Tomorrow*, arguing that this sequence uses its digital effects against continuity editing norms to imply that the ship is a mirage, which suffuses ambiguity into the film's optimistic ending. However, after Kee's point of view, when she spots the ship in the distance, the film provides us with a close shot of the ship, with its crew pointing to the rowing boat; the latter is not a character point of view but the film's own perspective, since it is not tied to human perception and can, through editing, travel rapidly from one point in space to another. The final shot reveals the ship still in the distance, but clearly approaching the boat. The ending is not as ambiguous as Purse suggests, as reinforced by the fact that we hear sounds of children's laughter over the closing credits, suggesting that this hope for humanity has succeeded. The film's innovative use of CGI lies not in its refusal of 'the seamlessness that contemporary digital can achieve' (Purse 2013: 17), but rather in its modification of backgrounds to make us perceive our reality differently, a device that is even more central to *Monsters*, where the illusion of continuity editing (such as eyeline match) and synchronised sound is harnessed to embed provocative CGI elements in recorded reality.

EXTRATERRESTRIAL BORDERLANDS: *MONSTERS* AND THE US–MEXICO BORDER

Monsters inhabits a world six years after the arrival of aliens. Its opening titles briefly gesture to events that resulted in the creation of this world. After the crash landing of a NASA space probe containing alien life samples, half of Mexico next to the US border was declared an 'Infected Zone'. The US and Mexican military are engaged in the struggle to contain the 'creatures' that now populate this borderland. The narrative takes the form of a travelogue: a US photojournalist, Andrew Kaulder, is asked to escort Sam Wynden, daughter of his boss, an American newspaper tycoon, back home. Sam and Andrew do not fall into the gender stereotype of a male rescuing a female in distress, as Sam's fluent Spanish makes her an equal partner as they travel across Latin America. Despite being privileged rich, white travellers, they find themselves marooned at the threshold of the 'Infected Zone' at the beginning of the aliens' mating season and are compelled to traverse it, like poorer migrants, in order to reach the USA. Although Sam is engaged to another man favoured by her father, she and Andrew fall in love as a result of being transformed by their journey through the cultures of this borderland. The film's director, Gareth Edwards, has described *Monsters* as 'a road movie for aliens'. Within its narrative, it symbolically inscribes another journey, that of undocumented migrants facing exclusion and expulsion from the USA.

Representations of the US–Mexico border have long been the province of both Hollywood and Mexican cinema. The border is a symbolic and literal preoccupation of Hollywood SF, horror and western genres, where it has traditionally functioned as part of a paranoid imagination: a safeguard against the Other, protecting the community from that which threatens it from without. However, some recent US–Mexican co-productions, such as *The Three Burials of Melquiades Estrada* (2005) and the 'Amelia' segment in the multiple-thread narrative *Babel* (2006), have begun to interrogate this idea of the border, and have portrayed the cultural life of the borderlands, the immigrant experience and undocumented migrants' risky journey across the frontier. A British SF film, *Monsters* can justifiably be discussed as belonging to this new border film genre, which criticises Hollywood's dominant tendency of confirming US border ideologies. It shares a great deal with recent Mexican and US–Mexican productions, including the narrative trope of the border as an obstacle to be traversed, usually from south to north. Focusing on the southern side of the US–Mexico border, the scenography of *Monsters* articulates both the horizontal and vertical axes of border representation: it explores the cultures and identities that populate the borderlands (horizontal axis) and the embodied perils of border-crossing (vertical axis).

Monsters' artful production design belies its extremely low budget of less than £500,000; but, in many ways, this minimalism is key to its thoughtful dramatic form. Its cast consists of two essentially unknown actors, who play the protagonists, and non-professionals, whom the filmmakers met while shooting in locations found 'on the fly' in Mexico, Guatemala, Belize, Costa Rica and Texas. Its border scenes are created through a montage of border zones in these different places. Using mostly handheld camera, available lighting and a small crew, with director Edwards (himself previously a special-effects designer) performing the roles of writer, cinematographer, effects designer and production designer, the film manages to achieve an intimacy with both the people and the locations it captures. The script was written during the course of filming, on the basis of a treatment and improvised dialogue.

The film's use of CGI – employing readily available software, Adobe Photoshop and Adobe After-effects – follows the same principle of building upon a 'found' reality. It creates an SF otherworld that is basically similar to our world, with certain elements that distinguish it from ours (namely, the aliens). But while the bioluminescent, octopus-like aliens remain mostly unseen (their off-screen presence is conveyed through their aquatic sounds and the characters' reaction shots), other CGI elements manifest in an unsettling way throughout the landscape: road signs warning of the 'Infected Zone' and helicopters and other military hardware. These 'fantastic' elements are casually alluded to in the dialogue and largely remain in the background. At several places where the characters stay, TV news footage of an alien 'attack' runs on a continuous loop, while murals illustrating confrontations between aliens and the US military are encountered en route. All along the US border looms the Wall, a massive construction designed to keep the aliens out – another CGI insertion, evoking the US–Mexico barrier to exclude another kind of alien in our own reality.

Monsters is a good example of how the SF genre is being redefined and viewed outside Hollywood – partly due to technology that makes it possible to create effects on a lower budget. But while it has been critically acclaimed for its special effects, receiving several SF and technical achievement awards, these have generally been viewed separately from its narrative and political meanings, or else its socio-political commentary has been deemed weaker than other films of a similar sort. For example, in his otherwise favourable review, Matthew Jones writes that though it 'clearly wants its audience to understand something about restrictive immigration policies . . . the film simply does not engage with its political aspirations enough to provide a coherent commentary on the issues it raises' (Jones 2011). However, this is the case only if one attends exclusively to plot rather than to how the film's genre, mise-en-scène and references to reality interact together. Through its location shooting combined with CGI, *Monsters* creates a politicised production design that enacts socio-political commentary. It generates a heightened experience of a securitised border that is simultaneously a war zone. The 'Infected Zone' maps a space of violence in the contemporary geopolitical world.

The US–Mexico border, almost 2,000 miles long, highlights the inequalities between north and south. Thousands attempt the journey across it every year in their bid to make a livelihood in the wealthier north. Yearly, hundreds of them die, mainly from dehydration, in the process of crossing. Dominant US political discourses typically raise alarms about undocumented migrants (known as *mojados*) infiltrating the USA from Mexico and other Latin American countries, although many of them have worked in the country for years, providing 'a supply of service employees, farm labourers and building workers' (Harding 2012: 89) and paying their taxes and social security contributions. Already an obsession before 9/11, the Mexican border is perceived as 'the greatest threat to homeland security' (ibid.: 109) and border control has intensified since 9/11, leading to even more migrant deaths. A partition, called 'the fence' or 'the barrier', has been erected along it in sections. Initially set up in the 1990s, it first took the form of military landing mats (corrugated steel mats approximately ten feet long) set vertically side by side and metal fences. Since then, it has been reinforced with triple-layered fencing, concrete-filled steel bollards and concertina wire, growing into 'a monumental declaration of intent' (ibid.: 91). In the immediate aftermath of 9/11, the Patriot Act expanded federal government powers to detain and deport aliens. Across US border states, particularly in Texas, Mexicans have been regarded as 'unwelcome guests, aliens, and illegitimate occupiers' (Talavera et al. 2010: 169). People in these communities are subject to racial profiling, as police tend to stop the darker-skinned, rather than those who are Caucasian-looking, more or less 'equating Mexicans with "illegal aliens"' (ibid.: 194).

The Mexican border is lined with checkpoints to inspect identity documents, border patrols seeking to entrap *mojados*, and prisons. The battle against 'illegal' immigrants has become the domestic front in the 'War on Terror', involving many of the same initiatives, including drone deployment for surveillance along the border as well as helicopters and other armoured vehicles. Drones have become integrated into the Department of Homeland Security's attempt to obtain 'operational control' of this border in the belief that terrorists use the influx of 'illegal' aliens as a 'cover' to enter the USA (Shapiro 2009: 29). Despite a reprieve for a certain group of undocumented migrants in order to win Latino/a voters in the run-up to the 2012 election, the Obama administration has invested heavily in border security, immigration detention and deportation. Militaristic methods have become standard in the attempted pursuit of aliens, along with punitive legislation, such as SB1070 in Arizona, which requires police to check the immigration status of anyone they stop or arrest, if there is 'reasonable suspicion' that they are in the USA illegally, a measure that legitimates racial profiling; similar laws have been introduced in other states.

As Gloria Anzaldúa remarks, borders are established 'to define the places that are safe and unsafe, to distinguish *us* from *them*' (1999: 25). Everywhere in the mise-en-scène of *Monsters*, signs warn of the 'Infected Zone' between the USA and Mexico in which it is unsafe to travel. Its SF cartography of the 'Infected Zone' makes visible the frontier mentality against Mexicans. Drawing imagery from the immune system, the 'Infected Zone' figures the nation-state as a body whose boundaries and territorial integrity are being threatened. Hence the efforts of the military to fortify and defend its boundaries, to contain and destroy the creatures in the border zone through aerial bombing. Donna Haraway has noted how the military imagery of 'extraterrestrialism, ultimate frontiers' and high-tech war are joined together in contemporary immunological discourse (1992: 320). Conversely, 'military cultures . . . draw on immune system discourse' (ibid.: 321). The creatures in *Monsters* are regarded as 'ET monsters of the immune landscape', as suggested by the terminology of infection and defence according to which the nation is in danger of being invaded by 'the threatening "not-selves" that the immune system guards against' (ibid.: 320).

In *Monsters*, the border is a space of attrition, evoking contemporary war zones as well as the US–Mexico frontier. Whereas in media and government rhetoric the aliens are simply dangerous and must be expelled, we later hear from people smugglers who help Sam Wynden and Andrew Kaulder across the 'Infected Zone' that the US military has been using chemical weapons although the aliens don't harm unless they are harmed themselves. Throughout, the aliens are referred to as 'creatures', rather than 'monsters'. In one scene, the protagonists attend a candlelit vigil for victims of the 'Infected Zone'. Among shrines adorned with photographs of dead relatives, we discover a placard – 'Que son los "monstros" [Who are the "monsters"]? No Bombing'. Filmed at a real Day of the Dead festival, the scene evokes historical state-sanctioned atrocities, and invites us to ask the same question, implying that the real monsters are the military.

At a ferry terminal, Sam is charged $5,000 for a ticket for the safer sea route to the USA. She is privileged because she has a passport, which she proudly holds up. In contrast, other people in the queue, the undocumented, without passports, are expecting to go by land across the 'Infected Zone' – a perilous journey to which a nearby advertisement gives the lie: 'Passage to America. Free gas masks! Tickets only $5,000. NO PASSPORT NO VISA required.' Those people are shown with weary expressions; the tiredness of their body language expresses their interminable waiting, qualities that the film absorbs and uses to gesture to the real socio-political conditions of the undocumented migrant. In the distance, the southern perimeter fence around the 'Infected Zone' is visible across the harbour, with helicopters hovering above it.

When the protagonists' passports and money are stolen, they suddenly become placed in a similar position to undocumented migrants, regardless of the $5,000 they paid for a ticket the previous day. So they decide to take the daunting journey by land, having to pawn Sam's engagement ring to bribe officials. They are accompanied by people smugglers to guide them across the border, echoing real-world migrants' practice of hiring *coyotes* – whom the authorities call 'alien smugglers' – in order to evade border police detection (Talavera et al. 2010: 182). Through its narrative, the film alludes not only to the difficulties of crossing the US–Mexico border but also the journey across Mexico to the border which, for migrants from Central America, is as perilous as the border crossing itself.[2] *Monsters* evokes that fraught experience by combining footage shot in different places. In a scene filmed at a real border (in Guatemala), the characters, now bereft of their passports, encounter real, armed immigration officials in a palpably edgy atmosphere; the scene was played 'for real', with actors attempting to cross the border without passports, emulating conditions faced by real migrants.

Whereas contemporary deportation takes place in a world divided into nation-states, expulsion once occurred across the space of empires. The colonial legacy of the expulsions of long-settled, indigenous populations can be felt in the present-day treatment of disadvantaged migrants. In this respect, it is not surprising that, in *Monsters*, the journey towards the US–Mexico border is imagined across the rainforest, mapping areas populated by indigenous people. This rainforest scenery includes a Mayan pyramid which is juxtaposed, in the same image, with the Wall looming in the distance; the characters use it as their vantage-point. This sign of the past, before the European conquest of the Americas, acts as a reminder of the violent expulsions that shaped the two continents, offering a different perspective on the border: the people of the borderlands don't cross it; rather, it crosses them. Indeed, the US–Mexico border cuts across the lands of a native people called the Tohono O'odham. Native American groups have opposed the creation of this international border and state immigration laws which use 'the category "illegal" for people crossing it without papers' (Harding 2012: 108). Albert Hale, a former Arizona state senator and President of the Navajo Nation, has declared: 'We have been subjected to undocumented immigration since day one, since 1492' (ibid.: 107).

Importantly, the space of the colonised tropics is not imagined as empty in *Monsters* – a land without inhabitants fit for conquest – but as a biosphere that is incredibly alive. The borderland is a 'contact zone' (Pratt 1992: 8) between disparate peoples, a space of alien encounters. Alien spores are witnessed growing on trees, glowing eerily. The place itself has a kind of sentience. In a fireside conversation with the people smugglers, Sam asks them whether they think the Wall will really keep the aliens out of America. Their response – that, although the USA has been putting in huge financial investment, it remains an inadequate solution to the problem – pertains to both actual and fictional border realities.

Through Andrew's role as a photojournalist, the film comments on the sentimental politics of representation which holds up endangered children as ideal images of victimisation. His newspaper company will pay $50,000 for a photo of a dead child, but nothing for one of a happy child. It is in the hope of getting such a shot that he has travelled to the borderlands in the first place. In the early part of the film, he exhibits a cavalier attitude about his role in photographing tragedy and profiting from others' suffering: 'I don't cause it; I just document it.' Later, after a creature 'attack', he stumbles across exactly what he has been looking for, a dead girl, apparently killed by an alien. However, he resists the acquisitive impulse to photograph her; taking his coat out of his bag instead of his camera, he tenderly covers her body – a gesture that is significant not only as a mark of his ethical transformation but also for the ethics espoused by the film, which does not exploit icons of victimisation, but rather invites viewers to make their own connections from signs in the mise-en-scène. *Monsters* doesn't need images of endangered children to convey its meanings.

That the Wall is an ineffective barrier is proven when the characters pass through a deserted checkpoint into a devastated and evacuated Texas neighbourhood. In the aftermath of what appears to be a military onslaught, dead aliens are slumped on houses, tentacles lolling from the rooftops. At a secluded gas station, two of the creatures arrive, not to attack but to copulate in mid-air, their luminous tendrils expressively curling around each other against the night sky. The humans look on, entranced by 'the creatures bonding in a world that, to them, is far more alien than the Zone to the humans' (Roddick 2011: 57). They are transformed by their encounter, resulting in their first on-screen kiss. When the military arrive to 'rescue' and separate them, they experience it as a disruption to their communion with the creatures and with each other.

The film's night-vision opening, showing the military's battle with the aliens and Sam's injury (maybe her death), is actually the story's conclusion. It begins with a soldier humming a tune from *Apocalypse Now* (1979) (Wagner's 'Ride of the Valkyries') as he and other marines charge along the highway in their armoured vehicle, gung-ho for a fight. Instead of ending with militaristic confrontation, the film opts to conclude with its penultimate scene, which places the emphasis on the transformative encounter. It challenges socially constructed boundaries between 'human' and 'non-human' and xenophobic discourses of nationhood, placing the ethical responsibility to change attitudes firmly on our shoulders, in keeping with its taglines: 'After six years, they're no longer aliens. They're residents' and 'Now, it's our turn to adapt'.

DISTRICT 9: GUESTS AND ALIENS

In *District 9*, an alien spaceship reaches Johannesburg in 1982, during the South African apartheid era, and lingers over the city like an ominous cloud. When the authorities decide to cut their way in, they discover numerous malnourished aliens in the ship's hold. With international human rights groups intently watching, South African aid agencies bring the aliens to Earth. But, despite initial attempts to give the aliens 'proper status' and 'protection', the temporary refugee camp in which they are housed turns into a slum, known as District 9, a 'fenced' and 'militarised' area. The aliens are associated with crime and discriminated against. After twenty years, anti-alien sentiment rises to an all-time high. The government outsources the task of evicting the aliens to a private firm, Multinational United (MNU), which plans to resettle them in a new compound, District 10, 200 miles away. During the evictions, MNU employee Wikus van de Merwe becomes 'infected' by his exposure to an alien fluid, and begins a painful transformation into an alien himself. Taking refuge in District 9, he befriends an alien whom he previously tried to evict, Christopher Johnson, in the hope of retrieving the fluid that transformed him, the only means of restoring his human form.

A US–New Zealand–Canada–South Africa co-production, involving the Hollywood studio Tristar Pictures, commissioned and backed by *Lord of the Rings* director/producer Peter Jackson, *District 9* was a box office hit, despite its lack of stars and (then) unknown director, Neill Blomkamp (who, like Edwards, comes from a visual effects background). Made on a relatively 'modest' US$30 million budget, which it recouped within its opening weekend, the film went to number one in the US box office and earned over US$200 million worldwide (Schalkwyk 2009; Jones 2013). As in other films in this chapter, the use of real locations plus CGI gives a gritty, lived-in feel to *District 9*'s alternative reality. It was mostly filmed in Johannesburg, including a real shanty town on the outskirts, where 'people had lived in shacks on landfill for years' (Worsdale 2009: 35). The digital elements – the spaceship, military vehicles and helicopters – were added to location footage in postproduction, along with the aliens, digital creations based on performance capture technologies.

In the moment of first contact, recalling discoveries of immigrants hiding in shipping containers, the film indicates what it is about. These are literally homeless, stateless aliens: refugees from another planet. On Earth, the aliens are treated in a similar way to today's asylum seekers: unwanted and unwelcome, reduced to abject and humiliating conditions. The film has been accused of reproducing stereotypes about immigrants. According to James Zborowski, '*District 9* is a movie whose "immigrants" objectively are . . . the threatening, marauding, uneducated, slum-dwelling, amorphous social problem of the xenophobic imagination . . . The film thereby justifies the reactions to immi-grants it ostensibly condemns' (Zborowski 2010). Similar criticisms have been levelled at its depiction of Nigerians, who mix with aliens in District 9, where they engage in illegally trading alien weaponry, interspecies prostitution and selling cat food (to which the aliens are addicted) at exorbitant prices.

What these debates miss is that *District 9* doesn't aim to make morally upright, politically correct pronouncements about immigrants. At a deeper and more ethical level of reflection, it provokes us to think about how stereo-types are formed. With a startling directness enabled by the SF symbolism of aliens, it confronts audiences with their own xenophobic attitudes, magnify-ing the stereotypes to make them recognisable. But it then exchanges those perceptions with another set of perceptions, bringing about a cognitive shift; the same is true, to a lesser extent, of *Children of Men* and *Monsters*. The aliens are constructed as a 'type', with 'a few immediately recognizable and defining traits', yet these change and develop in the course of the narrative (Dyer 1993: 13). In the early part of the film, the aliens are seen entirely through the filter of the host society, including the media and academic experts; its latter part, however, increasingly focuses on the aliens' own perspective, the pivot being Wikus's transformation. As Richard Dyer reminds us, the crucial point about stereotypes is not simply that they are wrong but, rather, in whose power interests they work (ibid.: 17). *District 9* demonstrates this very clearly.

District 9's mixed-media format, consisting of a corporate MNU video and faux news, documentary and CCTV footage, highlights how much we per-ceive the characters and their situation according to the medium in which they are presented; we are encouraged to see them as the medium, and the power interests controlling it, wish us to see them. The plethora of different speak-ers and pseudo-documentary footage not only heightens the film's realism, reminding us that these injustices are based in reality, but also emphasises the aliens as an object of competing discourses. The alien population is caught in the crossfire between different interest groups: the government, the media, academics, humanitarian agencies, MNU and local South Africans, most of whom regard the aliens as a social problem to be resolved for the humans' benefit rather than for the aliens themselves.

The film starts with the filming of a corporate MNU video following the protagonist as he embarks on the eviction operation he has been chosen to lead. We hear a lapel microphone being attached to Wikus's clothes, as he gar-rulously talks off camera. The image jerks into vision, revealing him as a non-descript desk bureaucrat in a mundane office setting. As we will see, Wikus's portrayal as an unsympathetic protagonist, played by a then unknown actor (Sharlto Copley), is crucial to his function in the narrative. The MNU logo occasionally appears at the corner of the screen, reminding us when we are watching the final, edited version of the corporate video. Documentary-style titles appear, identifying interviewees. We also see outtakes from this video, which form an insight into the mindset of the aliens' oppressors.[3]

Occasionally, the narration switches to news footage, with headlines scrolling at the bottom of the screen. When it shows locals rioting, in an attempt to force aliens out of the townships, actual archive images of rioting supplied by the South African Broadcasting Company are spliced into the film. Voices of news anchors ring through *District 9*'s world, giving the impression that what they tell us is lifted directly from reality. Nonetheless, it is a selective and highly mediated portrayal. News images link the aliens to criminality, emphasising their destructive behaviour. Commentary over images of burning shacks in District 9 names aliens as perpetrators of this act, rather than as targets of the local community's hate crimes. Media reportage is later proved to be unreliable when Wikus himself becomes the victim of a smear campaign during his transformation into an alien. On a TV at a fast-food outlet, a breaking news item declares him to be an escaped fugitive carrying a deadly contagion due to his 'prolonged sexual activity with aliens'. Upon these words, the news programme produces an evidently faked image of Wikus having sex with an alien. The film shows how the media influence our perceptions of social groups and expose processes through which stereotypes are peddled. As Lindiwe Dovey remarks about media images of terrorism, the visualisation of violence enacts political goals: 'In apartheid South Africa, this visualization involved the constant streaming on television of black South African "terrorism" to convince whites that the government was justified in its (racist) laws' (2009: 48). In *District 9*'s world, too, media manipulation is crucial to justifying a new apartheid system and promoting it to the public.

Inserted into the narrative are documentary interviews with Wikus's family and colleagues, academic experts and members of the public. Although some of the experts are sympathetic to the aliens' plight, they tend to exert their power-knowledge: the aliens are considered inferior, as immigrants often are by the dominant culture. One such expert, sociologist Sarah Livingstone, informs us that the aliens are known by 'the derogatory term "prawn"', which 'implies something that . . . scavenges the leftovers'. This provides the cue for an entomologist to comment on the aliens' insect-like community. Both physically and in their mannerisms, the aliens appear to the humans like insects, with segmented carapaces and tentacles hanging from their faces. The digital design of the aliens was based on 'cockroaches, dung beetles, goliath bugs' (Fordham 2009: 25). *District 9* engages with an SF convention of representing aliens in insectoid forms which evoke fear and dread; yet, in doing so, it reflects on processes of dehumanisation that enable others to be oppressed and destroyed more easily, recalling the Nazis' characterisation of Jews as vermin and Hutus' labelling of Tutsis as cockroaches, as well as news media attempts to convince us that immigrants are 'almost subhuman' (Hanson 2013).

In their interviews, members of the public express prejudices about the aliens, scapegoating them for social ills and supporting the government's policy of separation in the belief that this is for their own safety. It is mainly black South Africans who express greatest hostility towards the aliens, a provocative reference to the country's past. One declares emphatically: 'They should just go.' Another complains: 'If they were from another country we'd understand, but they are not even from this planet!'

The film evokes the history of apartheid to question the legitimacy of current practices used to deal with immigration in South Africa and elsewhere. Literally meaning 'separateness' in Afrikaans, apartheid was introduced in South Africa shortly after the Second World War, denying basic rights to the black majority population and forcing them to live in a state of physical, legal and political segregation, not regarded as equal to the ruling whites. The apartheid system was enforced through a series of laws designed to preserve white privilege and 'ensure that society remained segregated and unequal' (Durrheim et al. 2011: 4). Spatial segregation was the tool used to create racial inequality. As Kevin Durrheim, Xoliswa Mtose and Lyndsay Brown note, 'segregation is the socio-geographic form that perpetuates inequality' and 'keeps the poor trapped in poverty' (ibid.: 21). Under apartheid, towns and cities were organised into racially exclusive areas to reflect the racial hierarchy. In public places, signs like 'Whites Only' or 'Non-Whites Only' controlled access to amenities on a racialised basis.

The apartheid system was built upon a previous history of institutionalised socio-economic inequality under colonialism. Frantz Fanon observed that 'the colonial world is cut in two', its frontiers marked 'by barracks and police stations' (2001: 29). For him, 'apartheid is simply one form of the division into

Figure 4.2 The aerial shots of District 9 reveal its geography of exclusion.

Figure 4.3 In *District 9*, the city's spatial divisions mark social divisions, reinforced by signs.

compartments of the colonial world' (ibid.: 40). *District 9* reverberates with echoes of both colonialism and apartheid, including forced removals. Its title is reminiscent of District 6 in Cape Town, declared a whites-only area under the Group Areas Act, resulting in the expulsion of its multicultural community to racially designated townships. In addition, the planned eviction of aliens to District 10 recalls the Bantu Homelands Citizenship Act (1970), which displaced black populations to rural areas known as 'Bantustans' or homelands in order to deprive them of South African citizenship.

Apartheid legislation was dismantled in the early 1990s. However, socio-economic and racial inequalities remain as a legacy of that era. In the post-apartheid era, South Africa, now a 'magnet' for migrants from other African countries, has become wracked with xenophobia (Harding 2012: 125). Immigrants are known by the pejorative term *kwerekwere* and have become scapegoats when nobody else is left to blame under a black political leadership (Maharaj 2011: 368). Citizens have supported 'heavy restrictions on foreign nationals, or no foreign nationals at all' (Harding 2012: 69). Anti-immigrant riots broke out in May 2008, forming the immediate backdrop to the fictional-ised events in *District 9*.

As under apartheid, space is a mechanism of domination and control in *District 9*'s world. The aerial shots of Johannesburg reveal its geography of exclusion. Separated into zones of human and non-human habitation, the city's spatial divisions mark social divisions, reinforced with signs such as 'No non-human loitering'. The inner city is sturdily built of steel and concrete, full of skyscrapers and gated communities, lined with leafy, well-paved, clean streets, all the rubbish cleared out of sight. Its borders protect the privileged group from its others. In contrast, District 9 is built on a landfill site. The aliens live on top of each other, in low-lying shacks crammed together. It is a barren wasteland, where nothing grows except the refuse of the city – a place for beings defined as waste. The bleakness is intensified by its narrow colour palette, mainly dry earth-tones, obtained by filming during winter and draining colour in postproduction (Worsdale 2009). Aerial perspectives from circling helicopters emphasise District 9's status as a place of otherness that is constantly policed and under surveillance. Surrounded by razor wire, electrified fences and armed patrols, it is an imprisoning structure. Its borders construct the aliens as a security threat and keep them firmly segregated from the wider population – reminding us of the structures of apartheid violence.

In *District 9*'s fictional world, MNU is one of the world's largest weapons manufacturers, hence the implication that the real reason for the evictions is to find alien weaponry, despite the company's humanitarian pretext of resettling the aliens in a more comfortable place. MNU represents the murky world of corporate and other non-state actors deployed by states in pursuit of mercantile interests. Along with other MNU officers, Wikus serves eviction notices, acting condescendingly to the aliens, threatening them with his armed guard and bribing them with cat food. At one point he discovers a shed containing alien eggs and removes them from the source of their nutrient, then summons MNU forces to torch the whole nest. He does so without any moral qualms, because he does not regard the aliens as human, though we hear sounds of babies squealing. Afterwards, he even jokes about it, comparing the popping noise the infants make when they die to popcorn.

Excerpts from the MNU video picture District 10 with the caption 'Sanctuary Park'. Yet behind the barbed wire can be glimpsed countless, densely packed tents. Later in the film when Wikus finds Christopher looking at the promotional brochures, he warns him that the new camp is worse than District 9 – that it's basically 'a concentration camp'. Situated even further outside the city, District 10 condenses memories of historical atrocities, from the Nazis' resettlement programmes and 'Final Solution' through to one of the earliest uses of concentration camps, by the British during the Boer War in South Africa. As suggested in relation to *Children of Men*, the film highlights how the 'deportation of aliens' is imbued with echoes of these former practices.

MNU's nefarious activities, including the practice of torture and death squads, add to the already rich historical layering in *District 9*. When Wikus begins to transform into an alien, he is moved to MNU's laboratories, where secret genetic experiments on aliens are underway. Even Wikus is aware that these experiments, which also hark back to Nazi practices, are morally abhorrent, exclaiming: 'What are they doing to these prawns?' For MNU, what happens to the aliens (and now to Wikus) isn't important; it just wants to harvest their bodies in order to operate the billion-dollar alien weaponry it plans to sell to foreign governments. Due to the aliens' sophisticated biotechnology, which requires alien DNA to be activated, MNU cannot operate it itself, so it takes advantage of Wikus's transformation to test the weaponry.

Evoking sinister corporate and government forces, MNU is rendered more alien than the aliens – forging a moral allegiance with the aliens.

Our introduction to Christopher Johnson and his son is the point at which this perspectival shift takes place. We first encounter them when they, along with a friend, are scouring a waste heap for alien technology in order to collect the precious fluid that will enable them to start up the mothership and return home. They speak in their language, which is translated for us in subtitles, enabling us to comprehend the motives behind their actions, which, by itself, makes them more relatable. Christopher is the first alien who is seen to explicitly question the terms of the eviction order, instantly recognising its illegality. So Wikus attempts a different tack – muttering patronisingly in an aside to his colleague that this alien is a little smarter than the others – and threatens to take his child away to child services. Christopher, who wishes no harm to come to his son, then has no choice but to sign the order. From this point onwards, the film cements our allegiance with Christopher and his son. Throughout the film, aliens wear odd combinations of human clothing in an attempt to assimilate. Christopher's red jacket allows us to recognise and distinguish him from other aliens from scene to scene. Through conferring recognition upon and fostering allegiance with Christopher, the film gradually gives the aliens a 'human' face yet, at the same time, it highlights the failure to perceive it as such.

With their 'expressive eyes and brows', the aliens' faces are designed to elicit empathy, enhanced in close-ups (Fordham 2009: 25). When MNU shoots his friend, Christopher's large, soulful eyes widen in alarm and blink in despair – a representation that reflects anthropomorphic principles that the eyes are portals into inner subjectivity. This anthropomorphism can be explained by the structures of character engagement in cinema, as Neill Blomkamp remarks: 'for any form of sentient being that the audience has to relate to, our psychology seems to require aliens to be presented with a human face' (ibid.). Digital characters have to possess a 'human-like agency' in order for audiences to recognise and empathise with them (Purse 2013: 62). However, this anthropomorphic dimension works on a deeper level in *District 9*, where the alien appearance also represents the filter of popular perceptions through which refugees and immigrants are seen, including as lowlife scavengers and scroungers. The film shows us an internal world of emotions that the media, academic experts and locals fail to see – they just see the aliens superficially, from the outside, through the grid of their own prejudices. When Christopher encounters the MNU experiments undertaken by those who had no regard for alien life, he is rooted to the spot, displaying moral emotions lacking in the human characters. Later, he declares: 'I must save my people.' His pain confirms that they are *people* upon whom this violence is being meted out.

In contrast to the media and experts' portrayal of aliens as a threatening horde or insect-like colony, the film individualises Christopher Johnson. It gives him a name, a family and a story: a longing to go home. As a caring parent with a child, he evokes sympathy; he is shown to have desires for a better life similar to the local community. His son displays a young child's curiosity in trying to find out about his home planet and his roots, inviting empathy that only intensifies when Christopher tells him that they can no longer return home, since the flask of fluid they have painstakingly been collecting for twenty years has been stolen by MNU. The son's light, playful movements are like those of a human child. The scene where he is trying to hide from MNU is filled with both humour and suspense, as the film makes us feel and imagine the aliens' experience of danger. Humour is often used to enable an in-group bond against an out-group, who become the butt of the joke (Morreall 2009: 121). This reactionary type of humour denigrates others and 'serves to reinforce social consensus' (Critchley 2002: 11). It is the laughter of the powerful at the powerless. As Simon Critchley observes, 'the *ethos* of a place is expressed by laughing at people who are not like us', underlying the 'belief that "they" are inferior to "us"' (ibid.: 69). Jokes are therefore a good indicator of 'who a particular society is subordinating, scapegoating or denigrating' at any moment (ibid.: 76). In *District 9*, the aliens appear in the media and academic commentary as figures of fun – for example, being addicted to cat food or wearing odd items of human clothing. But in this sequence, the humour depends on our sharing a world with the aliens, laughing with them.

Here it is not the dominant culture claiming likeness in its own (selective) terms; rather, it is the other way round. The alien child tells Wikus 'We are the same', a proposition that he vehemently rejects, even though at this point his DNA is being altered into alien DNA. After his exposure to the alien fluid, the transformation causes his nails to flake off, his teeth to fall out and his skin to blister all over. He is shocked when the bandages of his injured arm are unravelled to reveal that an alien arm has grown in its place. As a result of his transformation, he is compelled to experience what the Other experiences – namely segregation, destitution, loss of safety and rights, and exploitation. Criminalised, then alienated by his family and society, he loses his place in the organisation of the city, ending up in the low space of District 9. With the media smear campaign against him, Wikus becomes a victim of hate propaganda. Sara Ahmed writes that 'hate has effects on the bodies of those who are made into its objects'. Moreover, 'if the effect of hate crime is affect, and an affect which is visceral and bodily', the victim's body becomes its testimony; in a circular effect, the victim's affected body is read as the 'truth' of the hate crime by its perpetrators (Ahmed 2004: 58). Wikus, the eviction officer, is forced to feel how racism and discrimination operate on his own body, the implications of the coercive measures that he carried out against aliens.

Through its expressive visual effects, the film dwells upon his physical transformation into an alien, simultaneously a moral and an ethical transformation.

Although earlier in the film we are aligned with Wikus – we hear his voice commentary and the camera follows him – we do not share his moral perspective. It is only when he transforms into an alien that we are encouraged to ally ourselves with him, especially when he sacrifices his longing to be 'fixed' to help Christopher and his son return to their homeland. Through his contact and positioning with aliens, he morally evolves. However, a distinction between the film's moral and ethical perspectives becomes crucial. After Wikus's transformation, the film focuses on another perpetrator, the sadistic MNU mercenary Koobus Venter. In the film's moral perspective, violence towards Koobus and MNU is made acceptable because by this stage we are rooting for the aliens, a limiting perspective that simply switches allegiance from one group to another, rather than fundamentally changing attitudes. The greater, ethical potential in *District 9* lies in its ability to make us infer connections between past and present wrongs carried out in the name of humanity and to assume responsibility for them, to imagine how this present state of affairs came to be.

But even if Wikus's journey is one of upward moral progress, the film refuses to reward him with an elevated, heroic status, according to narrative conventions. In media interviews, we hear people speculating about what has happened to him. Various conspiracy theories hold that MNU or a foreign government has captured him. The film shows us his wife Tanya holding an artificial flower that she found on her doorstep, though she doesn't believe it could be from him. Its final image is an alien crafting the same flower from a waste heap in District 9, implying that this is Wikus, still an alien outcast.

CODA: *ELYSIUM*

It would be impossible to end this chapter without mentioning *Elysium*, which Blomkamp made after the success of *District 9*, with a similar production set-up but now with a US$115 million budget and two Hollywood stars, Matt Damon and Jodie Foster. Its story is set in 2154 on an increasingly derelict and polluted Earth. In this future, Los Angeles has become a Third World city, filled with waste, poverty and a substantial Latino/a population. Everything here is grimy, weathered and dilapidated. Hospitals are overcrowded and underresourced. Everyone aspires to travel to Elysium, the wealthy elite's space station, a shimmering double halo visible in the sky.

Elysium is another world, a pristine habitat where the wealthy are able to maintain their standard of living, enjoying luxury and longevity in large suburban homes with neat lawns and swimming pools, and attended upon by droid servants. Every house has a 'med bay', a device combining medical imaging technologies with tissue regeneration, in which the patient can have cancerous cells instantly removed. Elysium's rich inhabitants are largely white, although their leader, President Patel, is South Asian. Some of them own terrestrial industrial plants like the droid production factory where the protagonist, Max, works, underlining that, even in a world where robot technology is super-advanced, Elysium's wealth is still fed by the labour of the wretched of the Earth.

When the poor and the crippled try to get a foothold into the rich world in order to obtain better healthcare, their shuttles are shot down as 'undocumented spacecraft' by Elysium's Defence Secretary, Delacourt, who seeks to protect the wealthy elites' privileges for themselves. The travellers are apprehended by Homeland Security droids and prepared for deportation. Those lucky enough to land and reach a med bay may find that they show up on its database as 'illegal' and are therefore refused treatment. This parallels measures to restrict 'illegal' immigrants' access to healthcare and other amenities in today's society, for example the Immigration Bill 2013–14 in Britain.[4] Through its mise-en-scène, *Elysium* pinpoints contemporary structural inequalities in a provocative manner – as a form of global apartheid.

Yet, unlike the other films in this chapter, the thoughtfulness of *Elysium*'s mise-en-scène does not extend very far into its narrative. Its story of Max as a heroic underdog destined to save Earth, and who must fight against Delacourt and her agent, Kruger, in order to do so, deflects the focus on material inequalities to a metaphysical struggle between good and evil. *Elysium* lacks both the moral complexity of *District 9* and the historical signposting of the other films, which provoke ethical scrutiny of the causes and contexts of their dystopian worlds. The casting of Matt Damon as Max furthermore underscores that *Elysium* deals with inequality in a profoundly unequal way, with bankable

Figure 4.4 Migrants from Earth are refused medical treatment when their 'illegal' status shows up on the database in *Elysium*.

Hollywood stars who guarantee a big box office return and who confirm the cultural domination of the rich, white world.

Despite these profound contradictions, which highlight cinema's complicity with global capitalism, I would still claim that SF films on this topic fulfil an important role. While most migrant-themed documentaries and realist dramas tend to be watched by a self-selecting few, these films, by harnessing the pleasures of one of the most popular genres, cross over to a wide audience. Although the SF genre is often denigrated as superficial, due to its extensive special effects, in this chapter I have suggested that the films are thoughtful events, neither merely spectacular fun nor merely moral vehicles. In fact, it is by means of spectacle, combined with narrative, that they raise the genre's critical threshold and subvert audience expectations established in promotional materials, which do not make reference to migrants' rights or histories of political violence. Through their evocative mises-en-scène, mixing digital and recorded reality, they create vivid images with powerful associations that linger in our memories, outlasting the rehearsal of facts and statistics in realist and documentary representations. They enable us to understand some of the implications of the deportation regime, playing out the consequences of excluding others from the sphere of the human and the predicament of people caught between borders in conditions of exacerbated and ever-increasing inequalities.

NOTES

1. The proximity between realist and SF representations is testified by Michael Winterbottom's SF film *Code 46* (2003), set in a future where entry into cities is strictly regulated by permits; the rest of the world is a desert filled with shanty towns where the undocumented are consigned. Winterbottom also directed *In This World*, which forms one of the stated inspirations behind *Monsters* (see Edwards et al. 2011).
2. See, for example, the documentary *No One* (*De nadie*, 2005), which follows a train journey by Central American migrants across Mexico, where they are vulnerable to injury or death on the tracks, assault by criminal gangs and robbery by corrupt police; fearing deportation, they are reluctant to file complaints, so the gangs and corrupt authorities act with impunity.
3. I am grateful to Alex Hunt for illuminating this point.
4. At the time of writing, the Bill is being debated in Parliament.

CHAPTER 5

Architectures of Enmity: the Israeli–Palestinian Conflict through a Cinematic Lens

In the critically acclaimed Israeli co-production *Waltz with Bashir* (*Vals Im Bashir*, 2008),[1] Zahava Solomon, a post-combat trauma expert, relates an anecdote about an Israeli soldier who survived the ordeal of the 1982 Lebanon War by looking at everything through an imaginary camera. 'Wow! What great scenes,' the soldier exclaimed. 'Shooting, artillery, wounded people, screaming. . .' With a series of still images, the film envisions the scene through his imaginary viewfinder that enabled him to experience the war like a movie or holiday snapshots, shielding him from its horrors. But, then, Solomon tells us, his camera 'broke', which the film renders with images of frames disrupted in a shutter gate, extending the metaphor of camera malfunction as previously still images become moving ones. Roving across the ruined landscape filled with wounded and slaughtered Arabian horses, the 'camera' finally rests on a close-up of a horse's eye, surrounded by flies, reflecting the soldier in its distended iris.

The film invites us to interpret the anecdote, as Solomon does, solely through the paradigm of trauma: the soldier's experience of war as 'a series of dissociative events'. In this chapter, I argue that the trauma paradigm forms part of a dominant discourse that co-opts morality to its own ends and deflects attention from the wider ethical and political issues of the Palestinian–Israeli conflict. Seen beyond the trauma paradigm, the anecdote reflects the 'derealization of military engagement' (Virilio 1989: 1) – the Israeli soldiers' ability to distance themselves from the consequences of military actions which they themselves are orchestrating. The 'abstractification' of reality through its representation in a frame is a way of alleviating moral anxiety about those actions. This abstractification persists even after the proverbial camera breaks, as testified by the image of Arabian horses rather than Arabs.

Like the imaginary viewfinder, Western news media construct perceptions of the Israeli–Palestinian conflict that usually do not provoke any moral problems. While Al-Jazeera and some other news networks provide alternative viewpoints, Western journalists tend to avoid areas perceived as controversial, such as alluding to colonial history as the basis of violence. In a survey of the UK public, the Glasgow University Media Group revealed 'little understanding of the reasons for the conflict and its origins', due to reliance on primetime TV news (Philo et al. 2003: 134). Seventy-nine per cent of respondents did not know who was occupying the Occupied Territories and ten per cent thought it was the Palestinians – one of many examples in the survey suggesting that perceptions of the conflict fostered by news media are the opposite to reality. One reason, as an interviewed journalist commented, is that the media cover dramatic action 'but not the human inequities, the essential imbalances of the occupation, the day-to-day humiliations of the Palestinians' (ibid.: 138). Everyday oppression is rarely broached in the media, and never with 'the intensity with which Palestinian terrorism is discussed' (Said 1984). Furthermore, with the USA as Israel's ally, powerful voices speak on Israel's behalf. Because of Israel's strategic importance in the Middle East, the USA provides it with billions of dollars' worth of annual military aid. Because of the UK's close relationship with the USA, British media also offer little criticism of US or Israeli policy, especially since 9/11, when Israel has tried to enfold its battle against Palestinian militants into the global 'War on Terror'. Israel's actions against Palestinians are facilitated by this Western economic, military and ideological support.

One story we are repeatedly told through the media is that Israel is under terrorist attack, for example by Hamas rockets fired into Israeli territory from Gaza, and is simply 'responding'. This moral rhetoric of self-defence is one that Israel constantly uses to allay international concerns about its actions. In following Israel's lead with the vocabulary of state retaliation to terrorist attacks, Western news media do not countenance that a blockaded and imprisoned civilian population (with Hamas as its democratically elected representative in Gaza) may be attempting to defend *itself*. In news coverage, the word 'atrocity' is habitually applied to Israeli casualties of Palestinian rockets and suicide bombings but rarely to the much larger numbers of Palestinian deaths from Israel's deployment of its vastly superior military capabilities (Philo et al. 2003: 144). Where criticism of Israel is offered, it is often in the rhetoric of 'disproportionate response', which, too, confirms the moral validity of the aggressor, which merely has to measure its response.

Israel habitually regards itself as the victim, invoking the past of anti-Semitic persecution under the Holocaust and pogroms in order to justify its aggression. That identity of victimhood is determined in advance, serving to cover up its brutal actions. The creation of Israel was regarded by the West as compensation for the Holocaust – thus making Palestinians 'expiate for the historical crimes committed against the Jews in Europe' (Said 1992: xxiv).

This moral guilt over the Holocaust, linked to discourses about it as an incomparable and 'unique' event, is another story that subtends Western perceptions of the conflict and that has allowed Palestinians to suffer undeservedly for so long.

The third form of moral rhetoric that one finds in Western news media is that of 'balancing' the Israeli and Palestinian narratives in a way that is thought to be objective, as in the BBC's famous rhetoric of 'impartiality'. The resulting images present the conflict as an ahistorical 'cycle of violence' and 'hatred' between two communities who 'can't get on' (Philo et al. 2003: 139, 141). This obscures the fundamental power asymmetry that underlies and upholds the conflict, in which one group dominates and controls the lives and livelihoods of another, albeit with some resistance. The attempt to take a position that is apparently midway between either 'side' effectively legitimates the state's moral right to persist in its violence. Historical evidence uncovered by Israeli New Historians, such as Ilan Pappé (1992) and Avi Shlaim (1990), on the origins of Zionist colonialism during the British mandate period (1920–48) and the ethnic cleansing that it introduced supports the Palestinian narrative of expulsion and dispossession, previously dismissed as 'propaganda'; moreover, Pappé argues that similar tactics underlie Israel's present-day actions (Chomsky and Pappé 2011: 136).

The problem confronting films about the conflict, then, is to find a way of representing it in the face of public conditioning by this distorted media coverage. This chapter adopts spatial mapping as an analytical tool to explore how films allow us to perceive the conflict differently from news media. Since space is the instrument through which the conflict's everyday violence is inflicted, spatial mapping subtly permits its causes and contexts to emerge. In some cases, those spatial meanings are part of a film's dramatic intent, as in the Israeli films *Close to Home* (*Karov La Bayit*, 2005) and *Lemon Tree* (*Etz Limon*, 2008) and the Palestinian film *Paradise Now* (2005), as well as various documentaries about the Israel–West Bank 'separation fence', known by its opponents as the 'Apartheid Wall'. In *Waltz with Bashir*, however, they derive from its mixing of the war genre and animation, which portrays war as a kind of video game.

This analysis relies on the notion of space because when the conflict is reframed in terms of colonialism, it is essentially spatial: Israel as a colonial state lays sovereignty claims to a territory to which it believes it has divine or historical (and exclusive) right, yet the same space is already inhabited by Palestinians. Hence, Israel's colonial enterprise of gaining land that does not have Arabs living on it has historically taken the form of mass expulsions, population transfer and resettlement in refugee camps, destruction of Palestinian villages, erection of Jewish settlements in their place, and establishment of new colonies in the Occupied Territories. The chapter's title is derived from

Michael Shapiro's term 'architecture of enmity', which he uses to describe an imagined geography, historically derived from colonial notions of identity and space, that divides the world into 'us' versus 'them' antagonisms in order to justify war and security policies (Shapiro 2009: 19). Resistance comes from critically tracing these architectures and mapping 'alternative imaginaries'. The term highlights the use of landscape to generate terror with 'visible signs' of military and sovereign power: for example, destroyed houses and villages as both the material vestiges and symbols of state terror, creating and exuding the sign of a 'space of death' from which people are incited to flee (Gregory and Pred 2006: 4). Spatial mapping shows state violence penetrating everywhere, pervading Palestinian lives at checkpoints and roadblocks that can materialise anywhere. Although he had French Algeria in mind, Frantz Fanon's spatial characterisation of colonialism – 'The colonial world is a world cut in two [with] the dividing line . . . shown by the barracks and police stations' (2001: 29) – accords well with Israel/Palestine, its internal frontiers governed by force, military surveillance and direct action capabilities. Fanon also identified the asymmetry between spaces on either side of the dividing line, and that the divide is, traditionally, fractured by the coloniser's need for cheap labour.

Newspaper journalists, political scientists, human rights activists, and even the former US President Jimmy Carter (2006) have employed the word 'apartheid' in this context. Designating a form of colonial control, the term highlights the separate and unequal lives of Palestinians within both Israel (where they constitute twenty per cent of the population, often treated as second-class citizens) and the Occupied Territories. It evokes comparisons with South Africa, which are justified by a similar history of conflict between settler and indigenous communities and reinforced by use of the label 'bantustans', by both Israeli authorities such as former Prime Minister Ariel Sharon and opponents, to refer to the fragmentation of the Occupied Territories under the quasi-autonomous Palestinian Authority. Like blacks relegated to marginal territories in South Africa, the bantustanisation of Palestine gives Palestinians a spurious independence, although it was advanced as part of the 'peace process' enshrined in the Oslo Accords. Since the two-state solution is widely perceived as having reached a dead end, an anti-apartheid-type struggle is advocated by some activist groups as a way of imagining a different future: one state with equal rights for all of its citizens.

For journalist and activist Ben White, the apartheid paradigm offers a crucial way of rethinking the conflict beyond 'occupation' discourse (2012: 85). This is a perspective broadly shared by Pappé: the conflict needs to be seen 'as a process that began in 1948 [when the state of Israel was created on Palestinian land], even in 1882 [when the first Zionist settlement was established in Palestine], and not 1967 [when Israel occupied the West Bank and Gaza]' (Chomsky and Pappé 2011: 136). Pappé qualifies the situation: 'Some aspects of the occupation . . . are worse than the apartheid reality of South Africa and some aspects in the lives of Palestinian citizens in Israel are not as bad as they were in the heyday of apartheid' (ibid.: 147). However, in the International Convention on the Prevention and Suppression of the Crime of Apartheid (1973), apartheid is defined as a crime in its own right. Though drawn up in opposition to South African apartheid, the Convention's wording clearly indicates that it applies to 'similar practices and policies of racial segregation and discrimination' (UN 1973). Among practices against racial groups it includes 'arbitrary arrest and illegal imprisonment', 'deliberate imposition . . . of conditions calculated to cause its or their physical destruction in whole or in part', denial of 'basic human rights and freedoms' and 'expropriation of landed property' – all of which describe Israel's actions against Palestinians.

A crucial characteristic of spatiality, Doreen Massey states, is that 'it is always being made', lending it 'its continual openness and, thus, its availability to politics' (Lury and Massey 1999: 231). Films map and produce space in a variety of ways, not only entering real spaces but also constructing imaginary ones. Through their shot compositions, they activate various on- and off-screen spaces, alluding to spatial tensions that characterise the conflict, sometimes as much through their omissions as by what is actually depicted. The following analysis explores how they configure some of the conflict's key territorial *topoi* – invasions, checkpoints, roadblocks and fortifications.

INVASIONS: LEBANON 1982 / GAZA 2008

In *Waltz with Bashir*, the director, Ari Folman, attempts to recover his and other Israeli ex-soldiers' post-traumatic memories of the 1982 Lebanon war – specifically, his vicinity to the Sabra and Shatila refugee camps, where Lebanese Christian Phalangists (allies of the invading Israeli army) massacred thousands of Palestinians in revenge for the assassination of their leader, Bashir Gemayel. While recovering his memories, Folman realises that he and other Israeli Defence Force (IDF) soldiers illuminated the night sky with flares to facilitate the massacre. However, this acknowledgement of complicity is tempered by the discourse of Israeli victimhood. As I show in this reading, the film's focus on Israeli soldiers' trauma avoids ethical confrontation with how the massacre happened, who gave the Phalangists access to the camps, and what the Israeli army was doing in Lebanon. In this way, the film circumvents issues of individual and collective responsibility for the Lebanon War and Israel's continuing actions against the Palestinians – the film's release coincided with the 2008–9 Israeli bombardment of Gaza.

Created from a mixture of hand-drawn and digital animation, *Waltz* is an aesthetic tour de force, with documentary-style interviews punctuated by reconstructions of dreams, hallucinations and flashbacks – all to a mesmerising composed score and 1980s pop tracks. Because of this, and its post-traumatic model of narration, the film tends to dazzle and deceive on first viewing. As Gideon Levy observes in his review, it requires repeat viewing to become aware of its other layers of meaning (2010: 127). The animation storyboard was based on filmed interviews with ex-soldiers, a therapist, the post-trauma expert and a journalist, whose voice testimonies are laid onto the soundtrack, along with Folman's voiceover, as dialogue for animated characters. Two ex-soldiers agreed to participate only on condition that their identities were concealed: Boaz Rein-Buskila and Carmi Cna'an, Folman's closest 'comrades' in the narrative, are two fictional characters with voices dubbed by actors.

Until its final scene, when animation yields to archival news footage, realist documentary conventions are discarded for a more subjective logic, marked by the displacements, denials and repetitions that feature in traumatic memories. Folman claims his film 'could only be done in animation with fantastic drawings' because 'war is so surreal, and memory is so tricky' (Sony Pictures Entertainment 2008: 4). He presents it as an anti-war film – nothing like Hollywood movies. Yet *Waltz* belongs to a wave of Israeli war films, including *Lebanon* (2009), that draw on the same winning formula as Hollywood films about the Vietnam and Iraq wars like *The Deer Hunter* (1978) and *The Hurt Locker* (2008). All these films attempt to enter the perspectives of soldiers as victims of the general horrors of war, which 'enables us to obliterate the entire ethico-political background of the conflict' (Žižek 2010). In *The Deer Hunter*, for example, the roles of victim and perpetrator are reversed, making US soldiers appear as victims of a random, senseless war. In *Waltz*, the war is the soldiers' terrible ordeal; they are its exemplary victims, rather than the Lebanese and Palestinian civilians whose cities and camps were being bombed and attacked.

The animation depicts the war 'like a bad acid trip' (Luciano-Adams 2009: 12), which imparts the altered reality that overcomes soldiers when they quit Israel for the Occupied Territories or Lebanon, colonial other spaces where different rules and norms seem to apply. A sequence set to the Hebrew rock song 'I Bombed Sidon Today' begins with a soldier playing his rifle as a guitar, while another surfs, dodging explosives sprayed into the sea. The lyrics boast: 'I bombed Beirut every day / At the pull of a trigger / We can send strangers straight to hell / Sure, we kill some innocent people on the way.' The helicopters dropping bombs on the countryside to a rock soundtrack evokes a fantasy of omnipotent control over the territory, with imagery reminiscent of *Apocalypse Now* (1979). The sequence inadvertently conveys the sheer arrogance of the war: Lebanon is reduced to a playground where Israeli soldiers can indulge their libidinal fascinations with their war machines. The popular soundtrack enhances pleasure at the spectacle of destruction; notably, music, along with alcohol and drugs, is a means used by perpetrators to suppress moral anxiety about the violence they are carrying out.

The way the film maps space is through the aggressor's perspective, through the grids of power, surveillance and control. The soldiers dominate and master Lebanese space on account of their military superiority. Ronny Dayag reminisces how in a tank you always feel safe, invulnerable, while visuals show a tank coursing through a street, reversing into buildings and trampling cars in its wake. War film iconography, combined with video-game-like animation, turns all Palestinians (and other Arabs) into anonymous and often faceless enemies or victims. Carmi, who now lives in Holland, where he has made a fortune selling falafel (originally an Arabic food), relates how he and his comrades used to fire indiscriminately, at whom they knew not. In the visualised recollection, they continue shooting relentlessly when a Mercedes comes into view, riddling it with bullets until the door opens and a dead Arab flops out. Also pictured is Shmuel Frenkel's war routine: get up, lie on the beach, get back into uniform, then 'go after some terrorists'. Over a drink with his friend Boaz, Folman reminisces: 'A new trend started at that time – car bombs – still popular today.' They joke about it: 'A real blast!' It is for just such a job (assassinating Palestinian leaders with booby-trapped cars) that Folman is called back to duty after his leave, though this is forgotten in the ensuing narrative.

After Solomon's anecdote about the soldier with the imaginary camera, the film transports us into Folman's own dissociated vision of Beirut airport, a hallucination in which he feels as if he is on holiday until he realises that jets on the tarmac outside are bombed-out shells, the shops are empty, and the flight schedule board has been unused for months. Emphasis on his traumatised trance state allows responsibility for the devastation around him – caused by Israeli bombing – to be denied.

'Suffering is not really suffering when it is drawn in lines' and 'even the blood is amazingly aesthetic,' Levy asserts (2010: 127–8). By this reckoning, *Waltz*'s animated approach to reality is 'a safer, psychologically and estheti-cally subjective transfiguration' (Murray 2009: 66). Although, as I have argued throughout this book, all images transfigure the reality they represent, anima-tion does appear to serve here as a kind of mask – a distancing device, like the imaginary camera in Solomon's anecdote or video game simulation. At one point, Carmi gives Folman permission to draw, but not to film; notably, he is one of the figures whose real identity is disguised. This need for disguise is in keeping with another genre to which the film belongs, the confessional, where perpetrators confess their atrocities. Israeli examples of the genre tend to be preoccupied with the moral dilemmas of the Occupation, wherein atrocities are regarded as anomalies rather than part of a systematic culture (see Alexander 2012). Similarly, in *Waltz*, we are summoned to ratify Folman's guilt (or, rather, lack of it) regarding the Sabra and Shatila massacres, and allow him to 'move on'. The film is both confession and therapy.

The confessional thread starts from the opening scene. To an unnerving synthesiser score, a Tel Aviv street recedes before us against an apocalyptic sky. From a side alley, a dog with fiery eyes suddenly springs into view and races menacingly towards us. Another dog joins the chase, then another, and so they multiply, causing havoc on the streets. Finally, they halt at the foot of a building, where their intended victim, Boaz, looks down from a top-floor window. Boaz relates this recurring dream to Folman; he believes it derives from his Lebanese war experiences, when he was ordered to shoot dogs to prevent them raising the alarm in villages where the army was hunting out 'wanted Palestinians'. He was assigned the task as he was unable to shoot people: the archetypal reluctant soldier, self-agonising over his 'duty'. His actions return to haunt him in dreams where roles of victims and perpetrators are reversed.

Boaz's dream triggers Folman's memory. That night he has a 'flashback' of a palm-tree-lined seaside promenade in Beirut (the Corniche). Flares blaze in the nocturnal sky, staining the landscape with their lurid shade of amber. Folman and other soldiers rise from the sea, their scrawny figures silhouetted against the sky. They get dressed and walk into the city, where they meet Palestinian women emerging from Sabra and Shatila. The film expresses its forces through the visual rhyme of its colours, with amber as its leitmotif, starting with the hellish glow of the dogs' eyes, which become the flares that run through the film, 'like a guilty secret' (Klawans 2008: 34). This is the sole image Folman initially 'remembers' from the war, an uncanny afterimage of Boaz's dream. His therapist suggests it might be a false memory; in Freudian terms, a screen memory standing in for another memory that is more difficult to recover (Freud 1962: 320). As the narrative progresses, we are led to believe that Folman's seaside memory screens out his own role in the Sabra and Shatila massacres. What is suppressed is eventually revealed in flashback: his presence on a rooftop with other Israeli soldiers, lighting up the sky with flares.

Waltz's post-traumatic narrative and title evoke the IDF's guilty association with Bashir's followers, who believed Palestinians were responsible for their leader's assassination (though his real assassin was a Lebanese pro-Syrian militant). The film imagines the junkyard where Phalangist militia kept tortured and executed Palestinians' body parts in formaldehyde jars along with pictures of Bashir, whom they worshipped as an idol, finding the source of violence in their unnatural eroticism for their leader. The Phalangists are portrayed as thoroughly barbaric and immoral. Meanwhile, Israeli soldiers are idealised as innocent and morally conflicted. In flashbacks, they sport a youthful appearance, traces of which, for purposes of character recognition, are inscribed in the animation of their older selves, resulting in a 'childlike vulnerability' being 'etch[ed] into the contours of grown men's faces' (Murray 2009: 66). That vulnerability aids the audience's identification of them as victims, bewildered by circumstances beyond their control, and supports their dissociated view of the war. Apart from Boaz's stated inability to kill people, there is Carmi's amnesia over whether he actually shot anyone, and Frenkel's waltzing into a sniper zone, spraying bullets into the air, apparently harming nobody. This dissociated portrayal of the war climaxes in the Sabra and Shatila massacres, for which the Phalangists take the blame, exonerating individual Israeli soldiers.

Waltz allows the possibility that the Israeli government may have known about the massacre in advance and had some responsibility. It figures this wider net of complicity when journalist Ron Ben-Yishai telephones Defence Minister Ariel Sharon, who nonchalantly thanks him for bringing the massacre to his attention. Ben-Yishai also reports Brigadier Amos's belated arrival at the camps, where he halted the killing with the command 'Stop the shooting! Stop the shooting immediately!' – another piece of evidence strongly implicating the army. An official 1983 Israeli inquiry held Sharon and some generals accountable for failing to prevent the massacre, and they were dismissed from their posts. Yet, Sharon's political career was far from over, and from 2001 to 2006 he was back in power as Israel's Prime Minister. An international commission stated its conclusions more boldly, charging Israel with 'genocide' of Palestinians in Lebanon as well as 'reckless', 'indiscriminate' bombing of civilian targets and use of 'forbidden weapons' (MacBride et al. 1983: 131).

An interview with tank commander Dror Harazi reveals that the plan was to allow the Phalangists to enter the camp and 'purge' it, while the IDF provided cover. 'Purge them of what?' Folman asks in voice-off. 'Palestinian terrorists,' Harazi answers. He reports that trucks and bulldozers went into the camps to evacuate the civilians. He was not bothered by the fact that the Phalangist militia ordered the civilians out because it was similar to IDF tactics of forewarning civilians about imminent attacks. These tactics persist to this day, except they have become more high-tech: the traditional 'knock on the door' has evolved through telephoning inhabitants to 'firing low-explosive "teaser" bombs or missiles onto houses' (Weizman 2012: 28) in order to scare people into fleeing, used during the Israeli bombardments of Gaza in 2008–9, 2012 and 2014). Those remaining are regarded as legitimate targets, either as 'human shields' for terrorists or as terrorists themselves – a tactic that criminalises by association, espousing the logic that anyone is a terrorist if they live in that neighbourhood or indeed if they are too old, sick or traumatised to leave. It relabels civilians as terrorists in order to justify acts against them.

However, *Waltz*'s ambiguous narrative is more interested in its central protagonist's trauma than in issues of accountability. It transpires that Folman's amnesia about the war, particularly the Sabra and Shatila massacres, is due

Figure 5.1 The line of women, children and elderly relatives returning to the Sabra and Shatila refugee camps is compared to the Warsaw Ghetto photograph in *Waltz with Bashir*.

to a layer of transgenerational memory. As a child of Holocaust survivors, his interest in the camps stems from the '"other" camps', his therapist, Ori, tells him. The massacre frightens him because he was close to it and helped those who carried it out, which, in his guilty conscience, makes him akin to a Nazi. The refugee camps' resemblance to Nazi death camps forms one of the film's several references to the Holocaust, starting with Folman's 'memory' of rising from the sea and getting dressed before going to the camps: the emaciated silhouettes recall starving concentration camp prisoners. When Ben-Yishai sees the line of women, children and elderly relatives returning to the camps, he is reminded of the famous Warsaw Ghetto photograph. With the image of Palestinians being driven out and boarding trucks, the film also alludes to the Nakba, the catastrophe of 1948, when Palestinians were expelled from their homes – layering different historical memories. However, when Ori suggests Folman's guilt is unwarranted, since it is a product of his inherited Holocaust trauma, unrelated to Sabra and Shatila, a genuine encounter between these historical memories is prevented. Instead, *Waltz* dehistoricises the massacre by psychologising it and insisting that Israelis carry the burden of an even greater trauma: the Holocaust, whose enormity cancels out all other events. This is an ideology that the film shares with the Israeli state, on behalf of whom appeals to the Holocaust are made to give moral legitimacy to its policies. As Slavoj Žižek declares, 'the very need to evoke the Holocaust in defence of Israeli acts secretly implies that Israel is committing such horrible crimes that only the absolute trump card of the Holocaust can redeem them' (2009: 95). This is not a question of asserting equivalences between the Holocaust and Israel's oppression of the Palestinians. Rather, family resemblances (which, I have argued throughout this book, are not the same as equivalences) between these events should call into question the cultural acceptance of Palestinians' expulsion to refugee camps and their ghettoisation in Israel/Palestine and elsewhere in the Middle East.

Evocation of Holocaust memory forms part of *Waltz*'s redemptive story structure, as the war's moral ambiguity is replaced by a sense of moral certainty about one incident within it. In its ending, we follow Palestinian women coming out of the refugee camps, with their actual cries laid over the animated images. On the other side of the street, we encounter Folman as a young man, manning an entrance to the camp, and recognise this as the place where his previous 'memory' ended. He breathes deeply, his eyes narrowing and widening in consternation at and sympathy with the suffering before him. The animation transforms into live-action archive footage of the women in their inconsolable grief. Afterwards, the ambient sound is cut, except for a throbbing beat as the film surveys the bodies of innocents on the ground, closing into a little girl's head in the rubble, before fading to black. Folman has explained his choices here by saying he didn't want audiences to think that this was just a '"cool animated movie" . . . I wanted people to understand this really happened' (cited in Murray 2009: 68). The live footage is intended to confront audiences with an uncomfortable reality – it is the moment when, in the film's own analogy, 'the camera' breaks, preventing the possibility of dissociation or denial. The use of archival footage, with its indexical properties, imparts a revelation of 'truth'. But the archival footage is taken from British news sources (BBC World and ITN) and, as we know from the foregoing discussion, news media do not signify unmediated 'truth'. Moreover, the film controls how we view it by not subtitling the women, who are speaking Arabic; one of them approaches the camera in order to demand: 'Film, film and send them [the images] to foreign countries.'[2] Instead of taking responsibility for his own and Israeli state actions, Folman through his expression of compassion allows Israelis to be absolved of culpability and regain moral credibility in the eyes of the international community. This permits them (and Western governments and public who support them) to assuage their bad conscience, suppressing moral anxiety about long-term and ongoing Palestinian suffering. Meanwhile, those left behind, the Palestinian women, have served their purpose as passive icons of suffering in this drama of moral conscience.

Just as the film was released, Israel was committing huge human rights violations in Gaza (with US support), which resulted in what was then the highest violence against Palestinians since the occupation began. As with the 1982 Lebanon War, there were no lawful reasons for this attack. Despite Israel's official 2005 withdrawal from Gaza, its colonial presence there is as strong as ever. With the blockade, imposed in 2006 as a punitive measure after Hamas won elections and tightened in 2008, sealing all borders and affecting vital supplies, followed by successive bombardments, destroying homes, livelihoods and civilian infrastructure, the population has been 'deliberately reduced to a state of abject destitution' (Chomsky and Pappé 2011: 198). In the 2008–9 attack, called 'Operation Cast Lead', Gaza's population, with nowhere to escape, was pulverised with the latest military technology, resulting in well over a thousand deaths and thousands more wounded in the space of twenty-two days.[3] Like the Lebanon War, it gave Israel the opportunity to test out new weapons on largely defenceless civilian populations, redefined as a terrorist entity. Such actions are enabled by the logic of abstractification that dehumanises Palestinians and holds their lives to little account, precisely the same logic as *Waltz*'s animated war game aesthetic.

Pointing to similarities between *Waltz*'s images and the destruction raining down on Gaza, Gideon Levy notes that when Folman collected his Golden Globe award for the film, he made no reference whatsoever to events in Gaza (2010: 125). This underlines another risk of the moral redemptive narrative, where moral dilemmas are neatly solved so that one may no longer have any regrets. The film's post-traumatic mode of narration and its manner of closure work towards this end.

CHECKPOINTS AND ROADBLOCKS

Surrounding Palestinian towns and villages, checkpoints are one of many forms of border, also including 'separation fences', 'roadblocks', 'special security zones' and 'closed military areas', that fracture Palestinian space, while also opening and closing the routes between Israel and the Occupied Territories and between the latter and the outside world. Their apparent purpose is to protect Israeli settlers and reduce the chance of suicide bombings in Israeli cities, yet they have 'brought the Palestinian economy to a virtual standstill' (Weizman 2007: 146). Restricting freedom of movement and social and institutional connections, they lay physical obstacles in the path of workers, traders, family visitors and suppliers (of goods including food, medicines and building materials). It has therefore been suggested that the main aim of these checkpoints and other border structures is not security but 'to harass the Palestinian population and fortify . . . the "matrix of control"' largely without the need to deploy physical force (Chomsky and Pappé 2011: 98).[4] In order to travel through checkpoints along the Israel–West Bank 'separation barrier', Palestinians must apply for a multitude of permits that are difficult to get, and wait in exhausting queues, while 'Jewish settlers cruise unhindered through separate gates and down protective corridors that lead to segregated Jewish-only roads' (Weizman 2007: 147).

Out of this matrix of borders, a new film genre has been born, the Palestinian 'roadblock movie' (Gertz and Khleifi 2008: 153). Such films, as Ella Shohat notes, 'look at the hyper-regulation of movement as a daily nightmare' and use the checkpoint *topos* to render 'visible the usually invisible abuse by a technocratic maze' (2010: 294). By 'foreground[ing] quotidian dehumanization' and 'pithily encapsulating the daily indignities borne by Palestinians', the checkpoint lends a concrete image of 'structural violence, even if no spectacular bloodshed unfolds on the screen', manifesting 'the total lack of indigenous sovereignty'. Checkpoints, borders and the compulsory carrying of permits for Palestinians passing into and travelling inside Israel (reminiscent of pass laws, one of the most abhorred manifestations of South African apartheid) all depend on 'the power of space to separate individuals from each other, to direct and control their movements, and to reinforce social distinctions' (Barnard 2007: 6). Although 'space is precisely the sphere of the possibility of coming across difference' (Lury and Massey 1999: 232), checkpoints set up physical and ideological borders between self and other, between Israelis and Palestinians, placing the two groups in opposition to each other. In Israel proper, unofficial boundaries are also set up between neighbouring Palestinian and Jewish towns and cities, sealing off the more affluent Jewish areas from Palestinian ones, resulting in 'further fractalization and fragmentation of the terrain into an archipelago of enmity and alienation' (Weizman 2007: 155). The checkpoint/barrier system embodies a key belief that state security lies in the segregation of Jews and Arabs. However, a challenge to this underlying premise is offered from an unusual source, an Israeli military genre film, *Close to Home*.

Unlike war films set in the past and in neighbouring Lebanon, *Close to Home* depicts Israeli soldiers confronting the civilian population in present-day Jerusalem. Its directors, Vidi Bilu and Dalia Hager, wanted to present a female perspective in this genre, where male perspectives have predominated. Its focus is on two eighteen-year-old Israeli-Jewish women, Smadar and Mirit, doing their compulsory national service. Their job is to staff checkpoints and patrol the streets, checking the ID of all Palestinians entering the city. Though the film was underrated as a 'rather slight' coming-of-age story (Klein 2005: 20) and it has not received extensive scholarly attention, it is exceptional in attempting to tackle everyday realities of occupation and apartheid, topics that are typically denied in Israeli fiction cinema.

As we saw in *Waltz*, the war genre revels in the violent spectacle of combat and mastery of outdoor space, which is intertwined with the colonial rhetoric of conquest and land appropriation. In contrast, *Close to Home* is shot in a modest, realist style, adopting a minimalist approach in which direct violence takes place off screen. Although primarily about a female army unit, it is also, in its narrative interstices, about Palestinian lives affected by the soldiers' daily duties: the mundane, humiliating rituals of military surveillance. The two stories are present in the same narrative space; although the camera does not follow the Palestinians, on one important occasion the soundtrack does.

The film begins in close-up on a Palestinian woman, waiting next to a curtain upon which opening credits are superimposed. From the off-screen area behind the camera, Smadar and her unit commander, Dubek, then invade her space, drawing the curtain behind them, revealing the location as an inspection booth at a West Bank–Jerusalem border checkpoint, where Palestinians are placed under Israeli security's direct gaze. Smadar is instructed to search through the woman's personal belongings. Harmless, everyday objects – lipstick, cigarettes, a letter and a toy car wrapped as a present – are scrutinised while the Palestinian woman and Dubek exchange wary glances. This near-wordless sequence is punctuated by Dubek's terse orders ('To the censor!' 'X-ray!'). Smadar looks away as the woman undresses in order to be scanned with a security device. Through its tight framings of objects and characters in a claustrophobic space, the film conveys 'the state's invasion of the very intimacy of life', a form of biopower that surveys bodies with 'a penalizing panopticon' (Shohat 2010: 294), and the humiliation caused by these harassing searches. The minimal dialogue reflects the coloniser–colonised relationship in which the Palestinian woman clearly understands Hebrew, while the soldiers do not understand Arabic.

Outside, in the corridor, another soldier, Dana, refuses to carry out searches. Throwing open the terminal doors, behind which Palestinian women are kept waiting, she allows everyone to freely enter and go home. Other soldiers emerge from the booths, more concerned about punishment from Dubek than the alleged security threat of letting Palestinians through the checkpoint. It is at this point that Mirit first appears, piping up that she wasn't involved when Dubek demands who is responsible, threatening them all with court martial.

This film's emotional perspective on the conflict derives from its focus on 'the individual, its desires and weaknesses in this political situation' (Hager and Bilu 2005: 2). We see Mirit via the film's 'thinking' of her, as small and timid, fearful of authority, always seeking others' approval. Smadar, on the other hand, is initially presented as impulsive, bunking off duty and shoplifting, another unruly subject, like Dana, who neither wants to follow rules nor believes in Israeli state ideology. Yet, later, at the same checkpoint, facing a crowd of frustrated Palestinian women, Smadar becomes a hardline enforcer, inadvertently perpetrating administrative violence by pointing to the notice 'Do not enter with food', when ordering a woman to throw away the pitta she has brought for her son, even though he hasn't eaten all day. The constant process of checking and searching, which dehumanises Palestinians, is also wearying (in another way) for her, increasing hostility and mistrust between the two groups. The checkpoint thus becomes 'a topos for the banality of evil' (Shohat 2010: 294). This is what makes *Close to Home* more than merely a drama about moral conscience: its interest in exploring the atrocity-producing situation at individual and collective levels.

The soldiers patrol the city in pairs, and are told to stop and register any 'Arabs' they find, noting down their names, addresses and ID numbers on a form. Purportedly, the rationale is security in the event of a terrorist attack yet, as the film conveys in several scenes, policing itself is a form of terror, power surveillance and intimidation. Moreover, it implies the racially discriminatory notion that every Arab is a potential terrorist: an Arab appearance signifies a possible security threat that requires policing. Therefore, it is an explosive moment when Dubek rebukes Smadar for her poor performance with the forms and she replies with the excuse 'Maybe I don't know what an Arab looks like'. For it is a claim that, along with her reluctance to carry out such work, declares her refusal to be caught up in the racism of the exercise and a state ideology that creates boundaries between Jews and Arabs.

How can you tell who is a Jew and who is an Arab? Despite the pitting of 'Arab' and 'Jew' in opposition, each against the other, as 'mutually exclusive and inimical identities', these categories do overlap (Shohat 2010: 303). Jewish-Israeli citizens are from diverse ethnic and national backgrounds, including Arab and other oriental lands. Israeli identity is multifaceted, also incorporating Palestinian Arabs (Muslim or Christian). However, Zionist-Israeli discourse attempts to imagine a single Jewish identity that does not acknowledge connections with other groups. Shohat's work shows how Arab Jews are repressed from Israeli public discourse, including cinema: 'Zionist discourse turned the concept of "Arab-Jew" into an antonym, an oxymoronic identity' (2010: 255).

Highlighting a hybrid entity in this context, as Shohat's work does, is truly radical, enabling of new political and spatial possibilities. *Close to Home* doesn't go as far, since it doesn't acknowledge the distinction, for example, between Mizrahi Jews (of Middle Eastern origin) and Ashkenazi (central European) Jews. Largely, it remains silent on the issue of Arab Jews. However, it does question 'the taken-for-granted master narrative of Arab versus Jew' (ibid.) and, with it, the Israeli state's underlying racism in its present formation. When Dubek patrols with Smadar and Mirit on a bus to 'show' them what an Arab looks like, the film also challenges Western (and Israeli) audience expectations of the Arab as a dangerous 'other', since such an audience may assume it has some idea of 'what an Arab looks like' or, rather, what an Arab is *imagined* to look like, as purveyed by Hollywood and other popular media stereotypes. As Shohat writes, 'unlike novels, cinematic narratives require complex choices involving complexion and facial characteristics' (ibid.: 261–2). Casting decisions are often based on racial conventions, including a chromatic range of complexions and physical types. The scene of having to identify an Arab on a bus forces the audience to confront this stereotyping. As some passengers come aboard, the film identifies which one is supposedly an Arab, with a panning action and then a tight framing behind his head. This catches out the spectator, who has been forced to apply the same racist assumptions. Both Dubek and Mirit glance at Smadar, who looks straight ahead without reacting to the new passenger. Dubek immediately perceives Smadar's pretence, ordering her to register the man, while Mirit witnesses the injustice of the situation, not only towards Smadar but also towards the man who has been singled out.

In border checkpoint scenes, Jewish women were cast as Palestinian women. Although the directors present this as an ethical decision, it actually follows Israeli cinematic convention of casting (oriental) Jews as Palestinians. However, Hager and Bilu's comment about audience reaction is telling: 'Everybody, even in Israel, is convinced that these women are Palestinians, because actually we all look alike' (Soda Pictures 2005: 5). Indeed, as we see when the camera focuses on her dark eyes and long black hair on removing her veil, the woman surveyed in the opening could be an older version of Smadar, whose own looks could be interpreted as Arab according to those codes. Furthermore, it may be significant that, unlike Mirit's family, whom we see regularly, we never encounter Smadar's parents, whose off-screen presence is communicated via answerphone messages, as they are away from home; Smadar's own cultural identity (as potentially an Arab Jew) is hinted at yet kept a mystery.

Rather than employing further extras, the filmmakers frequently made use of location shooting with a telephoto lens, enabling them to film passers-by 'who were crossing the frame' (ibid.). One of these fortuitous shots is presented as Smadar's point of view through the bus window, following a headscarfed woman crossing the road. A road sign with an arrow directs the audience's

Figure 5.2 A road sign with an arrow seems to identify a woman crossing the road as a subject of racial difference in *Close to Home*.

gaze towards her, seeming to identify her as a subject of racial difference and again confronting us with racial discrimination in an environment in which differences are continually policed and literally pointed out.

Back on the bus, an officious passenger upbraids Smadar and Mirit for not noticing an apparently unaccompanied bag – though it happens to be his own – in order to warn them about security risks and the need to do their job properly. Annoyed by his condescending behaviour, Smadar asks for his ID. He categorically refuses, demonstrating power inequities not only between this older Israeli male and the young female soldiers, but also between Israeli-Jewish citizens and Palestinian Arabs. While Israeli security can pursue Palestinians anywhere, submitting them to daily humiliations of identity checks in their homeland, Israeli-Jewish citizens are shown in the film to be above such searches, secure in their entitlement to be there.

In what seems to be the turning point, a bombing occurs in the sector next to the one that Smadar and Mirit are meant to be policing. Like mainstream news media, the film identifies Palestinian resistance as terrorism and suggests that the security threat is genuine. The next day, a male commanding officer voices his appreciation of the important job the soldiers are doing and informs them that the city's security alert level is to be increased, urging them all to be vigilant. However, the bombing doesn't significantly enhance the soldiers' form-filling performance nor change their attitude to their policing role. Rather, its narrative function is the bonding that it develops between Smadar and Mirit.

While on patrol, Smadar and Mirit stumble upon Commander Dubek kissing an Arab man in a side street. To their surprise, Dubek and the man greet them bashfully and the girls leave in a fit of muffled giggles. A kiss between a Jew and a Palestinian Arab is taboo-breaking in a segregated and conflict-stricken society, although it taps into an existing genre of films about 'forbidden love'. Being intimate with the 'enemy' suggests a crossing of ideological as well as physical borders between Israeli Jews and Palestinians and hints at a potential for a 'multicultural and binational identity' (Loshitzky 2001: xvii). Narratively, however, it shows that Dubek has a 'soft side'; henceforth, she is no longer presented as authoritarian. Similarly, the military barracks, initially a hostile and forbidding place of military discipline, is no longer so by the third time it is shown. Here it becomes the scene of a fellow soldier's farewell party. The scene ends with the soldier, Julia, alone in the frame with the balloons and leftover cake. Although she is starting a new life, leaving the military, it seems as if the others, who have important work to do, have left *her* and it's her loss – affirming group solidarity and commitment to the cause. In these respects, *Close to Home* appears to serve the ideological function of institutionalising young people into military service.

Such a reading of the film might be reinforced by the fact that it doesn't show the worst aspects of checkpoints. In one scene, a man misses his bus to work because he must present his ID and it is implied that he may lose his job. But we only view him walking off into the distance and don't see what happens to him, nor do we see the serious consequences of policing to any of the other Palestinians. Clearly, the female Israeli soldiers are the focus of the narrative and it is through their perspective that we are invited to see. That means the film doesn't foster intense identifications with the Palestinians, who appear only as minor characters, in brief appearances. It might be argued that, by depicting young women in the army, who look vulnerable when they confront people on the street, the film shows us a gentler face of Israeli occupation and apartheid, focusing on low-tech, small-scale activities without revealing their full horrors, including the tight turnstiles at border checkpoints that slow down the flow of crowds and crush them into narrow spaces.

Yet *Close to Home* is more complex than this. That complexity is encapsulated in its title (in Hebrew as well as English); the question is, what is close to home, or brought close to home? One of the title's predominant connotations is security and inhabiting the conflict at close range. The title is rationalised in the narrative as Mirit wishes to be posted far from home, away from her suffocating parents. But it also has a counterpart in the film's style, including use of the telephoto lens, which brings what is far away close up. For those who enjoy a comfortable living (as most of the film's target audience do), violence is usually positioned at a distance; this film finds ways of bringing that violence close to home, precisely through its focus on mundane routines.

This is particularly well realised in the final scene, when a Palestinian man objects to giving the girls his ID and is assaulted by some passers-by, who aggressively intervene. Instead of showing the assault, the film shifts to the girls driving away on Smadar's motorbike. It is implied, through sounds of the assault laid over the image of their faces, that Smadar and Mirit feel responsible for the beating of the Palestinian. The audio focusing gives clarity to those sounds, layered on top of the instrumental track that closes the film. The escalating violence, with Smadar screaming 'Leave him alone!' and crying in self-recrimination, is thus heard off screen. While they have initiated a situation that has spiralled out of control, which positions them as perpetrators, the girls are still shown as victims; nonetheless, the resulting effect for the audience is ethical as it is emotive, more so than it would have been had the camera stayed on the Palestinian and dwelt on the physical violence. It is ethical precisely because of the emotional identification the film has fostered with the girls, focalising events through them, including their realisation of the consequences of their actions and that even their small, minor harassments are part of a larger societal and systematic violence perpetrated daily against Palestinians.

In a statement that one could place alongside the film's ending, the directors claim that their focus on young women in the army is part of a gendered critique of the system: 'We can't see any feminist values in that military world. We don't think that the women's role is to fight for equality in the army, but to struggle against those values which turn Israel into a military society' (Soda Pictures 2005: 4). The statement questions the values of a society that accepts the army's dominance, the conflict's continuation and the oppression of Palestinians as 'the exclusive past, present and future reality of life in Israel' (Chomsky and Pappé 2011: 167). Like the film, it moves towards a questioning of the normalisation of violence towards Palestinians by suggesting that what appears to be distant suffering is caused close to home.

From the other side of the 'security' divide, *Paradise Now* is said to be the first Palestinian film (though, technically, it is a German, Dutch and French co-production) to tackle the subject of suicide bombers. Its fictional plot is set in the West Bank city of Nablus and concerns Said and Khaled, car mechanics who are childhood friends and who are summoned for a suicide mission in Tel Aviv. It follows the would-be perpetrators as, with explosives strapped to their bodies, they are escorted to the 'security fence' between the West Bank and Israel, but then things go wrong and they are parted, each having to deal with his own doubts and resolve about the mission. Separately, they each encounter Suha, who, despite being a famous Palestinian martyr's daughter, voices the opinion that resistance can take other forms.

Shot on location in Nablus, at a hair's breadth from missile onslaughts by the Israeli military and assorted Palestinian armed groups, and in Tel Aviv, the film was produced directly out of Israel/Palestine's material and historical conditions. Filming in the West Bank, where the IDF has a permanent presence, carrying out targeted assassinations, using tanks, guns and rockets, required the cooperation of the Israeli authorities as well as of Palestinian armed organisations, who were suspicious of how such a large, well-equipped film crew had been allowed into the area. Amid rumours that the film was against suicide bombers, one armed faction kidnapped the location manager. Although he was finally released (with the help of Yasser Arafat), shortly afterwards a land mine killed three people close to the shoot and forced the crew to relocate to Nazareth.

Like *Waltz with Bashir*, *Paradise Now* won a Golden Globe award and an Oscar nomination but, unlike the other film, this high-profile exposure resulted in attacks and lobbying against it. A petition against its Oscar nomination was launched. The controversy has revolved around its so-called 'humanizing' of suicide bombers with calls for 'the need to historicize terrorism from the point of view of its historical victims' (Gana 2008: 24). As Nouri Gana notes, these reactions 'decontextualize and dehistoricize terrorism' by portraying it as 'a moral aberration', rather than engendered by the state's colonial violence. Moreover, 'the concern over the humanization of suicide bombers betrays, wittingly or unwittingly, an interest in their dehumanization' – part of the dehumanisation of Palestinians 'in theory and practice' (ibid.: 25). The film has generally received short shrift from critics. Several reviewers were puzzled by the fact that its protagonists do not appear to be motivated by any kind of religious zeal, contrary to standard images of 'fundamentalist' violence: 'There are no flames of fanaticism burning in their eyes, no bloodthirsty rage, and no crazed ecstasy at the prospect of their imminent trip to heaven. Their gazes are blank' (Chahine 2005: 73). Even Nurith Gertz and George Khleifi, in their excellent book on Palestinian cinema, characterise *Paradise Now* as inferior to other Palestinian films and attribute its success (it was picked up for distribution by Warner Independent Pictures, an arm of Warner Bros) to the 'Hollywood chase structure' in its second half, when Said and Khaled are separated (Gertz and Khleifi 2008: 194).

What the extant criticism (apart from Gana's article) seems to miss is the film's satirical take on suicide bombers, through its occasional black humour, as well as its exploration of the West Bank's real and symbolic spaces, highlighting the banal violence of Israeli apartheid and occupation, which are, in its analysis, what produces violent resistance. In this way, *Paradise Now* confronts how Palestinian resistance is portrayed in mainstream media through the stereotype of terrorism, and invites its viewers to attend to its causes, namely state terror. It eschews familiar reportage of suicide attacks – TV news flashes of carnage and outpourings of grief, Internet postings by groups claiming they were responsible for the attack, and clips from martyr videos. Instead, it attempts to take us 'behind the scenes' in the suicide bombers' humdrum lives: firstly, in its foreground story which is concerned with their last twenty-four hours and, secondly, in spatial images that portray everyday situations in the background that motivate them to extreme actions. In interview, the director, Hany Abu-Assad, declared that audiences should see his film twice, as 'the first time you will be busy with your own prejudgments' (Georgakas and Saltz 2005: 19). As we saw with *Waltz*, he is right to encourage a second viewing in which other layers of meaning, overlooked on first viewing, become apparent.

A sense of stasis and interminable waiting pervades the film's portrait of the West Bank. For this, it utilises spatial symbols common in Palestinian cinema. The protagonists work at a repair yard, where wrecked cars are piled on top of each other, producing images of a wasteland of 'stranded or engine-less cars' and 'vehicles whose destination is unclear', representing a 'dead-end' (Gertz and Khleifi 2008: 137). Numerous roadblocks, arresting the traffic, figure literal and symbolic constriction within space. The checkpoint is an obstacle to be traversed even before the narrative can get under way. The film opens with Suha crossing a checkpoint, which she has to pass in order to return to her hometown. At another point in the narrative, a taxi drops its passengers before a roadblock so they can make their own way on foot, along dirt tracks. One roadblock after another continually rears up before the characters.

On a hill overlooking the city, Khaled and Said smoke water pipes, an image that evokes boredom and chronic unemployment since Israel largely ceased employing West Bank workers during the second intifada; their gazes are blank because of the imprisonment of the occupation and their lives' futility. As well as causing daily frustrations, roadblocks and other mobility restrictions prevent them from leaving their town, with devastating repercussions on the economy, now stagnant owing to a decrease in trade and movement. The film evokes day-to-day realities under Israeli occupation through these implied means.

Following the protagonists walking or driving around by car, the film exposes several places destroyed by Israeli bombing, as when Said and his handler Jamal pass a ruined ancient building on their way to the militia's headquarters: Israeli state brutality leaves its physical scars on the landscape. As Eyal Weizman writes, 'the visible ruin is an important symbol in the public display of occupation and domination; it demonstrates the presence of the colonial power even when the colonist is nowhere to be seen' (Weizman 2012: 28). Moreover, the land is envisioned as hot and dry, a tactile-visual referent reinforced by mention of water filters in the dialogue, once by a taxi driver in connection with Jewish settlements, raising issues of struggle over water resources and water purification. Khaled even interrupts his second attempt at the martyr video to pass a message to his mother about where to purchase better-value water filters – a moment of humour in the film, but also a life-and-death matter. With later scenes in Tel Aviv, the film unfolds two worlds on either side of the 'Apartheid Wall': one world gleamingly new, spacious, tidy, well supplied; the other cramped, old, haphazardly constructed, underresourced. Tel Aviv is a Westernised city filled with well-paved roads, skyscrapers and billboards; its beach, open horizons and well-connected communications contrast with the West Bank's parched, imprisoning, maze-like spaces, where there is no such freedom to roam.

The film parodies the genre of the martyr video, supposed to be a laudatory speech about a suicide mission, when Khaled is filmed for one in a tile factory (using an actual location where such videos are filmed). With a keffiyeh draped around his shoulders, he is pictured posing with a rifle in front of the militia's banner. In an impassioned speech, he names his suicide-bombing mission as an 'answer' to the occupation's injustices: Israel's continued building of settlements, confiscation of lands, 'Judaisation' of Jerusalem and 'ethnic cleansing'. With Israel's refusal to accept either a one-state solution, granting Palestinians equality 'under the same democratic system' (seen as 'suicide for the Jewish state'), or a two-state compromise (though this gives Palestinians 'unfair' terms), Palestinians 'are either to accept the occupation forever or disappear'. Trembling with emotion at the end of his speech, he asks his audience: 'How was it?' When the cameraman replies that the camera malfunctioned and didn't record the performance, the tone shifts to bathos and continues as such when the militiamen pass around pitta sandwiches and start munching while Khaled is forced to do it all over again.

What this approach does is communicate the verbal 'message' that it is the occupation which motivates suicide bombers; at the same time, its absurdist humour satirises suicide bombing and militia leaders and religious teachers who are prepared to send young people to their deaths, presenting the enterprise as a personal honour. Individually greeted by the 'legendary' leader Abu-Karem, ritually washed, feasted and photographed for posters to adorn the town after their deaths, the men are told they will be celebrated as martyrs, with angels escorting them to paradise. Yet the leaders care neither about them nor those destined to be casualties of the bombing; all they really care about is their own glory, their small victories in an ongoing struggle.

The satire is present again in a later scene, where videos of martyrs and collaborators are found for rent in a local shop; furthermore, the shopkeeper tells Suha and Said, videos of collaborator executions are in greater demand and he could charge even more for them. The video rental business thrives on the cult of martyrdom and helps propagate its perverse model of heroism. *Paradise Now* therefore reveals destructive forms of masculinity on the Palestinian side, too – part of the internal violence that results from colonial control and occupation, manifesting in increasingly militant groups. We find out that Said's father was a collaborator, executed when Said was ten, a history for which he suffers continual humiliation. Recovering his father's damaged masculinity through his own martyrdom becomes his motive for his suicide mission, along with revenge for growing up in a refugee camp. It is the fact of dispossession and unbearable living conditions that produces terrorist violence, all of which is presented without context in Western news media.

When Said and Khaled are separated during their mission, the film turns into a chase within the West Bank's roadblock-strewn environment. *Paradise Now* thus becomes a pastiche of mainstream thriller genres, precisely because the elements upon which they rely (namely, speed and mastery of space) are thwarted: movement is constantly arrested; action becomes inaction; and the pyrotechnics of explosion, promised in the title's allusion to *Apocalypse Now*, is deferred. The title also parodies Peace Now, a well-known left-wing Israeli peace movement, referring to the failure of the so-called 'peace process' to improve Palestinians' livelihood and welfare and revealing the 'rhetoric of "peace"' as 'a gigantic fraud' (Said 2004: 6).

During this chase, a heated argument between Suha and Khaled ensues. Suha points out that suicide bombing gives Israel the excuse to carry on doing what it is doing. However, Khaled believes that, even without suicide bombing, Israel will not stop. Suha implores: 'If you kill, there's no difference between victim and occupier.' To which Khaled replies that if they had aeroplanes, then they wouldn't need martyrs, pointing to the socially constructed nature of what are considered legitimate and illegitimate forms of violence, and suicide bombing as a product of power asymmetry between the two sides. Although the film does not endorse suicide bombing, it allows both their arguments to be aired. In the end, Khaled is persuaded by Suha, although Said is not, and resolves to go ahead with another mission.

The final sequence begins with solitary framings of those who remain: Suha, looking at a picture of Said, which she turns over; Jamal; Abu-Karem; Said's mother; and, finally, Khaled. Suha, Said's mother and Khaled are each shown in melancholy over a future they might have had but have now lost, the film dwelling in particular on the distraught Khaled, despairing at losing his childhood friend. We then move to the interior of a bus, filled with soldiers as well as civilians. The film picks out Said, sitting towards the back, framed between the bus bars, coincidentally in the same position as the 'Arab' on the bus in *Close to Home*. Here, however, Said, wearing a suit, has 'passed' as a Jew. The sounds of conversation around him fade as the film closes into his eyes, before the screen bleaches out.

The white screen leads us to assume that the mission has been completed, though this is left ambiguous. The predominance of soldiers on this bus contrasts with an earlier scene, during the botched mission, when a small child's presence deters Said from boarding a bus; it implies that, because they are soldiers, their deaths are more legitimate than those of civilians, although the violent resistance of non-state actors does not usually obey the 'rules of war', which forbid the deliberate killing of civilians, any more than state terrorism does. According to Raya Morag, the purpose of the white screen is to enable 'ongoing identification with Said and what he represents by abstaining from audio-visualization of the attack . . . if the film had shown results of the attack, the entire film would have had a different impact, a less sympathetic one' (2008: 14). For her, it makes the act seem more excusable, directing attention away from its violence. The film, however, wisely eschews images of explosions, which are in any case already overdetermined by media representations. Instead, it seeks, as Abu-Assad suggests, to shatter 'those prevailing perceptions . . . to build a new perception' (Georgakas and Saltz 2005: 17). That new perception has to do with who is the suicide bomber and their backstory. Additionally, there is perhaps an even more important point: if this final scene had focused on the bombing's abject outcome – the dead and maimed bodies – the activation of the viewer's visceral empathies would neutralise the foregoing narrative and images, which emphasise the violence of occupation and apartheid and present the Israeli state (not just Palestinian armed factions) as a terror organisation that causes suffering to civilians. In other words, it would cancel out the wider political and ethical point the film is making, in favour of a more commonplace one.

THE WALL

The 1948 expulsion continues by bureaucratic means, through a web of measures designed to harass, intimidate, and ultimately drive Palestinians away. (Shohat 2010: 295)

It is about those on the other side of the wall that we fantasise: more and more they live in another world, in a blank zone that offers itself as a screen for the projection of our fears, anxieties and secret desires. (Žižek 2009: 88)

In 2002, Israel began building a barrier through the West Bank ('the Wall'), designed to separate Israeli towns and settlements from Palestinian ones. The Wall has been the subject of several documentaries, including *Wall* (*Mur*, 2004), *Budrus* (2009), and *5 Broken Cameras* (2011), all of which transport viewers to the 'real' spaces of the conflict, often with events unfurling in real time. Taking the broadest view, *Wall* begins with an exchange in Hebrew between the filmmaker, Simone Bitton, and two children, heard off screen as the film glides along a painted section on the Wall's Israeli side. When asked what the Wall is for, one child answers: 'They shoot Arabs from here.' 'No, Arabs shoot at us,' the other interjects. 'So we hide behind the wall.' 'Who shoots whom?' Bitton asks. The children admit that they initially ran away from the film crew because they mistook them for 'Arabs' before realising they were 'Jews'. Bitton inquires how they can be so sure; unfazed, the children specify language and facial features as sure-fire means of distinguishing Jews from Arabs. It transpires their mother is from Morocco and speaks Arabic, so Bitton proposes: 'When she speaks Arabic, one might say she's an Arab, no?' The children titter in response. It is apparent from their conversation that the Wall taps into, and helps to maintain, a geography of fear based on fantasies of self and other, us and them. Jewish children are constantly told stories about 'the enemy' and how only the Wall can stop them. In her documentary, Bitton, herself an Arab Jew from Morocco, explores the ideology of the Wall, which segregates the population on a racial basis and is designed to keep the Arabs out of Israel, as well as its impact on people's lives on either side. It features interviews with Palestinians who live under its shadow, including those employed as its construction workers, together with the IDF's director general and Israeli settlers.

At a desk flanked by Israeli flags, Amos Yaron, IDF director general, states the official line on the Wall – that its purpose is, firstly, to reduce Palestinian capabilities of entering Israel to carry out terrorist attacks and, secondly, to reduce the threat of Palestinians stealing Israeli property. He outlines how the Wall functions both as a physical obstacle and as a complete surveillance system, activating an alarm relayed to a control room 'where everything is seen and heard' when anyone attempts to cross it. In urban areas, it consists of 25-foot-high concrete slabs. Elsewhere along its path, it is an electronic fence, fitted with high-tech sensors, surrounded by cameras, radar and watchtowers, and lined with supplementary barbed-wire fences ('the first obstacle'), ditches to prevent vehicle access, dirt tracks to register intruders' footprints and patrol roads to enable the military to respond speedily to contact with it. With its apparatus of remote sensors and fast-access highways, together with aerial strike capacities (Israel retains control of airspace above), the Wall is a method of controlling enclosed Palestinian populations from afar without the need for actual territorial presence.

Throughout his interview, Yaron refuses to acknowledge the Wall as an ideological enterprise, adhering to its official term, 'seam-line obstacle'. The film juxtaposes his commentary with views of the Wall painted with scenery of an idealised pastoral landscape, blending in with real trees and sky beyond it. The juxtaposition undermines his claim, offering a concrete image of the Wall as a 'solid, material embodiment of state ideology and its conception of national security' (Weizman 2007: 162), screening out the assumed threat that lies beyond it.

Although the Wall is touted as an emergency security measure, underlying it is a politics of separation. According to Yosefa Loshitzky,

> the 'security' rhetoric behind this monstrous monument . . . cannot mask its ideological agenda, which goes far beyond Israel's immediate 'political gains', such as confiscating the most fertile lands of the West Bank, separating Palestinian villagers and their lands, disrupting the day-to-day life of the Palestinian population and controlling water resources . . . Walls raise questions regarding the creation of the politics of otherness . . . The Israeli wall functions in this way by erecting a boundary between self and other, the 'civilised' (Israeli) and the 'barbarian' (the Palestinian), the coloniser (the Israelis masquerading as the righteous owners of Palestinian land) and the colonised (Palestinians 'contained' under curfews and locked behind electrified barbed-wire preventing them from 'invading' their historical homeland). (2006: 333–4)

Different ideological connotations are attached to the various terms applied to the structure, the sanitised phrase 'security fence' contrasting with other labels, such as 'the Wall' or 'Apartheid Wall', which have played a part in raising international awareness about its injustices. Moreover, in contrast to the 'mundane, almost benign' images of Israel's 'red-roofed suburban settlements' in the West Bank, the Wall's menacing physical appearance, with its 'barbed-wire fencing and high concrete walls cutting through pastoral olive orchards, wheatfields or vineyards, or through the fabric of towns and cities', has helped its opponents gain support from international NGOs and activists (Weizman 2007: 171). The Wall resonates as a 'powerful image within the media economy of the conflict', tapping into still-unresolved historical legacies of colonial and Cold War eras and evoking memories of the Berlin Wall and South African apartheid, 'although even at the height of its barbarity, the South African regime never erected such a barrier' (Weizman 2007: 171).

In real-time shots of concrete slabs being lifted by heavy machinery, Bitton's film documents the Wall's construction and the Palestinian labour upon which it depends: Jewish workers refuse to do such menial work, while West Bank Palestinians need the employment and pay. As one slab after another is heaved into place, obstructing the landscape behind it, the film highlights the irony that Palestinian labourers are literally building the wall around themselves. For the Wall does not advance along the Green Line, the internationally recognised border between Israel and the West Bank, but loops around several Jewish settlements in the West Bank, placing them on the 'Israeli' side, seizing more territory for Israel while cutting off Palestinians from their farmland, schools, services and water sources. The construction workers' village of Jabara is one of several villages trapped in an inter-border zone between the Green Line on the west and the Wall on the east, its inhabitants barred from entering either Israel or the rest of the West Bank, unless they have special permits; moreover, the gate in the Wall is opened only once daily. In Jerusalem, a Palestinian recounts how the fence encloses her community and prevents them accessing the bus network, while other vital municipal services like rubbish collection, to which they are entitled as tax-payers, have ceased. In its closing sequence, the film pictures people furtively crossing the Wall, temporarily defying this oppressive reality in their determination to continue their lives. Meanwhile, a helicopter passing above reminds us of the risks they are taking and that the Wall is a system of observation and control, not just a means of partition.

The documentary *Budrus*, directed by Brazilian filmmaker Julia Bacha, charts one village's popular resistance against the path of the Wall, planned to cut through its olive grove. It follows the story of community frontman Ayed Morrar, who leads a non-violent protest when soldiers declare the olive grove a closed military area and assume the prerogative to shoot any Palestinians who enter. The film takes the biblical David and Goliath motif, which Israel has traditionally adopted for its wars against its Arab neighbours ('tiny Israel / mighty Arabs'), and reverses it as the villagers take on the mighty Israeli army. The reversal also harks back to the largely non-violent first intifada, when stone-throwing became a weapon. But when Palestinian youths start throwing stones in *Budrus*, senior community members ask them to stop. The resistance is reinforced when Ayed's teenage daughter Iltezam mobilises a group of female villagers. Israeli and South African activists are also shown joining the Palestinians in a demonstration against Israeli occupation and apartheid. Like other films in this section, *Budrus* underlines the colonised's agency, locating the secret of success in their steadfastness in holding their ground, despite the odds against them, and their ability to mobilise international opinion.

Both *Budrus* and *5 Broken Cameras* are testaments to the physical risks that their filmmakers took, filming from the conflict's frontline, with dramatic images of Israeli soldiers attacking protestors with tear gas and live ammunition. *5 Broken Cameras* is created from footage shot by a Palestinian farmer, Emad Burnat, who shares the director's credit with Israeli filmmaker Guy Davidi. It captures several protestors' deaths, its blurred, pixellated images reminiscent of news footage but depicting what few news organisations broadcast to the world. During the filming, Burnat's cameras broke one after another in the onslaught from Israeli bullets. This provides the film with its central conceit and aesthetic structure, which further distinguishes it from both news footage and amateur films on the Internet that also rely on the rhetoric of the camera as a 'witness' to events. The narrative is divided into segments, corresponding to footage from the successive cameras and concluding with footage from the sixth, as yet unbroken, camera. At one point in his voiceover narration, Burnat remarks: 'When I'm filming I feel like the camera protects me. But it's an illusion' – a statement that could be in dialogue with the soldier's anecdote in *Waltz with Bashir*. In *5 Broken Cameras*, the poetic concept of the broken camera has additional poignancy because at one point the camera does literally protect Burnat: a bullet lodges within it, saving his life. Not merely a protective, distancing device, the camera as a fragile, material object is itself susceptible to the ravages of the conflict: a metaphor for bodily vulnerability and life.

Together with the 'self-governance' of the Palestinian Authority, the Wall with its heavy fortifications creates the illusion of a political border, dividing 'Israel' from 'Palestine'. This illusion obscures the ongoing occupation and the fact that 'Palestine' is not a separate country from 'Israel', but one group of people under the colonial rule of another. The Wall does not mark a recognised border; rather, it materialises 'the violent reality of a shifting colonial frontier', erupting into Palestinians' lives and ripping into their homes and lands (Weizman 2007: 179). Since the Wall was approved as a concept without a pre-planned route, Palestinian farmers, human rights activists, NGOs, Israel's Supreme Court, international courts, foreign governments, settlers and other interest groups have attempted to influence and alter its path. In *Budrus* and *5 Broken Cameras*, popular resistance combined with international attention results in rerouting the Wall's path further west, nearer to the Green Line. But while this is an empowering struggle, which has succeeded in reducing harsh conditions in surrounding Palestinian areas, it does so only incrementally, without contesting the principle and illegitimacy of the entire enterprise, campaigning instead for the least evil route the Wall can take.

Moreover, as Eyal Weizman notes, barriers deep inside the West Bank have not attracted the kind of international public attention of the more visible, 'exterior' Wall. He describes how the colonial enterprise of gaining land has 'operated by imposing a complex compartmentalized system of spatial exclusion' in three dimensions (ibid.: 10). In the Occupied Territories, this includes: the system of fast Israeli-only highways and tunnels that link settlements with Israel; airspace control using high-tech tools to police and kill from the air by drones, helicopters, and satellites; and a monopoly of underground aquifers as well as hilltops for settlements, affording strategic advantages for self-protection and resource extraction. The roads' spatial layout, one passing on top of the other, prevents 'cognitive encounter' between the two groups as well as enabling Jewish Israelis to enjoy superior infrastructure, freedom of movement and other privileges (ibid.: 181).

The Israeli–German–French co-production *Lemon Tree* dramatises this lack of cognitive encounter and the problems inherent in applying humanitarian discourse to the Wall. A fiction film directed by an Israeli, Eran Riklis, and co-scripted by an Israeli-Palestinian, Suha Arraf, it opens with removal truck drivers trying to find the town of Zur-Hasharon, 'right on the border with the Arabs'. The film flits to views of the 'security fence' before the van comes to rest in an upscale neighbourhood. Defence Minister Israel Navon is moving in with his wife, Mira, right next door to Salma Zidane's lemon grove, which was planted on ancestral land by her father fifty years ago. The Israeli secret service identifies the lemon grove as a security risk and persuades the minister that he should cut it down. Salma, a Palestinian widow who ekes out a living from the grove, decides to dispute the minister's order, taking her David-like battle for justice all the way to Israel's Supreme Court.

Well received internationally, though not in Israel, *Lemon Tree* has been interpreted as an allegory of the Israeli–Palestinian conflict, with the security fence between the lemon grove and the minister's house (and his name) serving as 'obvious' metaphors (Elley 2008b). However, the narrative is not *merely* allegorical, as it is situated within the spatial and material environs of a real, ongoing conflict. The film's security fence is presented as *literally* part of Israel's Wall, as reinforced by various cutaways to its construction and, finally, its revelation in the final scene. Moreover, the fictional story is woven around a common situation faced by Palestinians – namely, legal disputes with the Israeli state over plans for destruction of their olive groves, demolition of their homes and other land expropriations.

Lemon Tree brings these stories to light by adapting the genre of melodrama focused on one woman's plight. According to its director, *Lemon Tree* is an attempt 'to fight against ... global indifference' through an internationally accessible, emotionally moving story, without making an overt political state-ment (Bowen 2009: 65). At its centre is a cross-cultural encounter relayed through its dual focus on a Palestinian woman's legal battle, on the one hand, and, on the other, an Israeli woman, Mira Navon, in her first contact with the injustices of the occupation and subsequent rift with her husband. Giving equal share of screen time and resolution to both women, *Lemon Tree* is a rare film in that it successfully portrays a dual subject position – both sides of the colonial divide – and attempts to bridge the spaces of self and other. Yet it does not fall into the trap of sentimentalising or simplifying the potential for such a cross-cultural encounter. As I suggest below, that cross-cultural encounter is ultimately portrayed as a failed encounter in the plot, although it is success-fully bridged at the level of narrative form and use of both Arabic and Hebrew dialogue.

In its split-focus melodrama, *Lemon Tree* contains a number of images mir-roring the two women, while underlining the social hierarchy between them. It pictures both of them gazing across the fence, alone in bed, and climbing over the barrier in Salma's yard. At the same time, it emphasises the emotional and ideological distance between Mira and her husband. In a TV appearance, Israel declares his aim is to hunt down terrorism in whatever form. The film satirises the state's tendency to define its acts as responses to terrorist threats. Here that suspected threat takes the form of a lemon grove, believed to be a potential terrorist hideout, which therefore must be cut down. On a talk show, the audience cheers at Israel's every word, indicating that his views on defence, particularly about the Wall's necessity, are widely shared.

Mira is disgusted when she sees a news item on Israel's objection on humanitarian grounds to the destruction of Palestinian olive groves, when he has ordered his neighbour's lemon grove to be cut down. The film does not present this merely as personal hypocrisy (the public avowal of humanitarian-ism at odds with his violent policies and practices) but rather as part of what Weizman calls the state's humanitarian violence. This includes its tendency to negotiate humanitarian problems arising from the building of the Wall not out of any real concern for Palestinians, but to appease the international community of human rights watchers, invoking their 'legal-moral rhetoric' so that potential restrictions or delays to the project may be averted (Weizman 2007: 175). Significantly, the Defence Minister's surname, Navon, sounds like the Hebrew word *na'or* ('enlightened'), used in the context of the occupation to imply 'a humane administration of the Palestinian population' (Ben-Zvi-Morad 2011: 285). It reflects the state's moral, compassionate façade.

In a newspaper interview with her journalist friend Tamar Gera, Mira bravely takes a stand against her husband and the state's actions. But though she claims to her daughter that her life has been turned upside down by the lemon grove dispute, it is not her life but Salma's that has been completely overturned. Ultimately, Mira's world is not so different from her husband's world of war, security and state rhetoric. As an Israeli-Jewish woman, Mira is in an asymmetric colonial relationship with her neighbour, secure in her own sense of entitlement and bourgeois privileges. Ensconced in her high-security fortress, she can draw her blinds and block Salma out; Salma does not share these privileges, nor can she simply live her own life, which her neighbours control in every aspect, damaging her livelihood and means of income by preventing her from accessing her lemon grove. An architect by profession, Mira is the one who has designed the house, making her a wielder of spatial power, and, as its hostess, she decides who is welcome in it. At her housewarming party, the guests eat Arabic food but, unlike scenes with Carmi in *Waltz*, *Lemon Tree* highlights the irony, as they are unable to extend hospitality to their Arab neighbour – indeed, they behave in less than neighbourly ways by stealing lemons from her grove. Mira is also responsible for uprooting an olive tree, presumably from a Palestinian orchard, and transplanting it to her garden, yet she fails to connect her own and her husband's actions. Both the Defence Minister and his wife, like the rest of elite Israeli society with whom they mix, are shown to suffer from an unhealthy siege syndrome, barricading themselves behind defensive walls, fences and watchtowers to protect their own privileges. On the night of the housewarming, a rocket attack does happen, as if to confirm their need for security, yet, as representatives of Israel's dominant class, they benefit the most from its rapacious politics of separation.

In a press statement, Mira announces she would like to be a 'normal neighbour' to Salma but 'there's just too much blood and too much politics'. Israel proclaims that Salma 'strikes us as a very nice lady', yet he admits they have no contact with her. So, while there is an expression of aspiration for coexistence, there is a defeatist acceptance of enmity and violence as routine. As represented by Mira and the Defence Minister, the Israeli left and right alike are revealed to share the same worldview – historically, both have used settlement building to gain territory and have endorsed violence against Palestinians. They share an affinity in their underlying attitudes, including condescension towards Arabs, and harbour the same sense of entitlement. *Lemon Tree* thus highlights modes of unethical thinking and behaviour that help perpetuate the conflict. When Mira attempts to see Salma, the film emphasises how, though it is a small physical distance to cover, ideologically it is much larger, by the capturing of her movements on CCTV and later by the security guard, who follows her to Salma's doorstep. Even though Mira shows her solidarity for Salma by attending the Supreme Court on the final day, the two women never speak to each other. Afterwards, she leaves her home and husband, driving off in a car. Perhaps she finds her situation ethically untenable and decides to exit it, but it is left ambiguous where she is going or to what purpose, handing over to the audience the responsibility of finishing her story.

Unlike in conventional courtroom dramas, relatively little screen time is spent inside the courtroom itself or on legal minutiae. Instead, Salma's legitimate claim to the land is shown cinematically through her sensuous attachment to and association with abundance of growth. This is depicted from the film's opening shot, which fades up into a bountiful lemon tree and closes onto one luscious fruit. A montage focusing on Salma's activity of preserving lemons ensues, linking her to traditional food preparation as well as preservation of tradition. Her tender care of the trees, treating them as fellow sentient beings, caressing them with her touch, conveys her belonging to the space and soil, in contrast with Israel and Mira's sense of proprietorship and stealing produce from the land. When the lemons are left untended, the film empathises with Salma's sadness through sounds that convey heaviness as the fruits drop. The film stresses her 'generational continuity' (Ben-Zvi-Morad 2011: 290) with ancestral land belonging to her father, who planted the trees fifty years ago and tended them along with Abu Hassam, an old employee of the family; although her father is no longer alive, his legacy is represented by Abu's continuing presence. *Lemon Tree* thus evokes pre-1967 borders, but doesn't go as far as to evoke pre-1948 ones.

The film offers close-up details of Salma's everyday life – her long-distance relationship with her children and her complicated situation as a Palestinian widow, in which her behaviour is monitored by the community's patriarchs, who remind her of her husband's memory. Sometimes the film glances at his portrait, an overbearing presence that acts like an obstacle to her affair with her lawyer, Ziad Daud. The affair is only fleeting, unsentimentally concluded when the trial ends and Abu shows her the newspaper announcement of Ziad's engagement to a Palestinian politician's daughter – Salma tosses the paper into the incinerator. While the community patriarchs warn her against going head to head with Israel, Salma clings to the struggle to retain her land – superbly rendered in Hiam Abbass's dignified performance.

Since the film suggests a Palestinian woman can successfully take her case all the way to the Supreme Court, it might be interpreted as pro-Israeli, promoting a progressive justice system. Within the story, the media present the outcome (not to uproot all the trees, but merely to prune half of them) as a victory for Salma but she instantly knows it's an insult and stands up in court to say so. By this and other subtle means the film indicates the flawed, compromised justice system, and is not a simple confirmation of its virtues. Even the Supreme Court uses the rhetoric of security in its proposal to moderate state actions, weighing up protecting Palestinian human rights in the Occupied Territories with 'security needs'. The shortcoming here is failure to consider other unjust factors, including the illegality under international law of building the Wall and settlements on occupied territory. Because the Supreme Court accepts the logic of security with which the Israeli state justifies its actions, it confers a certain legitimacy upon those actions, ruling in real cases that the Wall should be rerouted according to the principle of 'proportionality'. In Eyal Weizman's view, even if its ruling in favour of 'better' paths for the Wall reduces the amount of suffering that the original plans would have caused, it has the effect of making it more acceptable: 'The "lesser evil" approach . . . thus allow[s] a "greater evil" to be imposed on the Palestinian people as a whole' (2007: 175). In *Lemon Tree*'s last scene, the Defence Minister, now alone in his house, unrolls the blinds to reveal that the fence has solidified into tall concrete slabs, completely barricading his Palestinian neighbour out of sight. The film glides over the top of the Wall and reveals Salma walking through the orchard's pruned section, tending the formerly glorious trees' wounded stumps. Its final images, therefore, are of compromise and loss, sadness and triumph: a bittersweet ending.

CONCLUSION

This chapter has shown that, unlike TV news, films have the capacity to register perceptions of the Israeli–Palestinian conflict's everyday violence through their mapping of real and imaginary spaces. In particular, *Close to Home*, *Paradise Now* and *Lemon Tree* portray some of the devastating consequences of Israeli occupation and apartheid, both to the colonised and to colonisers. However, films can also be complicit in perpetuating the violence, even when they bear a compassionate 'message', as we saw with *Waltz with Bashir*. There, compassion serves to mask the violence perpetrated by the Israeli army. In contrast, *Lemon Tree* offers an explicit reflection upon the state's 'humane' rhetoric and the dominant society's capacity to take for granted a system of inequality, since it maintains its privileges. We are invited to challenge Israel's brutal actions and the narratives that support them, which present everyday oppression and killing of Palestinians as moral through their association with terrorism and Israeli state motives and methods as legitimate.

NOTES

1. *Waltz with Bashir*'s co-production credits include Australia, Belgium, Finland, France, Germany, Switzerland and the USA.
2. I am indebted to Sabine El Chamaa for pointing this out to me and for translating the Arabic.
3. As the book went to press in August 2014, Gaza was in the middle of a new bombardment in which casualties had already far exceeded the level of the 2008 onslaught.
4. The phrase 'matrix of control' derives from Halper (2000).

Conclusion

As this book was being completed, an extraordinary and highly praised documentary was released in the UK. In *The Act of Killing* (2012), US filmmaker Joshua Oppenheimer follows Anwar Congo and his associates, gangsters who belong to a paramilitary death squad employed by the Indonesian army during the 1965–6 genocide in which an estimated one million people deemed to be 'communists' were killed, and there were many instances of torture and rape. A former cinema ticket seller, Anwar claims to have been influenced by Hollywood westerns and gangster movies. He also expresses admiration for the films of Elvis Presley and models himself after Hollywood stars. The film's distinctive approach is that it enlists the perpetrators' collaboration in re-enacting their past atrocities. Scenes of genocide are restaged as vignettes from gangster films and musicals or vérité-style improvisations with amateur actors who are coaxed into joining the film. The perpetrators relish memories of their own sadism and unabashedly boast about their acts, indicating the impunity they still enjoy today.

The Act of Killing serves to shed light on this book's main insights. Oppenheimer has called his film a 'documentary of the imagination', as it is concerned with how cinema is implicated in the performance of atrocity (Bradshaw 2013). However, as Tony Rayns has remarked, 'the near-total absence of context, either about the historical facts or about the production process itself, definitely doesn't help us understand what we're seeing or how we're seeing it' (2013: 70). Through its exotic mise-en-scène (involving a bevy of dancers next to a giant fish-shaped structure or before a waterfall) and its focus on sadistic killers, *The Act of Killing* largely presents the Indonesian genocide as something unique and faraway, thereby distancing its Western viewers and letting them off the hook with regard to their own implication in that history. In the context of the Cold War, the genocide is far from unique; it took place against the backdrop of the Vietnam War and also harbours many similarities to the events in Latin America covered in Chapter 3. In Indonesia, an attempted coup by left-wing army officers gave the army the motive to wipe out the Indonesian Communist Party (PKI). The army took power and waged a campaign of terror with the encouragement of both the US and the British governments under the belief that such a regime was preferable to a communist one. US government documents confirm that Indonesia was considered at least as economically and strategically important as Vietnam; the USA wanted Indonesia to remain within its sphere of influence and was also keen to tap into the large Indonesian market and obtain favourable conditions for Western businesses (Curtis 2003: 398). Western complicity in the Indonesian genocide received little Western news media coverage, either at the time or since, another instance of 'perception management', which *The Act of Killing* risks repeating.

According to the arguments I have put forward in this book, the film is problematic in its focus on sadistic killers, not simply because this is voyeuristic, but because it makes it easier to regard the events it shows as aberrant, only facilitated by sadistic people, rather than the product of systemic violence.[1] It does not convey the sense of what Hannah Arendt called 'the banality of evil'. By portraying perpetrators as sadistic Others, unlike 'us', the film does not really unsettle our complacencies, except in so far as it offers a general indictment of the cruelties of which humanity is capable, removed from the political and economic contexts in which violence is carried out.

A few scenes form an exception to this, however. These include the footage of present-day Indonesian shopping malls, gesturing to the free flow of capital enabled by genocide. In fact, the opening titles are laid over an image of a restaurant complex with a McDonald's sign looming at the edges and constitute the film's only direct reference to Western governments' aid to the Indonesian military. In another telling scene, Anwar discloses that he already harboured a vendetta against communists because the communists threatened to withdraw Hollywood movies, which were the most popular (and therefore the most profitable), from theatres. It reveals cinema itself as part of the global capitalist system that is always seeking new markets and profits, and the gangsters as beneficiaries of that system, via the black market. Among those caught up in the whirlwind were people loosely affiliated to the PKI, as well as some ethnic Chinese, showing 'communist' to be an expediently vague concept (like 'enemy combatant' in the 'War on Terror'). The gangsters also helped to clear land (and dispossess the people living on it) for capitalist development, another form of state terror that the film hints at but does not dwell upon.

The Act of Killing claims to use cinema to explore the imagination of violence as a way into exploring the conditions of violence – a laudable aim. But it does not offer much by way of analysis in this respect. If the cinematic imagination is implicated in atrocity, what is it about cinema that does this? It is not that all the movies that Anwar admires and seeks to imitate are violent, nothing as simple as that.

Dick Cheney's declared wish to 'work the dark side', which lends this book its central metaphor, itself draws on the imagination of the movies (*Star Wars*) and constructs a moral universe which positions the USA and its allies as the forces of good, obliged to go over to the 'dark side' to defeat their enemies, justifying the use of torture and other brutal methods. Such a moral universe promotes the view that it is necessary to act on these beliefs. This book has emphasised how atrocity is often justified by its perpetrators as a moral act; films collude in this by constructing a moral universe in which violent acts are made acceptable and lent a certain glamour, dependent on their structures of sympathy which encourage us to root for heroes and permit the death and suffering of others. Our consent to violence is thus achieved through managing our perceptions of that violence.

This is why any moral axis of interpretation has to be supplemented by an ethical axis, which reflects on the causes and contexts of violence, including how moral norms are constructed and reconstructed in the atrocity-producing situation, as demonstrated in Chapter 1, which focused on films relating to the 'War on Terror'. In this book, I have made the case that films take a largely moral or ethical approach in the creation of their cinematic world. Moreover, films can construct several kinds of moral universe. *The Act of Killing* itself is informed by a moral outlook that upholds Anwar and his associates as war criminals, suggesting that they have escaped justice and should be punished. It wants to admonish the killers. Its narrative structure is contrived towards this end as, in one of the final scenes, Anwar appears to demonstrate remorse. Through this narrative *telos* towards punishment, *The Act of Killing* is predominantly moral rather than ethical. Its offers a moral judgement about the evil of others which, as I have argued in this book, can prevent ethical reflection on how atrocities happen.

Yet, when Oppenheimer asserts that what they did would be considered war crimes under international law, one of Anwar's fellow killers, Adi Zulkadry, points out: 'When Bush was in power, Guantánamo was right . . . but now it's wrong.' Adi himself links this with the genocide of Native Americans, which was justified by the morality of its time and remains unpunished to this day, since '"war crimes" are defined by the victors'. He brazenly states: 'Geneva Conventions may be today's morality, but tomorrow we'll have the Jakarta Conventions and dump the Geneva Conventions.' This underscores my argument about the alteration of morality under different circumstances and the need for ethical reflection on how moral norms are constructed and reconstructed.

While debates about human rights representations have tended to revolve around questions of 'truth', this book has stressed the value of taking a different stance that emphasises the aesthetic choices that lead to either moral or ethical confrontations with atrocity events; in other words, what kind of viewing experience (moral or ethical) a film creates through its aesthetic choices. This moves away from blanket condemnations of the aestheticisation of violence to focus on the different kinds of aesthetic strategy that films adopt. Moreover, it expands the critical potential of film beyond that addressed by traditional human rights discourses.

As identified in this book, the main problem with human rights representations is their sentimental politics of pity, which relies on icons of spectacular violence and victimisation, positioning viewers as benevolent rescuers. Driven by the need to find shocking images, particularly these days of endangered children, to stir viewers into action, these images have little context and, as critics have pointed out, they can also activate a sadistic-voyeuristic gaze that aligns viewers with the perpetrators rather than the victims, even while pursuing a moral agenda. In this book, I have opposed the voyeuristic focus on the spectacle of physical violence with reflection on the causes and contexts of violence, to suggest the possibility of a new kind of human rights representation that is not only sensitised to these problems but also reorientates our relation to atrocity.

Reflecting on the causes and contexts of atrocity is an ethical way of representing and writing about atrocity, because it is about finding ways of breaking patterns of violence that persist to this day. One thread of argument running through the book has been that present-day practices of violence are shaped by and echo colonial violence, as certain groups of people are constructed as unworthy, their lives easily disregarded in the pursuit of power and economic gain. Human rights themselves carry the legacy of past colonialism and have sometimes been co-opted by present-day imperialisms. They need to take account of how human rights abuses are embedded in this longer history if their changes are to be truly transformative and not just incremental.

To this end, the book shows the limits of existing critical approaches to the representation of atrocity. For example, what we miss when interpreting solely through the paradigm of trauma is an analysis of why such events happened and their legacy on present-day forms of oppression. Moreover, the inward focus on individual traumatised subjectivity or the inherited trauma of a particular group can obfuscate the political context, as we saw with *Waltz with Bashir* in Chapter 5. Without wanting to be disrespectful to survivors and their families, much more is at stake in atrocity representation than traumatised societies 'working through' their past. Knowledge of those events can be made available to a wider public to find ways of resisting deadly repetitions of violence – this is a political and ethical endeavour since it involves making use of that knowledge in the present.

Exploring the causes and contexts of violence goes beyond merely advocating an embrace of otherness, as implied by Levinasian ethics, and instead foregrounds the socio-political conditions under which categories of people are othered in order to be dispossessed, mistreated or killed, usually so that elites can maintain and extend their privileges. The Levinasian approach cannot account for the production of otherness that serves political purposes. Abandoning the Brechtian approach, too, allows us to consider a larger, more diverse set of texts rather than just those that conform to a preferred aesthetic technique. Instead of Brecht, I have drawn on theories of embodied spectatorship to point to other ways in which films can be thought-provoking. I have suggested that our engagement with cinematic atrocity images doesn't take place only through optical point of view but through multisensory means. This representational approach is implicitly more ethical since it is less reliant on the intrusive gaze. Through their appeal to our own embodied histories as sites of reception and understanding, sensory images have the capacity to trigger and disturb memories that we hold as individuals and communities, as we saw in Chapter 3. They invite us to relate their images to our own memories, to place ourselves in relation to violent histories and reflect on how we might be part of the same system, not separate from it as the sentimental politics of pity allows us to believe.

In this book I have looked at films that are aimed at transnational audiences, who do not have a direct connection to the depicted events. By engaging us with events that we have never encountered firsthand and with memories that we have never had, films can make us realise that what seems distant and unrelated actually bears on us. One way in which they can achieve this is by taking the ethical risk of making comparisons between different types of violence, as a way of confronting us with what is still occurring and the need to reflect on links between past and present. Throughout the book, I have emphasised that these comparisons highlight family resemblances – not equivalences – between histories that are both similar and different. The film analysis in Chapter 2, for example, situates the Holocaust and the Rwandan genocide, which have each been conceptualised as exceptional and 'unique', in a continuum of violence that stretches from colonialism to present-day atrocities. Filmic images can enable us to situate attitudes that have relegated categories of people to disposable non-persons in a much longer history in which present-day violence is shaped by previous forms of violence.

I have argued that cinema has the ability, on the one hand, to create and confirm moral consensus about historical atrocities and, on the other, to disturb commonplace perceptions, including those purveyed by mainstream news media. Its capacity to disrupt normative perceptions and build new ones lies in its potential to make new connections. Though often context specific, films resonate beyond their immediate context. What is special about cinema is its ability to release powerful associations through its creative juxtapositions of montage and mise-en-scène. These can leave traces in our memories that outlive our remembrance of abstract facts and statistics. By this means, cinematic images are capable of producing thought-provoking connections between past and present, here and there. They can 'show the complexity of things through simple images' (Frampton 2006: 193). Although debates about digital images raise moral anxieties about their manipulation of reality, every image is a manipulation and an alteration of reality by its very nature. This book has argued for the digital image as an expressive tool that can refresh our perceptions of reality, extending and enhancing the existing possibilities of cinematic montage and mise-en-scène.

Since films map and produce space, by both entering into real spaces and constructing imaginary ones, I have advocated spatial mapping in Chapters 4 and 5 as a subtle way to allow causes and contexts of violence to emerge. Spatial mapping offers us a critical tool for analysis and a means of representing violence without resort to icons of spectacular violence or victimisation, capable of illuminating the structural violence of our contemporary world. With the use of spatial divisions to evoke social divisions, it is possible to produce images of everyday violence resulting from long-term oppression, which is otherwise difficult to convey.

To paraphrase Susan Sontag, neither compassion for victims nor outrage towards perpetrators alone can direct a course of action. Indeed, compassion can act as a mask for violence and enable the perpetuation of a system of inequality that maintains the rights of the privileged, as shown in Chapter 5. In this book, I have argued that film's ethical value lies in the extent to which it disrupts commonplace perceptions of how atrocities occur and invites us to consider links between ourselves and systems of violence. Atrocities happen as part of a system of global inequalities and relations of domination. At their most thought-provoking, films can illuminate these dark aspects of geopolitical realities and highlight our own complicity in atrocities that are being committed here and now. So, instead of looking away from cinematic atrocity images, we should look on, yet learn to interpret them differently, and foster more critical forms of human rights representations as the basis for breaking oppressive patterns of thinking and behaving.

NOTE

1. In interview, Oppenheimer articulates a similar perspective to this book: 'We tell ourselves stories about how the Nazis were defeated and the killers got their comeuppance – which I think primarily serve as escape from the reality that behind everything we consume there's been mass political violence' (Bradshaw 2013). However, this is not the perspective conveyed by the theatrical version of his film nor the longer director's cut.

Bibliography

Aaron, M. (2007), *Spectatorship: the Power of Looking On*, London: Wallflower.

Adorno, T. W. ([1966] 1973), *Negative Dialectics*, trans. E. B. Ashton, London: Routledge and Kegan Paul.

Adorno, T. W. ([1955] 1981), 'Cultural Criticism and Society', in *Prisms*, trans. S. and S. Weber, Cambridge, MA: MIT Press, pp. 17–34.

Adorno, T. W. (1982), 'Commitment', in *The Essential Frankfurt School Reader*, ed. A. Arato and E. Gebhardt, New York: Continuum, pp. 300–18.

Adorno, T. W. ([1996] 2000), *Problems of Moral Philosophy*, trans. R. Livingstone, Cambridge: Polity.

Agamben, G. ([1995] 1998), *Homo Sacer: Sovereign Power and Bare Life*, trans. D. Heller-Roazen, Stanford, CA: Stanford University Press.

Ahmed, S. (2000), *Strange Encounters: Embodied Others in Post-coloniality*, London: Routledge.

Ahmed, S. (2004), *Cultural Politics of Emotion*, Edinburgh: Edinburgh University Press.

Ahmed, S. (2006), *Queer Phenomenology: Orientations, Objects, Others*, Durham, NC: Duke University Press.

Alexander, J. (1993), *The Films of David Lynch*, London: Charles Letts.

Alexander, L. (2012), 'Confessing without Regret: An Israeli Film Genre', in *Screening Torture: Media Representations of State Terror and Political Domination*, ed. M. Flynn and F. F. Salek, New York: Columbia University Press, pp.191–216.

Amadiegwu, M. (2005), Interview with Fanta Nacro, *Black Filmmaker* 8.32: 20–1.

Andermann, J. (2012), *New Argentine Cinema*, London: I. B. Tauris.

Anzaldúa, G. (1999), *Borderlands/La Frontera: The New Mestiza*, 2nd ed., San Francisco: Aunt Lute.

Arendt, H. ([1973] 1979), *The Origins of Totalitarianism*, San Diego: Harcourt Brace.

Arendt, H. (1990), *On Revolution*, London: Penguin.

Arendt, H. ([1982] 1992), *Lectures on Kant's Political Philosophy*, ed. R. Beiner, Chicago: University of Chicago Press.

Arendt, H. (2003a), 'Personal Responsibility under Dictatorship', in *Responsibility and Judgment*, ed. J. Kohn, New York: Schocken, pp. 17–48.

Arendt, H. (2003b), 'Some Questions of Moral Responsibility', in *Responsibility and Judgment*, ed. J. Kohn, New York: Schocken, pp. 49–146.

Arendt, H. (2006), *Eichmann in Jerusalem: A Report on the Banality of Evil*, New York: Penguin.

Austin, T. (2011), '*Standard Operating Procedure*, "the Mystery of Photography" and the Politics of Pity', *Screen* 52.3: 342–57.

Banham, C. (2012), 'New war emerges, as seen on your television', *Sydney Morning Herald*, 10 February, <http://www.smh.com.au/opinion/politics/new-war-emerges-as-seen-on-your-television-20120209-1rwkw.html> (accessed 25 March 2014).

Barker, J. M. (2008), 'Out of Sync, Out of Sight: Synaesthesia and Film Spectacle', *Paragraph* 31.2: 236–51.

Barker, J. M. (2009), *The Tactile Eye: Touch and the Cinematic Experience*, Berkeley: University of California Press.

Barnard, R. (2007), *Apartheid and Beyond: South African Writers and the Politics of Place*, New York: Oxford University Press.

Barthes, R. ([1980] 1993), *Camera Lucida*, trans. R. Howard, London: Vintage.

Bathrick, D. (2007), 'Whose Hi/story Is It? The US Reception of *Downfall*', *New German Critique* 102: 1–16.

Baudrillard, J. ([1991] 1995), *The Gulf War Did Not Take Place*, trans. P. Patton, Sydney: Power.

Bauman, Z. (2000), *Modernity and the Holocaust*, Cambridge: Polity.

Baxi, U. (2008), *The Future of Human Rights*, 3rd ed., New Delhi: Oxford University Press.

Bazin, A. ([1958] 1967), *What is Cinema? Vol. 1*, trans. H. Gray, Berkeley: University of California Press.

Becker, J. and S. Shane (2012), 'Secret "kill list" proves a test of Obama's principles and will', *New York Times*, 29 May <http://www.nytimes.com/2012/05/29/world/obamas-leadership-in-war-on-al-qaeda.html>(accessed 25 March 2014).

Ben-Zvi-Morad, Y. (2011), 'Borders in Motion: The Evolution of the Portrayal of the Israeli–Palestinian Conflict in Contemporary Israeli Cinema', in *Israeli Cinema: Identities in Motion*, ed. M. Talmon and Y. Peleg, Austin: University of Texas Press, pp. 276–93.

Benjamin, M. (2013), *Drone Warfare: Killing by Remote Control*, London: Verso.

Bergson, H. ([1896] 1988), *Matter and Memory*, trans. N. M. Paul and W. S. Palmer, New York: Zone.

Beverley, J. (1996), 'The Margin at the Center', in *The Real Thing: Testimonial Discourse and Latin America*, ed. G. M. Gugelberger, Durham, NC: Duke University Press, pp. 23–41.

Blakeley, R. (2011), 'Dirty Hands, Clean Conscience? The CIA Inspector General's Investigation of "Enhanced Interrogation Techniques" in the "War on Terror" and the Torture Debate', *Journal of Human Rights* 10.4: 544–61.

Blakeley, R. (2013), 'Human Rights, State Wrongs, and Social Change: The Theory and Practice of Emancipation', *Review of International Studies* 39.3: 599–619.

Bloom, L. (2008), 'Regarding the Pain of Others: Errol Morris on *Standard Operating Procedure*', *Cinemascope* 34: 6–12.

Boltanski, L. (1999), *Distant Suffering: Morality, Media and Politics*, Cambridge: Cambridge University Press.

Bowen, P. (2009), 'Do Not Cross', *Filmmaker* 17.3: 62–5.

Bradshaw, N. (2013), 'Build My Gallows High: Joshua Oppenheimer on *The Act of Killing*', *Sight and Sound* web exclusive <http://www.bfi.org.uk/news-opinion/sight-sound-magazine/interviews/build-my-gallows-high-joshua-oppenheimer-act-killing>(accessed 1 April 2014).

Brecht, B. (1964), 'The Modern Theatre is the Epic Theatre', in *Brecht on Theatre: the Development of an Aesthetic*, ed. J. Willett, London: Methuen, pp. 33–42.

Browning, C. (1998), *Ordinary Men: Reserve Police Battalion 101 and the Final Solution in Poland*, New York: HarperPerennial.

Brownmiller, S. (1975), *Against Our Will: Men, Women, and Rape*, New York: Simon and Schuster.

Buss, D. (2010), 'Learning Our Lessons? The Rwanda Tribunal Record on Prosecuting Rape', in *Rethinking Rape Law: International and Comparative Perspectives*, ed. C. McGlynn and V. E. Munro, Abingdon: Routledge, pp. 61–75.

Butler, J. (2004), *Precarious Life: The Powers of Mourning and Violence*, London: Verso.

Butler, J. (2009), *Frames of War: When Is Life Grievable?* London: Verso.

Calhoun, C. (2010), 'The Idea of Emergency: Humanitarian Action and Global (Dis)order', in *Contemporary States of Emergency: The Politics of Humanitarian Interventions*, ed. D. Fassin and M. Pandolfi, New York: Zone, pp. 29–58.

Carroll, N. (2010), 'Movies, the Moral Emotions, and Sympathy', *Midwest Studies in Philosophy* 34.1: 1–19.

Carter, J. (2006), *Palestine: Peace Not Apartheid*, New York: Simon and Schuster.

Caruth, C. (ed.) (1995), *Trauma: Explorations in Memory*, Baltimore: Johns Hopkins University Press.

Césaire, A. ([1950] 2000), *Discourse on Colonialism*, trans. J. Pinkham, New York: Monthly Review Press.

Chahine, J. (2005), 'Paradise Now', *Film Comment* 41.5: 73–4.

Chaudhary, Z. R. (2009), 'Humanity Adrift: Race, Materiality, and Allegory in Alfonso Cuarón's *Children of Men*', *Camera Obscura* 72: 73–109.

Chen, A. (2013), 'Newly declassified memo shows CIA shaped *Zero Dark Thirty*'s narrative', *Gawker*, 6 May <http://gawker.com/declassified-memo-shows-how-cia-shaped-zero-dark-thirty-493174407> (accessed 25 March 2014).

Cheney, D. (2001), Interview by T. Russert, *Meet the Press*, NBC, 16 September.

Cheney, D. (2011), Interview by C. Wallace, *Fox News*, Fox News Channel, 8 May.

Chomsky, N. and I. Pappé (2011), *Gaza in Crisis: Reflections on Israel's War against the Palestinians*, ed. F. Barat, London: Penguin.

Claude, R. P. and B. H. Weston (eds) (2006), *Human Rights in the World Community: Issues and Action*, 3rd ed., Philadelphia: University of Philadelphia Press.

Cohen, S. (2001), *States of Denial: Knowing about Atrocities and Suffering*, Cambridge: Polity.

Cohen, S. (2006), *Deportation Is Freedom! The Orwellian World of Immigration Controls*, London: Jessica Kingsley.

CONADEP (Comisión nacional sobre la desaparición de personas) (1986) *Nunca más (Never Again): A Report by Argentina's National Commission on Disappeared People*, trans. Writers and Scholars International, London: Faber and Faber.

Conrad, J. ([1899] 1973), *Heart of Darkness*, London: Penguin.

Cooke, P. (2007), '*Der Untergang* (2004): Victims, Perpetrators and the Continuing Fascination of Fascism', in *A Nation of Victims? Representations of German Suffering from 1945 to the Present*, ed. H. Schultz, Amsterdam: Rodopi.

Critchley, S. (2002), *On Humour*, London: Routledge.

Crowdus, G. (2008), 'Speaking Documentary Truth to Power: An Interview with Alex Gibney', *Cineaste* 33.3: 28–36.

Curtis, M. (2003), *Web of Deceit: Britain's Real Role in the World*, London: Vintage.

Curtis, M. (2004), *Unpeople: Britain's Secret Human Rights Abuses*, London: Vintage.

Danner, M. (2004), *Torture and Truth: America, Abu Ghraib and the War on Terror*, London: Granta.

Dargis, M. (2008), 'Horror through a child's eyes', *New York Times*, 6 November <http://www.nytimes.com/2008/11/07/movies/07paja.html> (accessed 25 March 2014).

Dawtrey, A. (2003), 'Emma defends maligned "Imagining Argentina"', *Variety*, 29 September, pp. 16, 20.

Dean, C. J. (2004), *The Fragility of Empathy after the Holocaust*, Ithaca, NY: Cornell University Press.

Delage, C. and P. Goodrich (eds) (2013), *The Scene of the Mass Crime: History, Film, and International Tribunals*, Abingdon: Routledge.

Deleuze, G. ([1983] 1986), *Cinema 1: The Movement-image*, trans. H. Tomlinson and B. Habberjam, London: Athlone Press.

Deleuze, G. ([1985] 1989), *Cinema 2: The Time-image*, trans. H. Tomlinson and R. Galeta, London: Athlone Press.

Deleuze, G. (2000), 'The Brain Is the Screen: An Interview with Gilles Deleuze', trans. M. T. Guirgis, in *The Brain Is the Screen: Deleuze and the Philosophy of Cinema*, ed. G. Flaxman, Minneapolis: University of Minnesota Press.

Deleuze, G. ([1981] 2004), *Francis Bacon: The Logic of Sensation*, trans. D. W. Smith, London: Bloomsbury.

Desser, D. (1999), 'Race, Space and Class: The Politics of Cityscapes in Science-Fiction Films', in *Alien Zone II: The Spaces of Science Fiction Cinema*, ed. A. Kuhn, London: Verso, pp. 81–96.

Douzinas, C. (2007), *Human Rights and Empire: The Political Philosophy of Cosmopolitanism*, Abingdon: Routledge-Cavendish.

Dovey, L. (2009), *African Film and Literature: Adapting Violence to the Screen*, New York: Columbia University Press.

Downing, L. and L. Saxton (2010), *Film and Ethics: Foreclosed Encounters*, Abingdon: Routledge.

Dumas, H. (2013), '*Gacaca* Courts in Rwanda: A Local Justice for a Local Genocide History?', in *The Scene of the Mass Crime: History, Film, and International Tribunals*, ed. C. Delage and P. Goodrich, Abingdon: Routledge, pp. 57–73.

Durrheim, K., X. Mtose and L. Brown (2011), *Race Trouble: Race, Identity and Inequality in Post-Apartheid South Africa*, Scottsville: University of Kwazulu-Natal Press.

Dyer, R. (1993), *The Matter of Images: Essays on Representation*, London: Routledge.

Edwards, G., S. McNairy and W. Able (2011), Commentary, *Monsters*, DVD, Momentum Pictures/Vertigo Films.

Eghbal, A. and F. Gardiner (2011), Interview by G. Andrew, Human Rights Film Night, Tricycle Cinema, London, 22 September.

Ehrenreich, B. (2004), 'Feminism's Assumptions Upended', in M. Benvenisti et al., *Abu Ghraib: The Politics of Torture*, Berkeley, CA: North Atlantic, pp.65–70.

Elley, D. (2008a), '*The Boy in the Striped Pajamas*', *Variety*, 29 September, p. 59.

Elley, D. (2008b), '*Lemon Tree*', *Variety*, 18 February, p. 26.

Ezra, E. (2000), *Georges Méliès: The Birth of the Auteur*, Manchester: Manchester University Press.

Fainaru, D. (2003) 'Imagining Argentina: unsavoury political drama shames the memories of the disappeared', *Screen International* 1420: 27.

Fanon, F. ([1961] 2001), *The Wretched of the Earth*, trans. C. Farringdon, London: Penguin.

Feitlowitz, M. (1998), *A Lexicon of Terror: Argentina and the Legacies of Torture*, Oxford: Oxford University Press.

Felman, S. and D. Laub (1991), *Testimony: Crises of Witnessing in Literature, Psychoanalysis, and History*, New York: Routledge.

Finucane, B. (2010), 'Enforced Disappearance as a Crime under International Law: A Neglected Origin in the Laws of War', *Yale Journal of International Law* 35: 171–97.

Flynn, M. and F. F. Salek (2012), 'Introduction', in *Screening Torture: Media Representations of State Terror and Political Domination*, ed. M. Flynn and F. F. Salek, New York: Columbia University Press.

Fordham, J. (2009), 'Slumdog Aliens', *Cinefex* 119: 21–7, 31–4.

Foucault, M. (1997), 'Of Other Spaces: Utopias and Heterotopias', in *Rethinking Architecture: A Reader in Cultural Theory*, ed. N. Leach, London: Routledge, pp. 350–6.

Frampton, D. (2006), *Filmosophy*, London: Wallflower.

Freud, S. (1962), 'Screen Memories', in *The Standard Edition of the Complete Psychological Works of Sigmund Freud, Vol. 3: 1893–1899, Early Psycho-analytic Publications*, trans. J. Strachey, London: Hogarth Press / Institute of Psychoanalysis, pp. 303–22.

Freud, S. ([1901] 1989), *The Psychopathology of Everyday Life*, trans. J. Strachey, New York: Norton.

Freud, S. ([1899] 1991), *The Interpretation of Dreams*, trans. J. Strachey, London: Penguin.

Freyenhagen, F. (2013), *Adorno's Practical Philosophy: Living Less Wrongly*, Cambridge: Cambridge University Press.

Gana, N. (2008), 'Reel Violence: *Paradise Now* and the Collapse of Spectacle', *Comparative Studies of South Asia, Africa and the Middle East* 28.1: 20–37.

Georgakas, D. and B. Saltz (2005), 'This Is a Film You Should See Twice: An Interview with Hany Abu-Assad', *Cineaste* 31.1: 16–19.

Gerima, H. (1989), 'Triangular Cinema, Breaking Toys, and Dinknesh vs Lucy', in *Questions of Third Cinema*, ed. J. Pines and P. Willemen, London: BFI, pp. 65–89.

Gertz, N. and G. Khleifi (2008), *Palestinian Cinema: Landscape, Trauma and Memory*, Edinburgh: Edinburgh University Press.

Gibney, A. (2012a), 'Screen Talk', 56th BFI London Film Festival, BFI Southbank, London, 16 October.

Gibney, A. (2012b), '*Zero Dark Thirty*'s wrong and dangerous conclusion,' Huffington Post, 21 December <www.huffingtonpost.com/alex-gibney/zero-dark-thirty-torture_b_2345589.html> (accessed 2 April 2014).

Goldberg, E. S. (2001), 'Splitting Difference: Global Identity Politics and the Representation of Torture in the Counterhistorical Dramatic Film', in *Violence and American Cinema*, ed. J. D. Slocum, New York: Routledge, pp. 245–70.

Goldberg, E. S. (2007), *Beyond Terror: Gender, Narrative, Human Rights*, New Brunswick, NJ: Rutgers University Press.

Gourevitch, P. and E. Morris (2008), *Standard Operating Procedure: A War Story*, London: Picador.

Grant, C. (1997), 'Camera Solidaria', *Screen* 38.4: 311–28.

Grant, C. (2008), 'Questions of national and transnational film aesthetics, ethics, and politics in Costa Gavras's *Missing* (1982)', <http://catherinegrant.wordpress.com/links/questions-of-national-and-transnational-film-aesthetics-ethics-and-politics-in-costa-gavrass-missing-1982/> (accessed 27 March 2014).

Greenberg, R. (2011), 'The Animated Text: Definition', *Journal of Film and Video* 63.2: 3–10.

Gregory, D. (2004), *The Colonial Present: Afghanistan, Palestine, Iraq*, Malden, MA: Blackwell.

Gregory, D. (2010), 'Vanishing Points: Law, Violence, and Exception in the Global War Prison', in *Terror and the Postcolonial*, ed. Elleke Boehmer and Stephen Morton, Chichester: Wiley-Blackwell, pp. 55–98.

Gregory, D. and A. Pred (eds) (2006), *Violent Geographies: Fear, Terror, and Political Violence*, New York: Routledge.

Gugelberger, G. M. (1996), 'Introduction: Institutionalization of Transgression – Testimonial

Discourse and Beyond', in *The Real Thing: Testimonial Discourse and Latin America*, ed. G. M. Gugelberger, Durham, NC: Duke University Press, pp. 1–19.

Hager, D. and V. Bilu (2005), 'Directors' Statement', *Close to Home* presskit, Soda Pictures <http://www.sodapictures.com/media/CTH-press-kit.pdf> (accessed 1 April 2014).

Halper, J. (2000), 'The 94 Per Cent Solution: A Matrix of Control', *Middle East Report* 216 <http://www.merip.org/mer/mer216/94-percent-solution> (accessed 1 April 2014).

Hanson, M. (2013), 'The UK's approach to Bulgarian and Romanian immigration makes me sick with shame', *The Guardian*, 5 February <http://www.theguardian.com/uk/2013/feb/05/uk-bulgarian-romanian-immigration-shame> (accessed 31 March 2014).

Haraway, D. (1992), 'The Promises of Monsters: A Regenerative Politics for Inappropriate/d Others', in *Cultural Studies*, ed. L. Grossberg, C. Nelson, and P. A. Treichler, New York: Routledge, pp. 295–337.

Harding, J. (2000), *The Uninvited: Refugees at the Rich Man's Gate*, London: Profile.

Harding, J. (2012), *Border Vigils: Keeping Migrants out of the Rich World*, London: Verso.

Härting, H. (2008), 'Global Humanitarianism, Race, and the Spectacle of the African Corpse in Current Western Representations of the Rwandan Genocide', *Comparative Studies of South Asia, Africa and the Middle East* 28.1: 61–77.

Haynes, J. (2009), 'A Note on Quentin Tarantino's *Inglourious Basterds*', *The Holocaust in History and Memory* 2: 93–6.

Herman, E. S. and N. Chomsky (2002), *Manufacturing Consent: The Political Economy of the Mass Media*, New York: Pantheon.

Hesford, W. S. (2011), *Spectacular Rhetorics: Human Rights Visions, Recognitions, Feminisms*, Durham, NC: Duke University Press.

Heyman, D. (2008), 'I felt it was a story that needed to be told', Interview, *Empire*, October, pp. 30–1.

Higson, A. (1993), 'Re-presenting the National Past: Nostalgia and Pastiche in the Heritage Film', in *Fires Were Started: British Cinema and Thatcherism*, ed. L. Friedman, Minneapolis: University of Minnesota Press, pp. 109–29.

Hintjens, H. (2008), 'Post-genocide Identity Politics in Rwanda', *Ethnicities* 8.1: 5–41.

Hirsch, M. (1997). *Family Frames: Photography, Narrative, and Postmemory*, Cambridge, MA: Harvard University Press.

Hirsch, J. (2004), *Afterimage: Film, Trauma, and the Holocaust*, Philadelphia: Temple University Press.

Horeck, T. (2004), *Public Rape: Representing Violation in Fiction and Film*, London: Routledge.

Hron, M. (2012), 'Genres of "Yet an Other Genocide": Cinematic Representations of Rwanda', in *Film and Genocide*, ed. K. M. Wilson and T. F. Crowder-Taraborrelli, Madison: University of Wisconsin Press, pp. 133–53.

Human Rights Film Network (n.d.), 'Charter' <http://www.humanrightsfilmnetwork.org/content/charter> (accessed 24 March 2014).

Huntington, S. P. (1993), 'The Clash of Civilizations?', *Foreign Affairs* 72. 3: 22–49.

ICRC (1949), '1949 Conventions and Additional Protocols, and Their Commentaries' <http://www.icrc.org/applic/ihl/ihl.nsf/vwTreaties1949.xsp> (accessed 25 March 2014).

Jameson, F. (1992), *The Geopolitical Aesthetic: Cinema and Space in the World System*, Bloomington: Indiana University Press.

Jones, M. (2011), '*Monsters*', *Strange Horizons* <http://www.strangehorizons.com/reviews/2011/01/monsters.shtml> (accessed 31 March 2014).

Jones, E. (2013), '*Elysium*: a politically charged "popcorn sundae"', BBC News, 12 August <http://www.bbc.co.uk/news/entertainment-arts-23630488> (accessed 2 April 2014).

Kaufman, M. T. (2003), 'What does the Pentagon see in "Battle of Algiers"?', *New York*

Times, 7 September <http://www.nytimes.com/2003/09/07/weekinreview/the-world-film-studies-what-does-the-pentagon-see-in-battle-of-algiers.html>(accessed 2 April 2014).

Kemp, P. (2005), 'Blood Meridian', *Sight and Sound*, September, pp. 46–7.

Kershaw, I. (1983), *Popular Opinion and Political Dissent in the Third Reich: Bavaria, 1933–1945*, Oxford: Clarendon Press.

Khatib, L. (2006), *Filming the Modern Middle East: Politics in the Cinemas of Hollywood and the Arab World*, London: I. B. Tauris.

King, G. and T. Krzywinska (2000), *Science Fiction Cinema: From Outerspace to Cyberspace*, London: Wallflower.

Klawans, S. (2008), '*Waltz with Bashir*', *Film Comment*, November–December, pp. 34–6.

Klein, U. (2005), 'Current Cinema in Israel', *Film Comment*, September–October, pp. 19–22.

Kleinhans, C. (2009), 'Imagining Torture,' *Jump Cut* 51 <http://www.ejumpcut.org/archive/jc51.2009/imaginingtorture/index.html> (accessed 24 March 2014).

Koepnick, L. (2002), 'Reframing the Past: Heritage Cinema and the Holocaust in the 1990s', *New German Critique* 87: 47–82.

Korte, B. (2008), 'Envisioning a Black Tomorrow? Black Mother Figures and the Issue of Representation in *28 Days Later* (2003) and *Children of Men* (2006)', in *Multi-ethnic Britain 2000+: New Perspectives in Literature, Film and the Arts*, ed. L. Eckstein, B. Korte, E. U. Pirker and C. Reinfandt, Amsterdam: Rodopi, pp. 315–28.

Landsberg, A. (2004), *Prosthetic Memory: The Transformation of American Remembrance in the Age of Mass Culture*, New York: Columbia University Press.

Landy, M. (1996), *Cinematic Uses of the Past*, Minneapolis: University of Minnesota Press.

Lanzmann, C., R. Larson and D. Rodowick (1991), 'Seminar with Claude Lanzmann 11 April 1990', *Yale French Studies* 79: 82–99.

Lebeau, V. (1995), *Lost Angels: Psychoanalysis and Cinema*, London: Routledge.

Lefebvre, H. ([1974] 1991), *The Production of Space*, trans. D. Nicholson-Smith, Oxford: Blackwell.

Lesage, J. (2009), 'Torture documentaries', *Jump Cut* 51 <http://www.ejumpcut.org/archive/jc51.2009/TortureDocumentaries/index.html> (accessed 25 March 2014).

Levenson, E. (2009), '"A shame on all humanity"', *The Guardian*, 31 March <http://www.guardian.co.uk/education/2009/mar/31/rwanda-genocide> (accessed 25 March 2014).

Levinas, E. ([1961] 1969), *Totality and Infinity: An Essay on Exteriority*, trans. A. Lingis, Pittsburgh: Duquesne University Press.

Levinas, E. (1989), 'Ethics and Politics', in *The Levinas Reader*, ed. S. Hand, Oxford: Blackwell, pp. 289–97.

Levi, P. ([1986] 1988), *The Drowned and the Saved*, trans. R. Rosenthal, London: Michael Joseph.

Levy, G. (2010), *The Punishment of Gaza*, London: Verso.

Lewy, G. (2000), *The Nazi Persecution of the Gypsies*, Oxford: Oxford University Press.

Lifton, R. J. (1973), *Home from the War: Vietnam Veterans – Neither Victims nor Executioners*, New York: Simon and Schuster.

Lifton, R. J. (1986), *The Nazi Doctors: Medical Killing and the Psychology of Genocide*, London: Macmillan.

Lifton, R. J. (2004), 'Conditions of Atrocity', *The Nation*, 31 May <http://www.thenation.com/article/conditions-atrocity> (accessed 24 March 2014).

Limbaugh, R. (2004), *Rush Limbaugh Show*, NewsTalkRadio 77 WABC, 4 May.

Loshitzky, Y. (2001), *Identity Politics on the Israeli Screen*, Austin: University of Texas Press.

Loshitzky, Y. (2006), 'Pathologising Memory: From the Holocaust to the *Intifada*', *Third Text* 20.3/4: 327–35.

Lubell, N. (2010), *Extraterritorial Use of Force against Non-state Actors*, Oxford: Oxford University Press.

Lubezki, E. (2006), Interview by Benjamin B, 'Humanity's Last Hope', *American Cinematographer*, December, pp. 60–6, 68, 70, 72–5.

Luciano-Adams, B. (2009), '"Waltz with Bashir": The Fallibility yet Persistence of Memory', *Documentary*, Winter, pp. 12, 72.

Lury, K. and D. Massey (1999), 'Making Connections', *Screen* 40.3: 229–38.

MacBride, S. et al. (1983), 'Israel in Lebanon: Report of the International Commission to Enquire into Reported Violations of International Law by Israel during Its Invasion of the Lebanon', *Journal of Palestine Studies* 12.3: 117–33.

MacCabe, C. (1974), 'Realism and the Cinema: Notes on Some Brechtian Theses', *Screen* 15.2: 7–27.

McClintock, A. (2009), 'Paranoid Empire and Imperial Déjà Vu: Specters from Guantánamo and Abu Ghraib', *Small Axe* 28: 50–74.

Maharaj, B. (2010), 'Immigrations to Post-Apartheid South Africa: Critical Reflections', in *Immigration Worldwide: Policies, Practices, and Trends*, ed. U. A. Segal, D. Elliott, and N. S. Mayadas, Oxford: Oxford University Press, pp. 363–75.

Maltby, R. (2003), *Hollywood Cinema*, 2nd ed., Malden, MA: Blackwell.

Mamdani, M. (2001), *When Victims Become Killers: Colonialism, Nativism, and the Genocide in Rwanda*, Princeton: Princeton University Press.

Margolies, D. (2008), 'Earning his stripes: David Thewlis reaches a career pinnacle with "The Boy in the Striped Pyjamas"', *Back Stage: National Edition*, 13 November, pp. 10, 13, 51.

Marks, L. U. (2000), *The Skin of the Film: Intercultural Cinema, Embodiment, and the Senses*, Durham, NC: Duke University Press.

Marks, L. U. (2002), *Touch: Sensuous Theory and Multisensory Media*, Minneapolis: University of Minnesota Press.

Massey, D. (2005), *For Space*, London: Sage.

Matheou, D. (2011), 'The Body Politic: Pablo Larraín on *Post Mortem*', *Sight and Sound*, web exclusive, 11 September 2011 <http://www.bfi.org.uk/news-opinion/sight-sound-magazine/interviews/body-politic-pablo-larra-on-post-mortem> (accessed 28 March 2014).

Mayer, J. (2008), *The Dark Side: The Inside Story of How the War on Terror Turned into a War on American Ideals*, New York: Doubleday.

Mboti, N. (2010), 'To Show the World as It Is, or as It Is Not: The Gaze of Hollywood Films about Africa', *African Identities* 8.4: 317–32.

Moeller, S. D. (1999), *Compassion Fatigue: How the Media Sell Disease, Famine, War, and Death*, New York: Routledge.

Moeller, S. D. (2002), 'A Hierarchy of Innocence: The Media's Use of Children in the Telling of International News', *The Harvard International Journal of Press/Politics* 7.1: 36–56.

Mohanty, C. T. (1988), 'Under Western Eyes: Feminist Scholarship and Colonial Discourses', *Feminist Review* 30: 61–88.

Morag, R. (2008), 'The Living Body and the Corpse: Israeli Documentary Cinema and the Intifadah', *Journal of Film and Video* 60.3/4: 3–24.

Morreall, J. (2009), *Comic Relief: A Comprehensive Philosophy of Humor*, Malden, MA: Wiley-Blackwell.

Mosley, P. (2001), *Split Screen: Belgian Cinema and Cultural Identity*, Albany: State University of New York Press.

Mulvey, L. (1989), 'Visual Pleasure and Narrative Cinema', in *Visual and Other Pleasures*, Basingstoke: Macmillan, pp. 14–26.

Mulvey, L. (2006), *Death 24× a Second: Stillness and the Moving Image*, London: Reaktion.

Murray, J. (2009), '*Waltz with Bashir*', *Cineaste* 34.2: 65–6, 68.

Ndahiro, A. and P. Rutazibwa (2008), *Hotel Rwanda, or the Tutsi Genocide as Seen by Hollywood*, Paris: Harmattan.

NFTS (National Film and Television School) (2011), *Abuelas* press pack, Beaconsfield: NFTS.

Nichols, B. (1991), *Representing Reality: Issues and Concepts in Documentary*, Bloomington: Indiana University Press.

Nichols, B. (2010), 'Feelings of Revulsion and the Limits of Academic Discourse', *Jump Cut* 52 <http://www.ejumpcut.org/archive/jc52.2010/sopNichols/index.html> (accessed 25 March 2014).

Nora, P. (1989), 'Between Memory and History: *Les Lieux de Mémoire*', trans. M. Roudebush, *Representations* 26: 7–24.

Nowrojee, B. (2008), '"Your Justice Is Too Slow": Will the International Criminal Tribunal for Rwanda Fail Rwanda's Rape Victims?', in *Gendered Peace: Women's Struggles for Post-War Justice and Reconciliation*, ed. D. Pankhurst, New York: Routledge, pp. 107–36.

Noyes, J. (1992), *Colonial Space: Spatiality in the Discourse of German South West Africa, 1884–1915*, Chur, Switzerland: Harwood Academic Publishers.

Ortuzar, C. (2013), 'Visualizing "the Other 9/11": Memory of the Chilean coup', in *The Scene of the Mass Crime: History, Film, and International Tribunals*, ed. C. Delage and P. Goodrich, Abingdon: Routledge, pp. 179–86.

OSJI (Open Society Justice Initiative) (2013), *Globalizing Torture: CIA Secret Detention and Extraordinary Rendition*, New York: Open Society Foundation.

Osmond, A. (2008), 'The Boy in the Striped Pyjamas', *Sight and Sound*, November, pp. 51–2.

Page, J. (2009), *Crisis and Capitalism in Contemporary Argentine Cinema*, Durham, NC: Duke University Press.

Pappé, I. (1992), *The Making of the Arab–Israeli Conflict, 1947–1951*, London: I. B. Tauris.

Patterson, O. (1982), *Slavery and Social Death: A Comparative Study*, Cambridge, MA: Harvard University Press.

Peck, R. (2006), Commentary, *Sometimes in April*, DVD, Warner Home Video.

Peutz, N. and N. De Genova (2010), 'Introduction', in *The Deportation Regime: Sovereignty, Space, and the Freedom of Movement*, ed. N. De Genova and N. Peutz, Durham, NC: Duke University Press, pp. 1–29.

Philo, G., A. Gilmour, M. Gilmour, S. Rust, E. Gaskell and L. West (2003), 'The Israeli–Palestinian Conflict: TV News and Public Understanding', in *War and the Media: Reporting Conflict 24/7*, ed. D. K. Thussu and D. Freedman, London: Sage, 2003, pp. 133–48.

Pilkington, E. (2012), 'Senate under pressure to release mammoth report on CIA interrogation', *The Guardian*, 13 December <http://www.theguardian.com/world/2012/dec/13/senate-pressure-cia-interrogation-torture>(date accessed 25 March 2014).

Plantinga, C. (2010), '"I Followed the Rules and They All Loved You More": Moral Judgment and Attitudes toward Fictional Characters in Film', *Midwest Studies in Philosophy* 34.1: 34–51.

Podalsky, L. (2011), *The Politics of Affect and Emotion in Contemporary Latin American Cinema: Argentina, Brazil, Cuba, and Mexico*, New York: Palgrave Macmillan.

Pottier, J. (2002), *Re-imaging Rwanda: Conflict, Survival and Disinformation in the Late Twentieth Century*, Cambridge: Cambridge University Press.

Powell, A. (2005), *Deleuze and Horror Film*, Edinburgh: Edinburgh University Press.

Pratt, M. L. (1992), *Imperial Eyes: Travel Writing and Transculturation*, London: Routledge.

Prince, S. (2009), *Firestorm: American Film in the Age of Terrorism*, New York: Columbia University Press.

Purse, L. (2013), *Digital Imaging in Popular Cinema*, Edinburgh: Edinburgh University Press.

Rancière, J. ([2008] 2009), *The Emancipated Spectator*, trans. G. Elliott, London: Verso.

Rancière, J. (2010), *Dissensus: On Politics and Aesthetics*, trans. S. Corcoran, London: Bloomsbury.

Rayns, T. (2013), 'The Act of Killing', *Sight and Sound*, July, p. 70.

Rejali, D. (2012), 'Movies of Modern Torture as Convenient Truths', in *Screening Torture: Media Representations of State Terror and Political Domination*, ed. M. Flynn and F. F. Salek, New York: Columbia University Press.

Richards, J. (2001), 'Imperial Heroes for a Post-imperial Age: Films and the End of Empire', in *British Culture and the End of Empire*, ed. S. Ward, Manchester: Manchester University Press.

Robben, A. C. G. M. (2005), 'How Traumatized Societies Remember: The Aftermath of Argentina's Dirty War', *Cultural Critique* 59: 120–64.

Roberts, A. (2006), *Science Fiction*, 2nd ed., Abingdon: Routledge.

Roddick, N. (2011), 'Alien Nation', *Sight and Sound*, January, pp. 56–7.

Rosenheim, S. (1996), 'Interrotroning History: Errol Morris and the Documentary of the Future', in *The Persistence of History: Cinema, Television, and the Modern Event*, ed. V. Sobchack, New York: Routledge, pp. 219–34.

Rosenstone, R. A. (2006), *History on Film / Film on History*, Harlow: Pearson Longman.

Rothberg, M. (2000), *Traumatic Realism: The Demands of Holocaust Representation*, Minneapolis: University of Minnesota Press.

Rothberg, M. (2009), *Multidirectional Memory: Remembering the Holocaust in the Age of Decolonization*, Stanford, CA: Stanford University Press.

Rutan, J. S. and C. A. Rice (2002), 'Dreams in Psychodynamic Group Psychotherapy', in *Dreams in Group Psychotherapy: Theory and Technique*, ed. C. Neri, M. Pines and R. Friedman, London: Jessica Kingsley, pp. 37–45.

Rwafa, U. (2010), 'Film Representations of the Rwandan Genocide', *African Identities* 8.4: 389–408.

Said, E. W. (1984), 'Permission to narrate', *London Review of Books*, 16 February <http://www.lrb.co.uk/v06/n03/edward-said/permission-to-narrate> (accessed 1 April 2014).

Said, E. W. (1992), *The Question of Palestine*, London: Vintage.

Said, E. W. (2004), *From Oslo to Iraq and the Roadmap*, New York: Pantheon.

Saxton, L. (2008), *Haunted Images: Film, Ethics, Testimony and the Holocaust*, London: Wallflower.

Scahill, J. (2013), *Dirty Wars: The World Is a Battlefield*, London: Serpent's Tail.

Scarry, E. (1985), *The Body in Pain: The Making and Unmaking of the World*, New York: Oxford University Press.

Schalkwyk, K. van (2009), 'Applause for D9', *Screen Africa*, October, p. 32.

Scheffer, D. (2006), 'Genocide and Atrocity Crimes', *Genocide Studies and Prevention* 1.3: 229–50.

Scheper-Hughes, N. (1996), 'Small Wars and Invisible Genocides', *Social Science and Medicine* 43.5: 889–900.

Scheper-Hughes, N. and P. Bourgois (2004), 'Making Sense of Violence', in *Violence in War and Peace: An Anthology*, Malden, MA: Blackwell, pp. 1–31.

Seremetakis, C. N. (ed.) (1996), *The Senses Still: Perception and Memory as Material Culture in Modernity*, Chicago: University of Chicago Press.

Shapiro, M. J. (2009), *Cinematic Geopolitics*, Abingdon: Routledge.

Shaviro, S. (1993), *The Cinematic Body*, Minneapolis: University of Minnesota Press.

Shlaim, A. (1990), *The Politics of Partition: King Abdullah, the Zionists, and Palestine, 1921–1951*, New York: Columbia University Press.

Shohat, E. (2010), *Israeli Cinema: East/West and the Politics of Representation*, London: I. B. Tauris.

Singer, P. (2004), 'War, Profits and the Vacuum of Law: Privatized Military Firms and International Law,' *Columbia Journal of Transnational Law* 42.2: 521–49

Smith, M. (1995), *Engaging Characters: Fiction, Emotion, and the Cinema*, Oxford: Clarendon Press.

Smith, M. (1999), 'Gangsters, Cannibals, Aesthetes, or Apparently Perverse Allegiances', in *Passionate Views: Film, Cognition, and Emotion*, ed. C. Plantinga and G. M. Smith, Baltimore: Johns Hopkins University Press, pp. 217–38.

Sobchack, V. (2004a), 'Inscribing Ethical Space: 10 Propositions on Death, Representation, and Documentary', in *Carnal Thoughts: Embodiment and Moving Image Culture*, Berkeley: University of California Press, pp. 226–57.

Sobchack, V. (2004b), 'What My Fingers Knew: The Cinesthetic Subject, or Vision in the Flesh', in *Carnal Thoughts: Embodiment and Moving Image Culture*, Berkeley: University of California Press, pp. 53–84.

Soda Pictures (2005), 'Interview with Dalia Hager and Vidi Bilu', *Close to Home* presskit <http://www.sodapictures.com/media/CTH-press-kit.pdf> (accessed 1 April 2014).

Sontag, S. (2003), *Regarding the Pain of Others*, London: Penguin.

Sony Pictures Entertainment (2008), 'Interview with Ari Folman', *Waltz with Bashir* presskit <http://www.sonyclassics.com/waltzwithbashir/pdf/waltzwithbashir_presskit.pdf> (accessed 1 April 2014).

Sorensen, K. (2009), *Media, Memory, and Human Rights in Chile*, New York: Palgrave Macmillan.

Sosa, C. (2011), 'Queering Acts of Mourning in the Aftermath of Argentina's Dictatorship: the Mothers of Plaza de Mayo and *Los Rubios*', in *The Memory of State Terrorism in the Southern Cone: Argentina, Chile, and Uruguay*, ed. F. Lessa and V. Druliolle, New York: Palgrave Macmillan, pp. 63–85.

Sosa, C. (2012), 'Queering Kinship: The Performance of Blood and the Attires of Memory', *Journal of Latin American Cultural Studies: Travesia* 21.2: 221–33.

Suner, A. (2010) *New Turkish Cinema: Belonging, Identity, Memory*, London: I. B. Tauris.

Suvin, D. (1979) *Metamorphoses of Science Fiction: On the Poetics and History of a Literary Genre*, New Haven, CT: Yale University Press.

Talavera, V., G. G. Núñez-Mchiri and J. Heyman (2010), 'Deportation in the US–Mexico Borderlands: Anticipation, Experience, and Memory', in *The Deportation Regime: Sovereignty, Space, and the Freedom of Movement*, ed. N. De Genova and N. Peutz, Durham, NC: Duke University Press, pp. 166–95.

Taylor, D. (1997), *Disappearing Acts: Spectacles of Gender and Nationalism in Argentina's 'Dirty War'*, Durham, NC: Duke University Press.

Thompson, A. (ed.) (2007), *The Media and the Rwanda Genocide*, London: Pluto Press.

Thompson, A. (2009), 'The father and daughter we let down', *Toronto Star*, 11 April <http://www.thestar.com/news/insight/2009/04/11/the_father_and_daughter_we_let_down.html> (accessed 26 March 2014).

Torchin, L. (2005), '*Hotel Rwanda*', *Cineaste* 30.1: 46–8.

Torchin, L. (2012a), *Creating the Witness: Documenting Genocide on Film, Video, and the Internet*, Minneapolis: University of Minnesota Press.

Torchin, L. (2012b), 'Networked for Advocacy: Film Festivals and Activism', in *Film Festivals and Activism*, ed. D. Iordanova and L. Torchin, St Andrews: St Andrews Film Studies, pp. 1–12.

Traverso, A. (2010), 'Dictatorship Memories: Working through Trauma in Chilean Post-dictatorship Documentary', *Continuum* 24.1: 179–91.

Trinh, T. M. (1989), *Woman, Native, Other: Writing Postcoloniality and Feminism*, Bloomington: Indiana University Press.

Trinh, T. M. (2011), *Elsewhere, within Here: Immigration, Refugeeism and the Boundary Event*, New York: Routledge.

Tyler, I. (2006), '"Welcome to Britain": The Cultural Politics of Asylum', *European Journal of Cultural Studies* 9.2: 185–202.

Umutesi, M. B. (2004), *Surviving the Slaughter: The Ordeal of a Rwandan Refugee in Zaire*, trans. J. Emerson, Madison: University of Wisconsin Press.

UN (1973), 'International Convention on the Prevention and Suppression of the Crime of Apartheid' <https://treaties.un.org/doc/Publication/UNTS/Volume%201015/volume-1015-I-14861-English.pdf> (accessed 1 April 2014).

UN (1984), 'Convention against Torture and Other Cruel, Inhuman or Degrading Treatment or Punishment' <http://www.un.org/documents/ga/res/39/a39r046.htm> (accessed 24 March 2014).

UN (2006), 'International Convention for the Protection of All Persons from Enforced Disappearance' <http://www.ohchr.org/Documents/ProfessionalInterest/disappearance-convention.pdf> (accessed 27 March 2014).

UN (2010), 'International Convention for the Protection of All Persons from Enforced Disappearance', United Nations Treaty Collection <http://treaties.un.org/Pages/View Details.aspx?src=TREATY&mtdsg_no=IV-16&chapter=4&lang=en>(accessed 2 April 2014).

UNHCR (2010), 'Convention and Protocol Relating to the Status of Refugees' <http://www.unhcr.org/3b66c2aa10.html> (accessed 31 March 2014).

Virilio, P. (1989), *War and Cinema: The Logistics of Perception*, trans. Patrick Camiller, London: Verso.

Walters, W. (2010), 'Deportation, Expulsion, and the Internal Police of Aliens', in *The Deportation Regime: Sovereignty, Space, and the Freedom of Movement*, ed. N. De Genova and N. Peutz, Durham, NC: Duke University Press, pp. 69–100.

Ware, V. (2010), 'The White Fear Factor', in *Terror and the Postcolonial*, ed. E. Boehmer and S. Morton, Chichester: Wiley-Blackwell, pp. 99–112.

Weissman, G. (2004), *Fantasies of Witnessing: Postwar Efforts to Experience the Holocaust*, Ithaca, NY: Cornell University Press.

Weizman, E. (2007), *Hollow Land: Israel's Architecture of Occupation*, London: Verso.

Weizman, E. (2012), 'Short cuts', *London Review of Books*, 6 December, p. 28.

White, B. (2012), *Palestinians in Israel: Segregation, Discrimination and Democracy*, London: Pluto Press.

Williams, L. (1993), 'Mirrors without Memories: Truth, History, and the New Documentary', *Film Quarterly* 46.3: 9–21.

Williams, L. (1998), 'Melodrama Revised', in *Refiguring American Film Genres: History and Theory*, ed. N. Browne, Berkeley: University of California Press, pp. 42–88.

Williams, L. (2010), '"Cluster Fuck": The Forcible Frame in Errol Morris's *Standard Operating Procedure*', *Jump Cut* 52 <http://www.ejumpcut.org/archive/jc52.2010/sopWilliams/index.html>

Wittgenstein, L. (1969), *The Blue and the Brown Books: Preliminary Studies for the Philosophical Investigations*, 2nd ed., Oxford: Blackwell.

Wolf, S. (2010), 'No Turning Back', *Sight and Sound*, September, pp. 14–17.

Wood, S. (2012), 'Film and Atrocity: The Holocaust as Spectacle', in *Film and Genocide*, ed. K. M. Wilson and T. F. Crowder-Taraborrelli, Madison: University of Wisconsin Press, pp. 21–44.

Woodbridge, J. (2005), *Sizing the Unauthorised (Illegal) Migrant Population in the United Kingdom in 2001*, Home Office Online Report 29/05, <http://css.escwa.org.lb/SD/1017/MIGRANTpop_in_UK.pdf> (accessed 31 March 2014).

Worsdale, A. (2009), 'Joburg Inspired Blomkamp', *Screen Africa*, October, p. 35.

Young, A. (2010), *The Scene of Violence: Cinema, Crime, Affect*, Abingdon: Routledge.

Yúdice, G. (1996), '*Testimonio* and Postmodernism', in *The Real Thing: Testimonial Discourse and Latin America*, ed. G. M. Gugelberger, Durham, NC: Duke University Press, pp. 42–57.

Zborowski, J. (2010), '*District 9* and its World', *Jump Cut* 52 <http://www.ejumpcut.org/archive/jc52.2010/zoborowskiDst9/index.html> (accessed 31 March 2014).

Zelizer, B. (1998), *Remembering to Forget: Holocaust Memory through the Camera's Eye*, Chicago: University of Chicago Press.

Zimbardo, P. (2007), *The Lucifer Effect: How Good People Turn Evil*, London: Rider.

Žižek, S. (1992), *Looking Awry: An Introduction to Jacques Lacan through Popular Culture*, Cambridge, MA: MIT Press.

Žižek, S. (2005), 'The Obscenity of Human Rights: Violence as Symptom', Lacan Dot Com <www.lacan.com/zizviol.htm> (accessed 24 March 2014).

Žižek, S. (2007), '*Children of Men* Comments', Special Features, *Children of Men*, DVD, 2 Disc Special Edition, Universal Studios.

Žižek, S. (2009), *Violence: Six Sideways Reflections*, London: Profile.

Žižek, S. (2010), 'A Soft Focus on War: How Hollywood Hides the Horrors of War', In These Times, 21 April <http://www.inthesetimes.com/article/5864/a_soft_focus_on_war/> (accessed 1 April 2014).

Index